The Sassafras Science Adventures

Volume 7: Chemistry

Johnny Congo & Paige Hudson

THE SASSAFRAS SCIENCE ADVENTURES
VOLUME 7: CHEMISTRY

First Edition 2023
Copyright @ Elemental Science, Inc.
Email: support@elementalscience.com

ISBN: 978-1-953490-18-6
Cover Design by Paige Hudson & Eunike Nugroho
Illustrations by Eunike Nugroho (be.net/inikeke)

Printed In USA For World Wide Distribution

No part of this book may be reproduced or transmitted in any form or by any means, electronic or mechanical, including photocopying, recording, or by means of any information storage and retrieval system, without permission in writing from the authors. The only exception is brief quotations in printed reviews.

For more copies write to:
Elemental Science
PO Box 79
Niceville, FL 32588
support@elementalscience.com

Dedication

We dedicate this book to Brad and Shannon. Your support means the world to us!! Without the two of you, the Sassafras twins wouldn't exist because we would have given up long ago. Thank you for believing in us and encouraging us every step along the way.

MAKE THE MOST OF YOUR JOURNEY WITH THE SASSAFRAS TWINS!

Add our activity guide, logbook, or lapbooking guide to create a full science curriculum for your students!

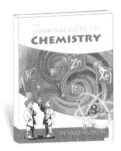

The Sassafras Guide to Chemistry includes chapter summaries and an array of options that coordinate with the individual chapters of this novel. This guide provides ideas for experiments, notebooking, vocabulary, memory work, and additional activities to enhance what your students are learning about the periodic table!

The Official Sassafras SCIDAT Logbook: Chemistry Edition partners with the activity guide to help your student document their journey throughout this novel. The logbook includes their own SCIDAT log pages as well as lab report sheets and an chemistry glossary.

Lapbooking through Chemistry with the Sassafras Twins provides a gentle option for enhancing what your students are learning about the periodic table through this novel. The guide contains a reading plan, templates and pictures to create a beautiful lapbook on chemistry, vocabulary, and coordinated scientific demonstrations!

VISIT ELEMENTALSCIENCE.COM TO LEARN MORE!

Table of Contents

Authors' Note — viii

The Sassafras Guide to the Characters — ix

Chapter 1: Celebrating at the Ambidextrous Octopus — 1
- Astronomical Bowling — 1
- Chemical Departure — 9

Chapter 2: 3 . . . 2 . . . 1 . . . Chemistry — 17
- Atomic Bits — 17
- Dancing Elements — 25

Chapter 3: Launching Lunar Adventures — 35
- Periodic and Romantic Tables — 35
- Fueling Hydrogen — 43

Chapter 4: Underground Siberian Science and Neon Joviality — 53
- Abundant Alkali — 53
- Shiny Sodium and Purply Potassium — 63

Chapter 5: Subterranean Dance-off — 71
- Extravagant Earth Metals — 71
- Magnesium and Calcium Mash-up — 79

Chapter 6: Oh Iceland, Oh Iceland — 89
- Three Transition Metals — 89

Fearless Gold   99

Chapter 7: The Three Metals Quest   107
Acquiring Zinc   107
Inquisitive Iron   117

Chapter 8: The Masaki-Do Dojo   127
Kihuping Lanthanides   127
Neodymium Ninja Magnets   139

Chapter 9: The Nuclear Rescue Mission   147
Actinide Bailout   147
Trapping Uranium   156

Chapter 10: Singapore's Merlion Fashion Extravaganza   167
Modeling Main Group Metals   167
Bisaam's Aluminum Cans   176

Chapter 11: Models and Mysteries   187
Observing Metals   187
Silicone Trends   197

Chapter 12: Britain's Carboxynitro Games   205
Menacing Nonmetals   205
Bubbles of Carbon   213

Chapter 13: The Three Challenges   221
Never Mind, Oxygen   221
Iced-over Nitrogen   229

Chapter 14: Iron Nails in the Chilean Desert 235
    Fortuneless Halogens   235
    Chemical Bonding   242

Chapter 15: The Desert Dune Buggy Race 249
    Chlorine Buggies   249
    Healing Iodine   259

Chapter 16: On to Morocco 269
    Mysterious Noble Gases   269
    Gaseous Helium   278

Chapter 17: Just a Bunch of Hot Air 287
    Neon Outbreak   287
    Air Below   296

Chapter 18: Zipping Back to Pecan Street 303
    Bonus Data   303
    A Periodic Setup   310

THE SASSAFRAS SCIENCE ADVENTURES

Authors' Note

The novel you hold in your hands is both a work of fiction and a teaching tool, which creates the need for a delicate balance.

We have taken fictional liberties when it comes to the story line—to our knowledge, no one is traveling around the world on invisible zip lines. But, when it comes to the information shared by our local experts, we have done our best to accurately reflect the current scientific knowledge at the time of writing this book.

We have drawn from our personal experiences and education, as well as the following resources:

- *Basher Science: The Complete Periodic Table*
- *Basher Science: Chemistry - Getting a Big Reaction*
- *Periodic Table by Scholastic*
- *DK Children's Encyclopedia*
- *DK Encyclopedia of Science*
- *Kingfisher Science Encyclopedia*
- *The Usborne Children's Encyclopedia*
- *Usborne Science Encyclopedia*

In addition to these books, we have drawn on the information found on many different websites.

Please keep in mind that science is ever-changing as our technology advances and our understanding deepens. If you find an issue in this novel, please let us know and take the opportunity to discuss these new developments with your students.

THE SASSAFRAS GUIDE TO THE CHARACTERS

CECIL'S NEIGHBORHOOD (CHAPTER 1)

★ **Tracey Sassafras**[§] – She is the female twin of the almost famous duo known as the Sassafras twins. She is an avid ambidextrous bowler and riddle solver. She is also known as Blaisey, Fish Hook, and Tracey the Plucky.

★ **Blaine Sassafras**[§] – He is the male twin of the almost famous duo known as the Sassafras twins. He is an aspiring break-dancer in his own mind, and his ambidextrous bowling record is average. He is also known as Train, Rowboat, and Blaine the Handsome.

★ **Cecil Sassafras**[§] – He is the one and only uncle to the Sassafras twins who will probably never get their names right. He is also the ambidextrous bowler responsible for the legendary octo-bowl. He is the inventor and scientist responsible for the twins' summer of science.

★ **Summer Beach**[§] – She is a most unique, sandwich-loving scientist! She has brought her infectious energy to every leg of the twins' journey so far. She's Cecil's schoolmate turned best friend and a *pro re nata* agent for the Triple S (Swiss Secret Service).

★ **President Lincoln**[§] – This legendary prairie dog serves as Uncle Cecil's right-hand paw. He is a reticent animal with a brilliant mind and is known as the second-best ambidextrous animal bowler. He is also known as The Prez and Linc Dog.

★ **Ulysses S. Grant**[§] – This mythical Arctic ground squirrel lends a paw to all that Summer does in her underground lab. He is a snappy inventor and holds the title of "Number 1 Ambidextrous Animal Bowler."

★ **Yang Bo**[§][*] – He is the astronaut who served as the twins' local expert on the International Space Station. He is also a former classmate of

---

[§] These characters appear throughout the novel. We have chosen to share about them in the chapter where they first appear.
[*] These characters are only mentioned in the text but are not a part of this leg of the journey.

THE SASSAFRAS SCIENCE ADVENTURES

Uncle Cecil and Summer from middle school.

☆ **Wiggles and Fidget**[§] – They are the museum security guards the twins first met on their astronomy leg.

☆ **Captain Marolf**[§] – He is the head of the Triple S. He also appeared in the twins' Earth science and astronomy legs.

Alaska and the Moon (Chapters 2-3)

☆ **Paul Sims**[§] – He is the museum curator at the National Air and Space Museum. He is also a friend and schoolmate of Cecil's and Summer's who is hiding quite a bit.

☆ **The Rotary Club** – This club is made up of the Slote siblings: Alexander, Graham, and Belle. They are against technology and will do almost anything to return the world to rotary phone usage.

☆ **REESE** – This joint invention of President Lincoln and Ulysses S. Grant is a robot whose name stands for Robotic Exploration, Entertainment, and Scientific Enhancement.

☆ **Jorgen Wuthrich** – He is the Triple S agent and partner to Agent DeBlose's whom the twins met on their Earth science leg.

☆ **Evan DeBlose**[*] – A lead Triple S Agent and earth science local expert. He was quite busy on the twins' astronomy leg taking down the rogue Agent Adrianne Archer and the nefarious Yuroslav Bogdanovich.

☆ **Mr. Womberfraggle**[§,*] – He was Uncle Cecil's and Summer's middle school chemistry teacher.

Siberia (Chapters 4-5)

☆ **Rodi Abramov** – He acts as the twins' local expert for their time in Siberia. He and his sister, Dina, were hired by the Turgenev Mining Company to bring science and joviality to the mining operation.

☆ **Dina Abramov** – She is Rodi's sister and sidekick in science and joviality.

☆ **Trof** – He is one of the miners who worked in the Siberian mine. He doesn't like science . . . or joviality.

☆ **Taras** – He is another of the miners who worked in the Siberian mine. He starts to see how amazing knowing about science can be!

★ **The Man With No Eyebrows**§ – He is the memory-erasing, disappearing cape-wearing, eyebrow-less man who has tried just about everything he can think of to stop the twins. His real name is Thaddeus, and it turns out that he was a schoolmate of Cecil's and Summer's.

★ **Sveta Corvette** – She is the neon-green punk-rocker who once traveled the trains as a stowaway, but now she is a star of the band Sveta and the Spark Plugs.

ICELAND (CHAPTERS 6-7)

★ **Ingrid the Hospitable** – She is the beautiful female member of the Kunningskapur, which is a guild of adventurers in Iceland who seek the three metals.

★ **Harland the Wise** – He is the blonde-headed male member of the Kunningskapur and the twins' local expert of their Iceland leg.

★ **Magnus the Brave** – He is the red-headed, short-tempered male member of the Kunningskapur.

★ **Dagfinn the Wicked** – He is the brawny, dark-haired opponent of the Kunningskapur.

JAPAN (CHAPTERS 8-9)

★ **Sensei Masaki** – He is the twins' local expert for their leg in Japan and the head of the Masaki-do Dojo.

★ **Haipa Yagi (or Hyper Goat)** – He is a member of the Masaki-do Dojo in Japan. His given name is Seth E. Prue, and he is the only non-Japanese student at the dojo.

★ **Hageshi Tora (or Fierce Tiger)** – She is a member of the Masaki-do Dojo in Japan. She's not afraid of anything.

★ **Chiteki Kirin (or Intelligent Giraffe)** – She is a member of the Masaki-do Dojo in Japan. Her proverbial mind can outsmart anyone.

★ **Attosuru Tonbo (or Overpowering Dragonfly)** – He is a member of the Masaki-do Dojo in Japan. He is short but incredibly determined.

★ **Sairento Sai (Silent Rhino)** – He is a member of the Masaki-do

Dojo in Japan. He doesn't speak, but he is one of the strongest ninjas in the entire dojo.

★ **Hayato Doi** – He is a rich, power-hungry businessman who has an army of evil ninjas known as the Jaken.

★ **Natsuki Saito** – She is the CEO of the A.B.G. Nuclear Power Plant.

SINGAPORE (CHAPTERS 10-11)

★ **Aishaanya** – She is a fashion icon and designer in the Singapore fashion scene who owns Aishaanya Inc. She is the twins' local expert for their time in Singapore.

★ **Brutus** – He is Aishaanya's bodyguard.

★ **Tamina** – She is a former employee of Aishaanya. She left under not-so-great circumstances and went on to start her own fashion business.

★ **Sadie Nichols** – She is a news anchor for THE DROP.

★ **Grady** – He is Sadie's cameraman.

★ **Bisaam** – He is one of the technology experts and conceptual artists at Aishaanya Inc.

★ **Rosemary Rajan** – She is one of Aishaanya's new and upcoming designers.

GREAT BRITAIN (CHAPTERS 12-13)

★ **The Unseen One** – He fulfills the role of the twins' local expert for their time in Great Britain. His voice is heard throughout the Carboxynitro Games but he's not necessarily seen.

★ **The Davies twins** – They are a blonde-headed set of twin boys participating in the Carboxynitro Games.

★ **The Edward twins** – They are a red-headed set of twin girls participating in the Carboxynitro Games.

★ **The Clark twins** – They are a set of boy-girl twins participating in the Carboxynitro Games.

★ **Tom** – He is a former colleague of the Unseen One.

CHILE (CHAPTERS 14-15)

★ **Rose Rock** – She serves as the twins' local expert in Chile. She is a chemist, a teacher, the daughter of the chief, and a strong supporter of the villagers.

★ **Ring Finger** – He is the War Lord King of the Atacama Desert.

★ **The Iron Nails** – They are a band of men who enforce the will of Ring Finger.

★ **Vicente** – He is Rose's good friend who also happens to be deaf.

★ **Maximiliano** – Another villager who is intent on beating Rose Rock.

MOROCCO (CHAPTERS 16-17)

★ **The SAM Collective** – They are a group of three scientists, activists, and mathematicians—Samir, Sami, and Samirah—who provide the local expert information for the twins in Morocco.

★ **The A.S.M. (Anonymous Snake-charmers of Morocco)** – They are a gang of hundreds of ruffians who charm snakes in Morocco.

Volume 7

Chemistry

Chapter 1: Celebrating at the Ambidextrous Octopus

Astronomical Bowling

"Spare!" Twelve-year-old Blaine Sassafras shouted in elation with a touch of cockiness as he turned from the knocked-down bowling pins toward his twin sister, Tracey. Tracey sported a good-natured smile as her brother walked past pantomiming pistol shots with his hands accompanied with shooting noises from his mouth like he was a sharp-shooting, cowboy-hero bowler. She grabbed her eight-pound, bright pink bowling ball from the ball rack and stepped forward to face the lane.

Tracey took a deep breath, lifted the ball underneath her chin and side-stepped a little to line her bowling shoes up with the arrows embedded in the glossy, polished wood flooring fifteen feet down the lane. Taking one more deep breath, she eyed the right edge of the number one pin that was her target. She envisioned seeing the pink bowling ball releasing from her hand and then hitting the front pin on its right side, causing it to wildly careen backward, knocking all the other pins down.

THE SASSAFRAS SCIENCE ADVENTURES

The good-natured smile remained on the girl's face. Surely a strike like she had imagined would cause Blaine to holster his pantomime pistols. After one more deep breath, Tracey stepped forward with purpose. She swung her arm behind her and brought it powerfully back to the front of her body in an inverted arch, releasing the fluorescent pink sphere with smooth, strong fluidity. Her bowling ball spun ahead, and to her surprise, it followed the mental trajectory she had traced in her mind.

Solid contact between the ball and the front pin. An explosion of white, red, and pink ensued. One last satisfied deep breath released itself from Tracey's lungs. Not one pin was left standing.

The twelve-year-old girl turned back toward her twin brother, who was now standing with zero elation and not an ounce of cockiness. Instead of pistols, his hands hung limply at his sides.

"Strike!" Tracey said with exclamation.

"Great job, Tracey Trace!" an excited female voice sang out. It was Summer Beach, and she was running toward Tracey with outstretched arms. "That strike puts us on top! That means the girls win and the boys lose! Oh, yeah! Girls rule! Boys drool! Animals schooled!" The female, white-coat-wearing scientist reached Tracey's spot and wrapped her up into a happy jumping dance-hug.

Blaine and his teammate, Uncle Cecil, looked on in dejection. So did the third team of President Lincoln and Ulysses S. Grant, who were a prairie dog and an arctic ground squirrel, respectively.

The group of six was at the bowling alley to celebrate. Blaine and Tracey had successfully finished their study of astronomy, and what better way to celebrate than to hit up the neighborhood's exciting new bowling alley, the Ambidextrous Octopus. It wasn't a big bowling alley; it had only eight lanes, but it was alive with glow-in-the-dark colors, happy electronic music, and decorations featuring its charming mascot, Ollie the Octopus. To everyone's delight, it only slightly smelled like feet.

It was a fantastic place to celebrate how far the twins had come. Last semester in school, Blaine and Tracey had failed science class. This had both disappointed and worried their parents. So, to address the situation, the twins' mom and dad had stuck them on a long-distance bus and sent them to their uncle's house for the summer. Their uncle, Cecil Sassafras, was a pseudo-famous research scientist, but by the twins' calculations the man was a crazy, mad scientist. When they had first arrived at their uncle's place, they thought he was a crazy, weird scientist. As they spent a little more time with him, their summation moved to a crazy, okay scientist. And now, after spending three-quarters of the summer hanging out with him and experiencing the science he was helping teach them, Blaine and Tracey thought he was a crazy, awesome scientist! They loved their quirky uncle with his wild uncombed red hair, messy lab coat, and bunny house slippers, which he was presently wearing at the bowling alley.

With the help of President Lincoln, his prairie dog lab assistant, Uncle Cecil had invented invisible zip lines that allowed the twelve-year-olds to travel anywhere on the globe at the speed of light. The key to connecting to these zip lines was a specially designed three-ringed carabiner. They needed to slip on a harness, don a helmet, turn the first ring of the carabiner to the desired latitude coordinate and the second ring to the longitude coordinate, and then let the carabiner snap shut. As soon as they did, the carabiner would automatically find the correct invisible zip line. The third ring would tighten and secure them to the line, they would hang with their feet dangling in the air for approximately seven seconds attached to the unseen line, and then they would zip off at the speed of light, traveling through swirls of bright color to their desired location.

At first, Blaine and Tracey had thought invisible zip-line travel impossible, too good to be true, or maybe even just a dream, but now after using this mode of travel for most of the summer, they were experiential believers. Under the direction and guidance of their uncle, the Sassafras twins had used the unseen lines to zip around the planet. At each location they had learned about fun scientific topics with the help of local experts. So far they had completed studies of zoology, anatomy, botany, earth science, geology, and most recently astronomy, where they were even able to use invisible zip lines to travel in outer space!

After they finished a subject and landed safely back in their uncle's neighborhood, they always spent some time celebrating the completion of a leg of learning with Uncle Cecil and President Lincoln, which is what they were doing at the Ambidextrous Octopus. The twins were enjoying themselves, even Blaine, who had lost the bowling match.

They were joined by Summer Beach and her animal lab assistant, Ulysses S. Grant, the arctic ground squirrel. Ulysses and President Lincoln were buddies. Summer and Cecil were buddies. However, it had become more and more apparent over the course of the summer that Summer was hoping to be much more than buddies with Cecil. To Blaine and Tracey's dismay, their uncle seemed totally oblivious to this fact. The twelve-year-olds really liked Summer. She had served as a local expert on every leg of their adventure so far. She was always overflowing with joy, kindness, and knowledge, and they each had gone so far as to imagine a scenario where Summer would need to change her last name to 'Sassafras' in the future.

Another way they celebrated their science-filled victories was by watching a brief review of what they had learned on the recently completed leg. As strange as it sounded, the one who orchestrated these reviews was President Lincoln, the prairie dog. Normally, they happened in Uncle Cecil's basement lab over in his house on 1104 North Pecan Street, but to the twins' surprise, it looked like this time the presentation was happening right here, right now, in the bowling alley.

President Lincoln scurried to the top of a ball return rack with a small clicker in his paw. After a tap here and a tap there, a projector screen lowered over the bowling lanes, immediately illuminated with a bright, colorful picture of Lincoln himself with words over his head that read, "President Lincoln's Ever-so-brief Presentation on Astronomy."

Uncle Cecil stood and made his way to the center of the lanes. The man was usually eccentric, but not when he was doing these presentations on behalf of his lab assistant. When Cecil was orating for these presentations, he was as serious and put together as a royal butler. He stood, back straight with hands folded in front of his chest, white lab coat flowing above pink bunny house slippers, looking as refined as possible.

The twins smiled as they watched their uncle, anticipating the start of the presentation. Summer Beach also smiled as she watched, her eyes enraptured.

"'President Lincoln's Ever-so-brief Presentation on Astronomy,'" Cecil started in a voice that could have won accolades on Broadway.

Lincoln clicked the clicker, the image on the screen changed, and Uncle Cecil continued, "A solar system includes the sun and anything that orbits around it. This includes the planets, asteroids, moons, comets, and any space debris."

The image on the screen showed a dome-shaped room the Sassafras twins had found themselves inside of in Poland—the Copernicus Code Escape Room—which had proven to be challenging and educational. Embedded in the walls, floor, and ceiling of the room had been moving and sparkly lights that represented many of those things that make up a solar system. The image was a picture the twins had captured using the cameras on their smartphones. Indeed, all the photos they would see during this presentation were images either Blaine or Tracey had captured with their phones while zipping around the solar system studying astronomy.

President Lincoln clicked again. The next image came up on the screen. Cecil again orated with vigor, "The inner planets, those closest to the sun are Mercury, Venus, Earth, and Mars. The outer planets, larger and out beyond the asteroid belt are Jupiter, Saturn, Uranus, and Neptune."

The picture on the screen now was one the twins had taken while floating out in space a safe distance from the planet Mercury. It had been amazing for the twins to get into their space suits and travel on the zip lines out into outer space.

Click. Next image.

This one was REESE the Robot with the lyrics of a hip-hop song showing on his data screen. The letters of the robot's name stood for 'Robotic Exploration Entertainment, and Scientific Enhancement.' To the twins' delight, REESE had more than lived up to his name.

"On Earth," Uncle Cecil continued, "our closest space neighbor is the moon. As the moon moves, part of it is 'lit' by the sun, which makes it look like the moon is changing shape. We call these different shapes phases, and we call the pattern they follow the lunar cycle."

"Lunar cycle, wooka, wooka, wooka, lunar cycle!" Blaine suddenly shouted the chorus to the hip-hop song that REESE had taught them.

The outburst didn't seem to bother Summer or Cecil at all. But everyone else in the bowling alley, including Tracey, glanced at Blaine as though he were a little crazy.

"Wooka? Wooka?" Blaine sang out a little quieter this time, more as a question, as though asking if anyone wanted to join in with him. No one did, and the presentation continued.

"Stars go through a life cycle," Cecil narrated. "They are born; they burn brightly for a long time; and when their fuel is burned up, they die."

Now the image was of Starship Ishani, and in a huge window located on her bridge, bright and beautiful constellations of stars shown. In actuality, the window was a green screen, and the starship was the set of a Bollywood TV show. Nonetheless, it had been a perfect location for the twins to learn about the constellations.

President Lincoln used the clicker once more, and the picture changed from a pretend spaceship to a real one. It was a picture the twins had taken on the bridge of the International Space Station. In the picture were six real-live astronauts, one of whom was Yang Bo, a Chinese astrobiologist who had been their local expert.

"Astronauts travel in space with the use of special suits," Cecil spoke in his well-mannered voice. "There is no gravity in space, so life is very different. Astronauts live on the International Space Station to research space."

"*Au la vache!*" This time it was Tracey suddenly blurting out.

"*Au la vache?*" Blaine questioned.

"*Au la vache,*" Tracey confirmed and then translated the phrase into English. "Oh, my cow."

It was a statement the French astronaut, Bayard Clemence, had often used in their interactions with him on the International Space Station.

"And last but not least," Cecil stated stately, "we have learned many things about space using telescopes, which magnify faraway objects. We have also gained knowledge about space by using satellites and space probes that travel into space and send information back to Earth."

The last image to come up on the projector screen was one of the telescopes on the summit of Mauna Kea. This picture immediately brought reverent pause to Blaine and Tracey's hearts. They had hiked to the observatory on the summit with their local expert, an elderly gentleman by the name of J.P. Jungos. Mr. Jungos had used all the energy left in his frail body to make the journey, and then he died peacefully while gazing at the stars.

Both twins wiped away tears from the corners of their eyes as the ever-so-brief presentation concluded. President Lincoln hopped down from the ball return rack, the projector screen rolled back up into the ceiling, and Uncle Cecil reverted from a refined orator to his normal self. "Welly, welly, willikers, these scientific adventures of yours have been amazing-riff-tastic, have they not? There have been so many high-up highs, and I know there have also been some low-down lows."

As the red-headed scientist said this, he wrapped up his niece and nephew in a kind and empathetic hug. He had sensed their sadness over the loss of J.P. Jungos and had responded with compassion. Call the man crazy, but he was a wonderful uncle, and the twins loved and appreciated him.

"And these phones of yours!" Cecil exclaimed as he released the two twelve-year-olds. "They sure do take some fantabulous pictures. The pristinely clear images we saw on President Lincoln's presentation were out of this world!" He said this with big, waving arms like he was reaching for the edge of the atmosphere. Then he brought his arms close to his chest to ask a question, "Are the phones still functioning correctly? All of the doodads, whatchamacallits, ringdingers, whirligigs, doohickeys, gadgets, gizmos, levers, bells, and whistles are still working fine, right?"

"You mean the applications?" Blaine and Tracey asked together.

"Persactly, Train and Blaisey. Persactly."

"Yes, our smartphone applications are working great," Blaisey (Tracey) confirmed.

At the beginning of the summer, Uncle Cecil had given each of the twins a smartphone to take on their science-learning adventures. The phones were inherently tied to the invisible zip lines and so were the apps on the phones. The Sassafras twins were required to gather data as they rode the invisible lines to locations where the zip-lining coordinates on their three-ringed carabiners would land them as closely as possible to their local expert without being detected.

The application that gave them the correct latitude and longitude coordinates to those locations as well as the topics of study and the names of the local experts was called LINLOC, which was short for line locations. Next was an app called SCIDAT, which stood for scientific data. This was the application Blaine and Tracey used to record everything they learned about the scientific topics. They simply texted the information into SCIDAT and pressed "send." That information would then electronically make its way to a data tracking screen in Uncle Cecil's basement laboratory, where he could monitor not only what they were learning but also where they were located.

Additionally, there were a few other applications on their phones. There were the microscope app and the archive app. Along with the high-resolution cameras, these two apps were designed for the purpose of capturing images needed to complete their SCIDAT data at each location. Finally, the last two applications were the compass app and the taser app. These served to keep the twins from getting lost and as a last resort of protection, respectively.

Satisfied that his niece and nephew's handheld devices were working properly and their science-learning adventures were progressing smoothly, Cecil let his shoulders fall in a moment of contentedness and leaned over, putting his weight on a shelf full of fluorescent bowling balls. As he did, all eight of the balls clinked to the floor and sprawled in all directions.

Chemical Departure

Bowling balls rolled in multiple directions. The Sassafras twins were tempted to feel embarrassed, but as they watched, the eight careening spheres spread. They saw the balls bounce around off chair legs, return racks, and people's feet. Amazingly, every ball somehow found its own lane and then started rolling toward the pins.

Everyone stopped to watch what the bowling balls would do. Slowly, each ball rolled, each ball managing to avoid a tumble into a gutter. Each ball was met by a crescendo of excited cheering.

The balls rolled on. The cheering got louder. The lights of the bowling alley flashed with zeal.

Then, to everyone's amazement—each runaway ball bowled a strike in its adopted lanes—one, two, three, four, five, six, seven, eight in succession. Every cheering voice ceased for a stunned second. Every eye sparkled with silent awe and found its way to Cecil Sassafras.

"Well, golly, golly, goodness!" Cecil exclaimed, surprised at what had occurred. "That was highly improbable."

After one more stunned second of silence, the Ambidextrous Octopus crowd burst forth with uproarious cheers for the striking scientist. Cecil was immediately surrounded by his fan club and greeted with happy handshakes and fervent high fives. The music in the bowling alley got louder. The lights shone brighter. The cheers rang on. And a fluffy, life-sized mascot of Ollie the Octopus ran out to give Cecil Sassafras a merry high forty.

Blaine and Tracey jumped in to celebrate their uncle, adding their own cheers and high fives!

Summer Beach celebrated the man she liked more than anyone else in the solar system in her own unique style. The frizzy blonde-haired, lab-coat-wearing scientist squealed with delight, waved her arms wildly around in the air, and skipped through the small crowd toward Cecil with the intention of wrapping him up in a happy jumping dance-hug. She dodged a fan here, side-stepped a fan there, ducked under the tentacled arms of Ollie, and collided into Cecil. The two friends, colleagues, and former junior-high classmates laughed, jumped, danced, and hugged, hardly noticing that Blaine and Tracey had somehow gotten tangled up in the hug with them.

The Ambidextrous crowd laughed and watched in fondness, slowly backing away from the quartet. Even Ollie, with his permanent smile, stepped back in appreciation of the man and the moment. The lights slowly dimmed, and the music dropped from a fast song to a slow ballad.

The twelve-year-old Sassafras twins noticed the change immediately and quickly pulled out of the dance-hug, but Cecil and Summer continued hugging. They danced on. Their jumping turned into slow steps. Their slapdash hug turned into a meaningful embrace, and as a slowly spinning disco ball lowered out of the ceiling; the dancing duo's eyes matched its sparkle.

Blaine and Tracey looked at each other with mouths open. Was this actually happening? Were Uncle Cecil and Summer . . . falling in love? Summer had never been too shy about her feelings for Cecil. However, with Uncle Cecil it was a different story altogether. The twins weren't sure if he was even aware at all that his old classmate was crushing on him. But right now, as the two danced under the sparkling glow, and Summer gazed dreamily at Cecil, the twelve-year-olds wondered if possibly their uncle was just now seeing it for the first time. Maybe he was now comprehending and maybe even . . . reciprocating . . . the same feeling.

"Summer, I . . . I . . ." Cecil started to say, rather shakily.

The twins looked at each other again. Tracey reached over and tugged excitedly at her brother's arm. Blaine let his mouth drop open even wider in anticipation. What was Uncle Cecil trying to say?

"Well golly, golly, goodness, Summer, I just . . . well . . . welly . . . I think maybe . . . Summer you are the most . . . whoa . . . wow . . . wow . . . I've . . . Summer, I just wanted to let you know that . . . manny-oh-manny . . . I . . ."

Summer waited, googly-eyed and expectant for her friend's forthcoming words.

"Summer Beach, I . . . it's . . . equation . . . science . . . focus!" Cecil took a deep breath. "I'm feeling a reaction—a bit like a chemical reaction. You know two compounds coming together. A reaction occurs and yields two new compounds, ones that are permanently changed to something new. Molecules are rearranged."

"RING!" The ring of a cell phone suddenly burst unwelcome into the middle of the scene.

"Summer, I'm saying . . . the equation . . ."

"RING!" Again, the phone rang.

"Whose phone was that?" the twins wondered as they instinctively reached for their own smartphones to see if it was them.

"Summer, welly-well, I think it's time to share the equation . . . $CS + SB \rightarrow L_2F_2$. It means . . ."

"RING!" Summer realized it was her phone that was doing the ringing. "Oh, Cecil, I'm so sorry. I have to get this," the female scientist said as she pulled away from Cecil and looked at the screen of her phone. "It's Wiggles and Fidget."

"Wiggles and Fidget?" Blaine and Tracey wondered silently. "The two short, stocky security guards they had met at the National Air and Space Museum in Washington, DC?" Both were curious why those two might be calling Summer.

"Oh, my," Summer answered as she held her phone up to her ear. "Uh huh, uh huh, I understand."

Now not only Blaine and Tracey but the whole crowd of bowlers at the Ambidextrous Octopus were leaning in to hear what the conversation might be about.

"Well, that's not good," Summer said with a sad sigh. She paused again and then said, "Okay, you two. Thanks for letting me know. I'll see if there's anything I can do to help. Bye."

Summer let the phone fall from her ear.

"It's the *Ranger* spacecraft," the female scientist shared with everyone listening. "It's been stolen."

A gasp released from the small crowd.

"You mean the one that was on display at the museum?" Tracey asked.

Summer nodded her head.

"Why would anyone want to steal that?" Blaine questioned.

Summer shrugged her shoulders and looked like she was about to say something when suddenly her cell phone rang again. Back to her ear the device went, and she immediately nodded in response to whoever was on the other side of the line.

"Yes, sir, I understand, sir," Summer replied respectfully and then listened for another while before responding again. "Yes, sir, I think we can do that, sir." There was more listening by Summer and more listening and curiosity from the Ambidextrous spectators.

"Yes, sir, I understand completely, sir. We will get right on it, sir," Summer confirmed. "Thank you, Captain, sir. Goodbye."

The female scientist again holstered her phone and looked at everyone. "That was Captain Marolf."

"Captain Marolf?" Blaine asked, surprised. "You mean Captain Marolf from the Swiss Secret Service? You know him?"

"Well, of course I do," Summer responded with a laugh. "He's the one who funded the space-worthy science lab you have been to several times on your journey."

"He did?" Blaine blubbered.

"Yes. My underground science lab—the one that doubles as a spaceship—was completely funded by the Triple S, also known as the Swiss Secret Service. At first Captain Marolf wanted to name the craft either *Triple S-2* for Summer's Spaceship or *Triple S-3* for Summer's Science Station. I thought that was too confusing; plus, I wanted to name it after my stellar lab assistant, Ulysses S Grant!"

At the mention of his name, the arctic ground squirrel puffed his chest out a little.

"So, as you already know, the name of my Swiss-funded labship is *Ulysses-1*."

"Yes," Tracey cut in, somewhat flustered and trying to get to the main point, "but why did he call you, Summer? What did Captain Marolf say?"

"He said Triple S spotted the stolen *Ranger* spacecraft via satellite."

Another gasp escaped from the crowd of bowlers.

"He said it looks like it's headed to the moon and . . ." Summer paused and turned toward Cecil. "He asked me to go after it, to use *Ulysses-1* to see if we can stop whoever it is who has stolen the *Ranger* spacecraft to retrieve it. Cecil, will that ruin our plans?"

Cecil stared blankly at Summer for a few long seconds as if he were still thinking about what he had previously been trying to say. Then he suddenly shook his head with red hair shaking and blue eyes beaming. "No, no, no. I don't think so, sweet Summer Thyme. I think we can movity-move forward with our plans . . . for the twins, right? Our plans for the next leg of their summer science learning—those plans?"

Summer nodded yes with frizzy hair bouncing and her own blue eyes beaming. All at once, Ollie the Octopus realized that the group of six needed some space to finish their conversation. He, along with the Ambidextrous Octopus patrons, who had been enthralled by the miracle bowler, the possible romance, and the unfolding spacecraft mystery, was realizing that the group needed to hash the rest of their plan out alone without the eyes and ears of a crowd of kind but curious bowlers. The mascot used all eight of his tentacled arms to slowly usher the onlookers away, leaving the six standing alone under the still-twirling disco ball.

Summer, who was still looking at Cecil, now asked her friend, "But Cecil, if I now have to go to the moon, how will I be able to . . . you know . . . and teach the twins about . . . all that?"

"I think it will still work fanterrifically!" Cecil answered again, full of his usual excitement. "Because you'll still be in your lab, you know, where you were going to go to do the topic-talking and all. So you can still do that! And what better place than the moon to talk about hydrogen! And because the twins have already earned their space legs, we can be sure that they'll do just fine on the moon!"

Growing excitement now began to bubble over in Summer. "Yes, Cecil, you're right! This could work out perfectly!"

Even President Lincoln and Ulysses S. Grant were nodding in agreement now.

"So, can I tell them, Cecil? Can I tell these two cutie-frasses what we'll be studying next?"

"Of coursety-course, Summer! Gopher it!"

"Chemistry!" Summer blurted out with more than a little energy. "And I get to be your first local expert on this leg!"

A lot of big things had happened today at the Ambidextrous Octopus bowling alley, and Blaine's and Tracey's heads and hearts were reeling, but they were both more than a little excited.

Blaine and Tracey let out squeals of excitement accompanied by a round of clapping.

"During your study of chemistry, you two will get to zip-line all over the globe studying the basics of chemistry solutions, properties, bonding, and more! You'll learn about the elements that make up our world, where they are found, and what they do! You'll learn about how most of the elements are not found in their purest form but instead in compounds. And you'll learn how compounds are substances composed of two or more elements. You'll learn about the two types of compounds found on Earth: organic compounds and inorganic compounds. Organic compounds are those that support life and contain carbon. Inorganic compounds are salts, metals, and so on. Isn't this all so exciting?"

The twins nodded and jumped along with their clapping.

"And as you two super-frasses probably gathered, the original plan was to start chemistry by zipping to my underground lab in Alaska, but now we'll get to do that *and* go to the moon!"

The twins, along with Summer, Cecil, and the two animals, entered a full-on happy jumping dance-hug. There were still quite a few unknowns about what was coming, but the Sassafras twins were starting a new subject of science, and they were beyond happy about that fact. One could even say they were "over the moon" about it.

Chapter 2: 3 ... 2 ... 1 ... Chemistry

Atomic Bits

Swirls of breathtaking exhilarating light surrounded them. The Sassafras twins were traveling on the invisible zip lines with huge smiles on their faces. Summer T. Beach and Ulysses S. Grant were with them, traveling at the speed of light from Uncle Cecil's neighborhood to Summer's lab.

The coordinates the LINLOC app had given them were familiar—longitude 67° 3' 58.91" N, latitude 163° 4' 12.24" W. Alaska had been a learning destination several times this summer. The local expert listed on LINLOC was also familiar because the local expert herself, Summer Beach, had spilled the beans about that already. The four topics for study, however, were not familiar—atoms, elements, the periodic table, and hydrogen. Blaine and Tracey could tell by looking at these topics that the subject of chemistry was going to be much different than anything they had studied thus far.

Suddenly, the four high-flying zip-line riders reached their destination with a jerk. Their carabiners automatically unclipped from the invisible lines, and all four slumped to the ground with tingling bodies, devoid of sight and strength. These sensations were all typical for landing after invisible zip-line travel. Slowly but surely, the normal physical faculties returned to the four travelers.

Blaine and Tracey picked themselves up from the ground.

Chapter 2: 3 ... 2 ... 1 ... Chemistry

They looked around, took in deep breaths of fresh air, and smiled. They were in a wide-open field with nothing but trees and mountains in the distance. It looked like the middle of nowhere, but they knew exactly where they were. In a minute, the Earth was going to open up, and they would fall onto a spiral slide that would gently glide them down to the underground lab. Summer and Ulysses also knew what was about to happen, as evidenced by the matching smiles on their faces.

Sure enough, within moments, the ground opened, and down the curves of the slide the four went, smiles intact, laughing. Each hit the bottom of the slide, skipped across a padded landing area, and careened to smooth stops on the glossy, clean, white floor of Summer's lab.

"Home sweet science-y home!" Summer exclaimed in joyful contentment as she jumped to her feet and smoothed her lab coat.

Blaine and Tracey got to their feet and let their eyes take in the familiar amazing space they were in. The circular underground lab was pristinely clean with smooth surfaces and shiny equipment. It was full of cutting-edge technology and eye-catching scientific displays like the cylindrical specimen tubes perfectly spaced out, showcasing their contents with bubbles and LED lights. There was also the floor-to-ceiling translucent data screen on which information could be read from both sides. Even now, the twins could see data about atoms being displayed on the screen.

"Oh, Summer, it's so good to be back in your lab. And it's so good to be starting another subject!" Tracey swooned.

Blaine agreed with a big nod of the head and then pointed at the data screen, asking excitedly, "What's all this about atoms? Wait, that's our first topic, right?"

"It sure is!" Summer shouted with a smile and outstretched arms. "This info about atoms is going to kick off the super fantastic and adventurous study of chemistry! Do you guys want to jump right into it?"

"Sure!" The Sassafras twins chorused in unison.

"Yay-yay-yay! Okay then! Yay!" Summer exclaimed at a happy shouting volume as she skipped to the data screen. "Okay, cutie-frasses, I'll read the information about atoms that we can see here on the screen, and when I'm finished, I'll make sure the data is uploaded straight to your smartphones!"

Blaine and Tracey nodded, knowing that as they progressed through their study of chemistry, they would send their Uncle Cecil data and images for each topic studied. He would view their information on his data screen in his basement, making sure they had learned what they needed to at each scientific stop.

"The Greeks are credited with being the first to come up with the concept of an atom," Summer read the data on the translucent screen. "They believed that matter could be cut into smaller and smaller pieces but that eventually you would get to a piece that could not be cut. So the word 'atom' comes from the Greek word '*atomos*,' which means 'uncuttable.'"

Usually, the twins had to add the data into their phones from memory. It was a nice break in Summer's lab because the data could be directly shared to their phones. However, they still made an effort to commit the information to memory as Summer read it.

"In 1808, John Dalton, an English scientist and schoolteacher, developed a theory about how atoms behave. His theory said that an element is composed of these tiny particles, and that in an ordinary chemical reaction, no atom of an element disappears. He also thought that compounds were formed when atoms of two or more elements combine. On the basis of his theory, scientists said that the atom was the smallest particle that makes up an element. The modern atomic theory is very similar to what Dalton proposed, except now we know the structure of an atom as well as the fact that there are sub particles that comprise an atom."

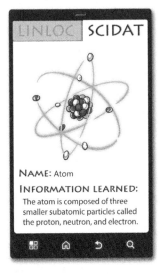

NAME: Atom
INFORMATION LEARNED: The atom is composed of three smaller subatomic particles called the proton, neutron, and electron.

"Wow, the theory all started with a schoolteacher?" Blaine mused.

Summer nodded.

"That's amazing," Tracey said, impressed. "Maybe when we get back to school after summer break, we should show a little more respect to our teachers."

Blaine agreed as Summer smiled.

"Now, let's take a closer look at the structure of an atom," the scientist started again. "The atom comprises three smaller subatomic particles called the proton, neutron, and electron. A proton is a positively charged particle that resides in the nucleus at the center of an atom. A neutron is a particle with no charge that also resides in the nucleus of an atom. An electron is a negatively charged particle that resides in a cloud around the nucleus, which is called and electron shell."

"And lastly," Summer paused for a breath and then read the information displayed on the floor-to-ceiling data screen, "atoms have an equal number of protons and electrons, which gives them no net charge. In other words, normally the positive charges from protons are canceled out by the negative charges of the electrons. Regarding protons and neutrons, generally an atom of an element has the same number of neutrons as protons. Of course, there are exceptions to these two rules, called ions and isotopes. Ions are atoms or groups of atoms that have become charged by gaining or losing one or more electron. Positive ions have lost one or more electron, and negative ions have gained one or more electron. Isotopes are . . ." Summer started to say but then she paused and moved in front of the text on the screen, smiling and waving her arms.

"Actually, I'm going to save isotopes for one of your friends to share about later! Even so, let me upload this to your phones." Summer Beach turned and pushed the upload button on the large screen. Immediately, the twins' phones buzzed as the information about atoms was uploaded directly. They resisted the urge to peek at the last bit of SCIDAT and turned to receive the happy jumping dance-hug they were sure was coming.

But before it did, Summer turned and shared more about atoms, "And here's another thing that's cool about atoms—they combine to make molecules and compounds! Molecules are formed when two or more atoms of an element join together. Compounds are formed when two or more atoms from different elements join together. For example, H_2 (hydrogen gas) is a molecule because two atoms of hydrogen are joined together. However, because there is only one type of element present, H_2 is not a compound. In contrast, H_2O (water) is a molecule because the three atoms, one oxygen atom and two hydrogen atoms, have been joined together to form it. It is also a compound because it contains two different elements, hydrogen and oxygen. So, all compounds are molecules, but not all molecules are compounds!"

Now, the twins knew a happy jumping dance-hug was coming their way. However, before it did, Summer's phone rang . . . again.

"Goodness me, this thing is awfully noisy today, isn't it?" Summer said as she answered the call. "Hello? Well, hi there, Paul! I would ask how you're doing, but I heard from Wiggles and Fidget about the stolen lunar module, so I assume you're not doing as great as you could be . . . uh huh, uh huh . . . yes, well, we are actually going to go after it ourselves using *Ulysses-1*…uh huh, uh huh . . . okie dokie, friend, we'll keep you posted! Okay, you too… bye."

"Was that Paul Sims from the Air and Space Museum?" Tracey asked Summer as she hung up her phone.

The scientist nodded in confirmation. "Poor guy," Summer said with a rare frown. "First there was the attempted heist of the guidance component from that old Soviet rocket, and now the lunar module has been stolen. So many unfortunate things have happened to my old buddy and junior high classmate as of late. He's such a nice guy."

In Washington DC, Paul Sims hung up the phone, and immediately the big fake smile on his face faded away completely. His countenance now scrunched up into a mixture of concern and spite. Summer probably thought he was a nice guy. Little did she know how malicious he was.

The door to his office was already closed, but he locked it now for good measure. He didn't want anyone walking in on him as he stewed—especially not those two annoying security guards, Wiggles and Fidget. He stalked from the door to his large mahogany desk and flumped heavily down onto his plush, black leather swivel chair.

"So now Summer knows about the lunar module," he angrily whispered. "And she's going after it. I doubt there's anything she can do to stop them, but she has surprised me before."

Paul began to nervously wring his hands. "Have I gone too far? No, no! It's totally worth it. I'm rich now, but I'm only going to get richer—so much richer."

The thought of money brought a smile to his face, but it was fleeting as anxiety returned. "But are those three trustworthy? More than that, are they capable? Can they pull off this master scheme?"

He threw back his head into the headrest with a thud as he thought about the Rotary Club—not the group of little old neighborhood ladies who met for the purpose of good will and philanthropy but the other Rotary Club, the one made up of the three sinister Slote siblings—Alexander, Graham, and Belle. The two brothers and one sister had joined together to form an evil club, one bent on destroying all the world's cell phones, forcing everyone to go back to using rotary phones.

The wicked trio had attempted to take the guidance component of an SS-20 Soviet missile that was on display right in this museum where Paul sat as curator. Evidently, they were going to use it to complete a missile they were going to launch into space—one that would destroy a satellite, rendering cell phone use impossible. This would usher in the glorious rebirth of rotary telephone use. Their attempt had been thwarted by Summer, the security guards, those kids, the janitors, a few animals, a robot, and himself.

However, the failed heist had given Paul's greedy mind an idea. He knew how wealthy the Slotes were. He knew how badly they wanted that guidance component. And he knew that the destruction of only one satellite would not take out all of the world's cell phones. So he had bailed the Rotary Club out of jail. They had been more than happy to pay him a ridiculous amount of money for the guidance component, which he had secretly taken after the failed heist.

"But why stop there?" Paul had thought. There were many more things at the Air and Space Museum the Rotary Club might be interested in. If they were ready and willing to fire a missile at a satellite, why not fire multiple missiles? Or, better yet, why not travel to the moon and set up a remote station from which to launch their attack against cell phones? They could establish an attack station, while he made a lunar fueling station—that's right, a fuel station on the moon.

Paul had recently heard about the hypothetical idea to establish a fueling station on the moon. He didn't completely understand it, but basically, it's known that sections of the moon are covered in ice, which, of course, is frozen water. Water, H_2O, is made up of two parts hydrogen and one part oxygen. If you split hydrogen and oxygen, and then liquefy those constituents, you have rocket fuel. If there was a station on the moon that could provide rocket fuel for spacecraft, it would significantly lighten the needed fuel loads of the different crafts leaving Earth, greatly cutting costs for the entire space industry and making that fuel station owner mega-rich!

It had been a calculated risk to steal and sell the guidance component to the Rotary Club, but that was small in comparison to the risk of stealing and selling the lunar module. On top of that, he had sold a lunar rover vehicle to them! That act should go unnoticed longer because the rover had been in storage. The Rotary Club, who already had a working and space-worthy rocket, now had a working missile, a way to land on the moon, and a way to travel on the moon. Unfortunately, if you looked hard enough, pretty much everything led back to him. The probability of him being caught was much higher now than it had been when the guidance component had been the only missing item, but even with the raised stakes and anxiety, he still thought it was worth the risk. He was going to be so, so, rich. And, as far as he could tell, everyone around him still thought he was a responsible, law-abiding, nice guy.

Dancing Elements

"So as you two already know," Summer was saying in review, "the invisible zip lines work a little different in space than they do here on Earth. Here you two cuties use longitude and latitude coordinates and specially designed three-ringed carabiners, but in space you'll use astronomical units (AUs) and zip-zop cuffs. The astronomical units help us measure distances in space for the zip-zop cuffs, which are digital carabiners of sorts. Also, the invisible zip lines can't be traveled on through the Earth's atmosphere. However, once this wonderful spacecraft we are in breaks through the atmosphere, the lines can be freely traveled on throughout space."

Blaine and Tracey smiled, remembering all of these details.

"But what about our Linc 2.0 IEVA spacesuits?" Blaine asked. "We can't travel in space without those."

"You're absolutely right. And that's why…" Summer started a response but was interrupted by the sound of the room's large, egg-shaped door sliding open. To their immense joy, in rolled the Sassafras twins' favorite electronic friend. Here was REESE the robot carrying with him the spacesuits Blaine had just mentioned.

"REESE!" the twelve-year-olds exclaimed as they rushed to

give him a hug. The twins had met him at the beginning of their study of astronomy, and he had been all those things and more. He was about four feet in height. He had a trapezoid-shaped head that was topped with small antennae; had speakers in place of ears; two big, round eyes; and a light box that served as a sort of mouth. His torso was oval-shaped and housed both a data screen and a storage compartment. He had two flexible yet strong metallic arms and was supported at his base with a swiveling, oblong wheel with tank-like treads.

"Blaine and Tracey Sassafras," REESE vocalized in his robotic voice. "So very good to see you again. I am so excited we will be traveling to the moon together. Here are your spacesuits."

"REESE is going with us?" Tracey asked happily, looking to Summer for confirmation.

"He sure is!" the female scientist responded. "REESE will be along for the ride as we travel to the moon and as we study the remaining topics for this location—elements, the periodic table, and hydrogen. Oh! Oh! And I believe he has prepared a little ditty about isotopes."

"Isotopes?" Tracey asked.

"Little ditty?" Blaine added.

Summer laughed instead of answering and then started danced to a song that was evidently playing in her mind. "Whatcha think, REESE?" Summer asked as she enthusiastically completed dance moves probably only ever attempted at awkward junior high dances back when the twins' parents were young. "You ready to bust out the wicked-cool hip-hop song you prepared about isotopes?"

Now REESE also danced—his moves were much better than Summer's in that they looked less like convulsions. He answered her in the affirmative with an explosion of light and sound from his trapezoid head. REESE started his rap.

> *Wooka, wooka, wooka.*
> *Isotopes add it up,*
> *Add it up.*
> *Wooka, wooka, wooka.*
> *Isotopes add it up,*
> *Add it up.*

"This must be the chorus," Blaine and Tracey thought as they started dancing their own, not robotic, not jerky, but a cool, modern style of dance. REESE continued with the song.

> *Hey, y'all, step on over, step on up and*
> *Look at this! Look at this!*
> *Some atoms have additional neutrons in*
> *Nucleus! Nucleus!*
> *And we call these atoms isotopes of an*
> *Element! Element!*
> *Learning chemistry can be cool, but can you*
> *Handle it? Handle it?*
>
> *Wooka, wooka, wooka.*
> *Isotopes add it up,*
> *Add it up.*
> *Wooka, wooka, wooka.*
> *Isotopes add it up,*
> *Add it up.*

Not to be outdone by the robot and the humans, Ulysses S. Grant, the arctic ground squirrel, was busting moves at a frenetic pace. REESE started the second verse.

> *Same atomic number but a different*
> *Atomic mass, mass, mass!*
> *Please, y'all, remember this in case you are*
> *Asked in class! Asked in class!*
> *Atomic mass and atomic number, are*
> *They the same? They the same?*

THE SASSAFRAS SCIENCE ADVENTURES

CHAPTER 2: 3 ... 2 ... 1 ... CHEMISTRY

Nope! Not always! When if differs, isotopes
Are to blame! Are to blame!

Wooka, wooka, wooka.
Isotopes add it up,
Add it up.
Wooka, wooka, wooka.
Isotopes add it up,
Add it up.

As cheesy as this moment was with the dancing, lights, and subpar hip-hop, it was moments like this that had wooed the Sassafras twins into loving science. Even in the silliness, they appreciated Summer, Ulysses, and REESE. They sure had a unique way of presenting scientific information! So the twelve-year-olds danced on as the robot began his third and final verse.

So, the figures of an element, let us
Break it down! Break it down!
Atomic number is how many protons
Can be found! Can be found!
Atomic mass is a bit different, it
Deals with weight! Deals with weight!
Protons, neutrons, electrons—add 'em up, you've
Got it great! Got it great!

Wooka, wooka, wooka.
Isotopes add it up,
Add it up.
Wooka, wooka, wooka.
Isotopes add it up!
Add it up!

At the conclusion of the rap, a final spray of exciting lights and sound came from REESE. Summer completed the lawnmower, the sprinkler, and the shopping cart dance moves in succession. Ulysses S. Grant skittered onto the shoulders of Blaine and Tracey, and the trio struck a pose.

"Wowie!" Summer exclaimed. "That was awesome! Great job, REESE! My, oh my, what a great song!"

The scientist reached over and gave the robot a fist bump. "So, what did you think, twinkie-frasses? Do you feel like you know all about isotopes now?"

Blaine and Tracey both nodded, but the female Sassafras had a question. "I feel like we know about isotopes, and atoms too because of the SCIDAT you read on the screen earlier, but what about elements? You mentioned elements but didn't explain them."

Even though REESE's song was over, and the lab was absent of music, Summer answered Tracey's question by firing back up the lawnmower dance as she made her way to the floor-to-ceiling data screen.

"Good point, Tracey, good point! Why don't we hop on the data screen here and see what we can find?" Upon reaching the screen, Summer switched her dance moves to the shopping cart. She was dancing in place, motioning like she was pushing the cart. Then, instead of pantomiming that she reached for groceries, as the second part of the dance required, she was reaching over and tapped the data screen to pull up information about elements.

"Ahhh, here it is," the scientist said as data about the desired topic popped up. "Elements are a type of matter that cannot be broken down into two or more substances," Summer immediately read the data even as she continued dancing.

"For instance, when you hold a lump of iron ore, you are holding the element iron, which contains billions and billions of iron atoms. More precisely, elements are substances made up of one type of atom that cannot be broken down by a chemical reaction to form a simpler substance." At the mention of chemical reactions, Summer got a far-off, dreamy look on her face.

Tracey noticed the pause. Blaine didn't. He was in his own world doing his own silent version of the shopping cart, which looked to Tracey more like something that should've been called the dying flamingo.

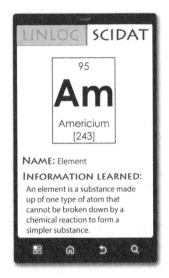

Tracey cleared her throat, and Summer shook her head, beginning again, "In 1661 Robert Boyle showed that there were more than just the four classical elements. "However, it was not until 1789 that Antione Lavoisier wrote down the first list of elements, which contained only 33. Eighty years later, Dimitri Mendeleev was the first to organize the 66 known elements of his time into a table that displayed the relationships among those elements. His table became the basis for our modern periodic table. As the field of science moved into the modern era, new instruments such as the spectroscope, have allowed for more elements to be discovered. At the time of this article, there are 118 known elements, 92 of which can be found naturally. The remainder must be synthetically produced, usually by man-made nuclear reactions."

Tracey noticed Blaine's dance moves had progressed, well maybe regressed was a better word, from the shopping cart to the dying flamingo to what she would now call earthquake in the city. She was tempted to roll her eyes at her brother, but she found herself dancing her own little shimmy and shake as Summer Beach finished up the SCIDAT data about elements.

"Gold was one of the first elements to be discovered and used. It has been used for much of recorded history and was used extensively by the ancient Egyptians in the tombs of their pharaohs. Biblical records show that Tubal-Cain used the element iron. However, the first concept of an element was described by the ancient Greek philosophers, who said there were four elements: fire, earth, water, and air. They believed all substances were a combination of these four elements. Today we have come a long way in our knowledge of the elements. Elements, like gold, copper, and iron, are familiar to us. Other elements are necessary to life, such as oxygen, nitrogen, and phosphorous. Then there are elements like aluminum, which is used for foil and other products, and silicone, which is used in nearly every electronic product on the market. Each and every element can be found arranged according to atomic number on the periodic table."

Summer had read to the bottom of the screen, completing the information that was there. She pushed the upload button, and immediately the entire data set found its way to the twins' phones. Blaine and Tracey sent the data they had so far to Uncle Cecil's data screen located in his basement. They were happy about getting all this new information but somewhat sad it meant the dance party was probably over. However, knowing Summer, there were sure to be more dance parties in the future! In addition, the next thing on the docket was . . . traveling to the moon . . .

"We've landed," the dark, scratchy voice of Alexander Slote came through the satellite phone, the irony of which was not lost on Paul.

"Good," the museum curator responded. "But you better get right to the main mission because you now have a tail. You've been spotted, and they're coming after you."

"What? Who?"

"Evidently the Swiss Secret Service spotted you on satellite, and they don't like space flights and moon landings that are unsanctioned. They're sending a craft after you."

Alexander responded to that with a snarl of disgust and then spat out, "The faster we start blasting satellites, the better."

"Fine, you do that," Paul agreed. "But don't forget about staking a claim for the fueling station and all the reconnaissance that action will require. You owe me."

"Yeah, yeah, yeah. We owe you. We know. We'll do all that we discussed. You can be sure of it."

"You'd better! And you better do it quick because they're coming!" Paul said a little more threateningly than he would have liked. He was purposefully leaving out the fact that it was Summer who was coming after them because he didn't think that would add any motivation for the three.

"Reading you loud and clear, Paul. We'll get right to it," Alexander shouted through the sat phone and then hung up.

Paul hung up his end and leaned back in his chair.

The barrel-chested man ran his fingers across his thick, white mustache and sighed. Maybe he had been too hasty in sending DeBlose on sabbatical. Sure, Evan deserved it. He was exhausted after apprehending Bogdanovich and Archer, as well as traveling to space to repair the satellite, but Evan DeBlose was also his best agent. He'd never told Evan that, but he had a feeling the agent knew it.

Yes, Evan deserved the sabbatical, but he sure could use him right now. Not only did DeBlose have the most time in space out of all his agents, but he also seemed to perform the best under pressure.

Captain Marolf moved his fingers from his mustache to his perfectly cut flattop and sighed again. He knew he needed to perform under pressure. He couldn't let his agents see him like this—not even one sigh. He needed to lead them as they attempted to stop this unsanctioned spacecraft.

While looking at information from the newly repaired satellite, they had spotted the craft. As soon as they had, the captain had gotten a lump in his throat. This craft was up to no good. He could feel it.

He knew Triple S needed to go after it. But with Evan DeBlose on sabbatical, it would have to be the next agent up.

Who was that? Summer T. Beach.

She wasn't a full-blown agent. She was more of a freelancer, but she had a craft worthy of space and hours in space herself. So he had sent Summer to the moon after the rogue craft.

Captain Marolf now went from sighing to chuckling. Why was he so worried?

Yes, Evan was out of pocket, but Summer had never let him down. Triple S had invested millions into Summer and her lab/craft there in Alaska, and she had always delivered. Plus, the woman had more energy and joy than anyone he had ever met.

Sure, he wasn't the biggest fan of her happy jumping dance-hugs, but the work ethic and expertise she brought to the table far outweighed any awkwardness.

She could do this.

She'd be able to go nab this mystery craft.

The big captain stood from the chair in his office, walking through the door out into the control room, where everyone was awaited him. "Okay, people," he boomed, full of confidence. "Let's go get this rogue spacecraft!"

Chapter 3: Launching Lunar Adventures

Periodic and Romantic Tables

"Golly gee, whiskered willikers, President Lincoln!" the red-headed scientist exclaimed as he looked at the data screen in his basement. "I sure am proud of that niece and nephew of mine! They've gotten through six subjects of science with flying colors, and here they are on a seventh subject, soaring yet again! They've already sent in their SCIDAT data and pictures for atoms and elements." President Lincoln nodded.

"Lookie here now! Look what's popped up on the data screen. Here is their SCIDAT data and a wonderiffic picture from the archive app about the periodic table!" Cecil exclaimed.

The prairie dog lab assistant responded by dropping a bag of macadamia nuts he'd been snacking on, skittering up to the messy desktop, and looking with twinkly eyes at the new SCIDAT the Sassafras twins had sent.

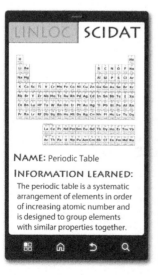

"Yessity yes, sir, the periodic table," Cecil said as he sidled up next to his rodent buddy. "Let's read what they sent—the periodic table is a systematic arrangement of elements in order of increasing atomic number and is designed to group elements with similar properties together." Cecil read the data aloud as it had come in on his screen. He didn't always read it out loud, but when he did, he did it with enthusiasm because, man oh man, he loved science. And he loved his niece and nephew. And he also loved Sum…Summ . . . somebody else too.

"The periodic table gives the following information for each element: the atomic number, the atomic mass, and the symbol. As you move from left to right on the table, the atomic number and atomic mass of the element increases. The same is true as you travel down the periodic table. The atomic number is the number of protons found in the nucleus of an atom. The atomic mass is the total weight of the protons, neutrons, and electrons in each atom. Sometimes this can vary if there are isotopes of the element, so the atomic mass given on the periodic table is an average of those varying weights. The symbol is the 1-, 2-, or 3-letter code that scientists use for the element. These codes are accepted internationally to remove language barriers when discussing chemical compounds. Some are easy, like O for oxygen. But some make less sense like Pb for lead. This is because the symbol is typically based on the Latin name for the element, which in the case of lead is *plumbum*. Chemists use the symbol of an element when referring to it in a compound or equation, so the symbols are important to know."

THE SASSAFRAS SCIENCE ADVENTURES

Cecil Sassafras was indeed full of love as he read the SCIDAT aloud, and although he was coming to grips with the fact that love was more than an equation. He still had a chemistry-like equation running through his head—CS + SB -> $L_2 F_2$. Could it be? He hoped so.

"The original periodic table was created by Russian chemist Dmitri Mendeleev," Cecil continued enthusiastically reading. "He wrote it almost 30 years before J.J. Thomson discovered the electron, close to 45 years before Ernest Rutherford found the nucleus of an atom, and more than 50 years before scientists determined the proton and neutron made up the nucleus of the atom. Mendeleev proposed a primitive version of today's periodic table as he was writing a textbook about general chemistry. Through his research, he was struck by the fact that elements' chemical properties varied with the atomic mass. So he drew up a table to show these relationships. In a stroke of genius, he left gaps for elements that had not yet been discovered and even went so far as to predict the properties of those missing elements when they were finally discovered. Their properties were remarkably similar to what Mendeleev had predicted. Even though our modern-day table looks quite a bit different from what Dmitri drew up, we still give him credit for the original idea of the periodic table."

As Cecil finished reading the freshly sent SCIDAT, he also had a stroke of genius. If it was truly possible that CS + SB -> $L_2 F_2$, that Cecil Sassafras plus Summer Beach yields Lifelong Love and Forever Friendship, then, like Mendeleev, he also needed to come up with a table. Dmitri Mendeleev set up the periodic table. Cecil would set up a romantic table. Dmitri's table helped everyone better understand elements and their properties. Cecil's table would help Summer better understand his love for her.

His recent epiphany at the Ambidextrous Octopus had changed everything. Standing under the bowling alley's slowly spinning disco ball face-to-face with Summer, Cecil had suddenly realized that he loved the woman. He didn't only like her as a friend. He didn't only appreciate her as a colleague. He loved her.

"I love her, Linc-Dog, I surely durely do. I love Summer Thyme Beach!" the red-headed scientist announced to his lab assistant. Then, as he twirled around his basement, his mind twirled around memory lane.

Cecil had first met Summer in junior high school chemistry class. Cecil had annoyed most of his teachers, especially the science teacher, because he asked so many questions. That, combined with the fact that he was both forgetful and dyslexic, didn't make him a popular pupil. None of his classmates seemed to get him either, mostly because they thought him so strange.

Then one day, in walked Summer T. Beach to his first-hour chemistry class. She was a pretty little girl who had just moved to the states from Switzerland. The chemistry teacher, Mr. Womberfraggle, paired Summer and Cecil as lab partners. It was an immediate friendship with instant chemistry. Unlike Cecil, Summer was neither forgetful nor dyslexic, but like him, she was brilliant and passionate about all things science.

The two were like peas in a pod all the way through junior high and high school. They attended separate universities for their undergraduate degrees, their master's degrees, and their doctorates. Even so, they remained friends and always kept each other in the loop on any and all projects they were doing. Through it all, not once had Cecil ever thought about Summer in a romantic light—until now.

When Summer had gone to space with Train and Blaisey for their study of astronomy, Cecil had realized how much he missed Summer. He had taken it to heart when Summer had defended him and spoken such kind words about him at the Left-Handed Turtle when Adrianna Archer had tried to "transform" him. However, the true epiphany hadn't come until yesterday when he and Summer had slow danced under the disco ball at the Ambidextrous Octopus. It was as factual as two parts hydrogen plus one part oxygen yields water. He loved her. Cecil Sassafras loved Summer Beach. He probably had all along.

Now, he would jump to the joyful task of setting up a table for her right here in his basement. It would be a romantic table. It would be an inviting table. And it would be set and ready for Summer's return at the end of the twins' study of chemistry. Cecil was a man floating way up on that ninth cloud.

However, he did have one question nagging his mind. So, he stopped twirling and memory-lane walking and came back down to Earth. He asked the question out loud.

"But does Summer love me, Linc-Dawg?"

"Yes!" Summer Beach shouted in elation as *Ulysses-1* touched down safely on the moon. "We have successfully landed!"

Blaine and Tracey's eyes were wide with wonder. Yes, they had previously traveled all over the solar system, but that had done nothing to dull the sheer awe they were experiencing right now as Summer's spaceship touched down on the moon. They knew they were here to retrieve a stolen lunar module, to apprehend the burglary suspects, and to study hydrogen. However, right now they were enjoying this thrilling moment. They were actually on the moon!

They had donned their space suits. They had launched from the field in Alaska. They had broken through the atmosphere and they had landed on the moon. Is this what Neil Armstrong, Buzz Aldrin, and Michael Collins had felt way back in 1969 when they had been the first humans to land here? Wow, this was amazing!

Summer and Ulysses were excited too, and even REESE,

who in theory couldn't feel emotions, was sporting a big smile. In her extreme excitement, Summer wrapped everyone in a happy dance-hug of sorts, but it was more of a happy, floating dance-hug because of the lower level of gravity on the moon.

In a matter of minutes, the group of five found themselves standing at the craft's open door, about to step out onto the surface of the moon.

"Summer, I think you should take the first step," Tracey offered.

"Really?" Summer giggled with a big smile that could be seen through the circular, transparent helmet of her space suit.

"Really," Tracey answered. "You've taught us so much, you've been the best local expert, and we appreciate you!"

Blaine, Ulysses, and REESE nodded in agreement. Summer giggled some more then turned from the craft toward the expanse of the moon. She lifted her space boot into the air, and then planted it firmly down on the lunar surface.

"One small step for a scientist, one giant leap for science . . . and the Sassafras twins . . . and studying the topic of hydrogen . . . and apprehending some bad guys . . . and . . ."

"And let's go," shouted Blaine happily because he couldn't stand waiting anymore.

The boy bounded onto the dusty surface of the moon, and his companions followed. They bounced and took big leaps across the barren yet magical landscape. They were laughing, smiling, and enjoying every moment of the experience until they saw it.

There, off in the dusty distance, stood the stolen lunar module.

THE SASSAFRAS SCIENCE ADVENTURES

"The claim is staked, boss man," Alexander Slote's scratchy voice informed over the satellite phone.

Paul smiled. He couldn't tell if Alexander was being sarcastic or not by calling him "boss man," but that didn't matter because his claim for the lunar fuel station site was staked!

"Excellent," Paul responded, trying not to sound as excited as he was. "And what about the site? What's it like? Did you have to travel all the way to the moon's south pole to find a suitable location?"

"We nearly did," the oldest Slote answered. "The spot we landed the lunar module in was fairly flat with no signs of ice at all. But as we traveled southward in the lunar rover, we began to encounter more and more craters, deep, dark craters that never see the light of the sun. They look to be filled with endless ice."

"Endless ice?"

"Yeah, boss man, endless ice."

"And that's where you staked my claim? Right there in the middle of all those deep, dark craters?"

"That's right, Sims. That's where we staked your claim. We planted a flag deep in the soil right at the edge of the biggest one. It's a crater as big as a lake, blanketed in darkness and filled with ice."

Paul's smiled as he thought to himself, "Endless ice. That meant rocket fuel, endless rocket fuel. But more than that, it meant riches, endless riches." His smile got even bigger before he said out loud, "And what about the surrounding area? You said there are numerous craters in that location?"

"Yeah, boss man, that's what I said. There are lots of craters, lots of ice, but that's not why we, the Rotary Club, signed up for this mission, remember?"

"I remember."

"We did what you asked us to do. We staked your claim for the fueling station. We're done with that. We're moving on to our job. We're going to launch a missile from this spot. And with that missile, we will begin the destruction of all the world's cell phones!"

Paul was about to make a quip in response to Alexander's last statement, but before he could, the wild, rotary telephone-using man erupted in an explosion of evil laughter. The museum curator knew that was the end of the conversation, so he hung up the satellite phone.

Soon, it would no longer work if the Rotary Club's wicked plan was carried out successfully.

"Okay, people," the captain's big voice boomed. "We know they found the lunar module, and we know it was empty. Now the team has found tracks leading away from the module. I know we're looking at satellite images here, not live video, but we want to offer as much help as we can to Summer and her team."

"Agent Jorgen Wuthrich," Captain Marolf barked in the direction of a dark-haired, short, well-built male agent. "Can you tell us anything about those tracks?"

Swiss Secret Service Agent Wuthrich carefully looked at the image displayed on the large screen here in command central in front of the scores of tense yet hopeful Triple S agents.

"Yes, sir, Captain Marolf, sir," Agent Wuthrich responded after concentrating a moment. "Those appear to be tracks left by a lunar rover vehicle."

"Okay, good, Agent Wuthrich," Marolf affirmed, putting his fists on his hips. "And in which direction are those tracks headed?"

"South, sir. Toward the dark side of the moon."

Fueling Hydrogen

"How is everyone's ride experience so far?" REESE the robot asked as his treads churned skillfully and effectively over the surface of the moon.

"We're doing great, REESE!" Summer responded. "You keep chug chug chugging away and follow those tracks!"

"My pleasure," the robot answered as he leaned forward a bit more to pick up speed.

The group of five had found the lunar module, but it was empty. Additionally, they had found tracks leading away from the stolen craft. Captain Marolf, from Triple S headquarters, had given them instructions to follow the tracks, which appeared to have been made by a lunar rover vehicle. The big captain had warned them to use caution but to proceed. Here they were now, traveling away from *Ulysses-1* toward the lunar horizon.

The three humans and the one ground squirrel were very thankful for REESE, who was such an amazingly versatile robot. The storage compartment in his torso was filled with all kinds of hand attachments designed for a variety of purposes. Right now, the robot was pulling his four companions behind him on rollerboards that were connected via a hand attachment to his long and strong flexible metal arms. Blaine and Tracey sat on one; Summer and Ulysses were on the other. The whole scenario reminded the Sassafras twins of their escapades on Mars. There they had followed footprints from a module to find a lost space tourist. That story had turned out okay. The twins hoped this one would as well.

As they rolled quickly forward, Blaine and Tracey noticed

the ground becoming rougher. They saw craters everywhere. Many were quite large and looked deep and dark. If the twins were honest, they looked kind of creepy. The light cast over the moonscape around them felt eerie because the sun looked like a small dot barely peeking up over the horizon. It wasn't setting. It wasn't rising. It was resting, refusing neither to disappear nor to shed ample light. "This phenomenon must have something to do with the moon's orbit around the Earth," both twins thought in sync.

REESE was doing a great job maneuvering through the terrain as he continued to follow the tracks of the rogue rover. However, it was evident to all that from here on, it would not be a smooth ride. The roller-board riders were finding it more difficult to hang on as they hit bigger bumps and swerved around bigger holes. Still, the robot designed for exploration, entertainment, and scientific enhancement whirred on—over and around every obstacle until they reached the biggest crater they had seen yet by far.

"Whoa!" Blaine exclaimed. "This thing's as big as a lake! A huge lake!"

Tracey agreed. "And it looks deep! Deep and dark. Like maybe it's filled with ice."

"That's exactly right," Summer confirmed Tracey's suspicions. "The moon has incalculable amounts of ice all over, hidden in its numerous craters and chasms." Even though the facts were somewhat ominous, the jolly female scientist had a way of saying things that made them sound happy and exciting. However, the twins weren't ready to be happy or excited. Even as Summer finished the statement, they both spotted something that made their stomachs drop.

Blaine managed to point, and Tracey managed to speak. "Look," she whispered loudly. "There it is . . . up ahead—the lunar rover we've been tracking!"

Sure enough, a hundred yards or so in front of them at the crater's edge, almost hidden in the shadowy light, they could barely make out the outline of the mysterious vehicle. However, that's not all they saw. Standing upright next to the rover was what looked like, quite possibly, a . . .

"Missile?" Tracey asked out loud, while Blaine managed only to point.

Summer studied the distant scene for a moment, then nodded. "Well, golly, I think you two are right. That does look like a missile."

"But why would anyone put a missile on the moon?" Tracey asked with a whisper.

"I don't know," Summer answered with no fear at all in her voice. "Let's go find out."

REESE turned his treads again, a little slower this time. The five Triple S representatives cautiously began their approach toward the insidious location. Rolling through the shadows as quietly as possible, the group reached the spot.

REESE stopped. None of the roller-board riders moved a muscle. All remained still and silent. Here was the lunar rover, whose tracks they'd been following. Here was the tall, upright object they'd seen from afar, which indeed looked like a missile. But where were the burglars? The thieves? The masterminds who had brought this stuff to this spot? There was no one here. Or at least, that is what it appeared to be at first.

Suddenly, seemingly out of nowhere, there was a stick of dynamite laying on the ground in front of them.

"Where did that come from?" Blaine shouted.

"Look, the fuse is lit, and it's burning down quick!" Tracey added details in horror.

REESE cranked his treads to life and quickly whipped around

in an attempt to flee the danger and protect his companions, but it was too late. The dynamite's sparkling wick had already burned down to its end. A violent explosion was inevitable.

The twins instinctively ducked their heads.

"Ahhhh!" Tracey shrieked.

"Eeeek!" Blaine squeaked.

"Mmmmmmm, curious," Summer mused, her voice still absent of fear.

Blaine and Tracey waited . . . and waited some more. There was no explosion.

"Oh, man, that was a dud," a female voice said.

"Wait," the Sassafrases thought. "That's not Summer. Where did that voice come from?"

The twins raised their heads again and immediately saw who the new female voice belonged to.

"Belle Slote?" Tracey exclaimed, still whisper-asking.

"And look," Blaine added with a point. "Alexander and Graham, too!"

The three members of the infamous Rotary Club, decked out in space suits, emerged ominously from a hidden spot to face the five.

"A dud," Belle repeated, referring to the stick of dynamite that had been lit but not exploded, "a big fat dud. C'mon, Graham, why did you bring the dynamite all the way to the moon if you were gonna bring duds?"

"Because I like blowing stuff up, Belle!"

"Well, you can't very well blow stuff up if you're using duds, now, can you?"

"How was I supposed to know that stick was going to be a dud? Sometimes they just . . ."

"Enough, you two," Alexander spoke authoritatively, interrupting the argument. "Drop the bickering, and let us get reacquainted with these who've come to apprehend us . . . again." Alexander looked menacingly through his helmet directly toward the five. "That is why you've come, is it not? To apprehend us?"

"It is," Summer stated.

"Now why would you want to do that?" Alexander mused, dropping the menace from his voice, replacing it with obviously fake kindness. "We became such good friends after you prohibited us from acquiring the guidance component and got us thrown in jail."

"That's just it," Tracey spoke up, now talking at a normal volume. "How did you guys get out of jail? And what are you doing here on the moon?"

Alexander's response at first was just a scratchy laugh, which crescendoed into an answer with menace. "We got out of jail. We got our hands on the component. We got to the moon! Now everything's in place to destroy all the cell phones in the world, ushering in the dawn of a new age of rotary telephone use!"

At that all three Slotes threw back their heads in guttural laughter. All the wicked plans the Sassafrases had thought they had halted at the museum had, in the end, actually been realized.

"Why? How?" Tracey asked desperately.

"Why? How?" Alexander repeated Tracey's questions. "Why of course it's because we have a racket on rotary telephones. And how will we pull off this great cell phone destruction? We are going to set up a station on the moon from which to launch missiles into space, targeting satellites. Take down the satellites. Take down the cell phones!"

The gravity of the situation suddenly hit the Sassafras twins like a ton of bricks, an 80s-style ton of brick phones, that is. If the Rotary Club was successful in taking down satellites, not only would that devastate the entire world as it currently operated, but it would also prohibit them from studying science as they were trying to do right now. The gathering of data and the sending of images would all look different. The logistics of how they zipped around the world on invisible lines would be rendered impossible. No cell phones meant none of their apps would be usable: no microscope app, no archive app, no compass app, no SCIDAT app, no LINLOC app, and no taser app.

"Taser app . . ." Blaine's mind latched onto the thought of that application. However, his forthcoming question was seemingly not related. "What about that flag over there?" The boy pointed at the six-foot flag the Slotes had planted in the ground. "What's that about?"

"Oh, that's nothing important," Graham answered.

"Not important to us, anyway," Belle added.

Alexander seemed to agree with his brother and sister, but then he felt obliged to give Blaine a better answer. "That is a claim staked for an associate. This will be the future sight of the moon's first fueling station."

"Fueling station?" Blaine asked.

"That's right," Alexander confirmed. "Something about converting ice or hydrogen or something into rocket fuel."

"Yes! Exactly!" Summer suddenly cut in. "Hydrogen!"

"What?" Blaine and Tracey joined the Slotes in asking.

"There are some interesting ideas and theories about the hydrogen that's on the moon. That's why your uncle thought this would be such a good place to study the topic."

Everyone's faces still looked baffled, so Summer explained. "Hydrogen is the most abundant element in the universe, and it is key to life and energy. It's the fuel that makes it possible for the sun to burn so brightly. It's the first element on the periodic table. As such, the normal state of the hydrogen atom has one proton and one neutron in the nucleus and one electron soaring around the nucleus. The symbol for hydrogen is H. Its atomic number is 1, and its atomic mass is 1.008."

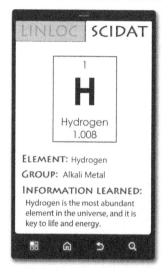

There was still nothing but dumbfounded looks on the faces of the female scientist's audience, so she continued. "On Earth, it exists as a gas, which consists of a pair of hydrogen atoms. Hydrogen gas is extremely flammable. But it is lighter than air and can escape the Earth's atmosphere. It was used to fill airships, until the Hindenburg disaster. Hydrogen on Earth can also be found bonded to other elements in compounds such as water, hydrocarbons, acids, and bases. These days, hydrogen is being looked at as an option for a clean and efficient fuel cell. These vehicles would have a fuel cell where hydrogen and oxygen combine to form water, producing electricity and heat. The main problem with these fuel cells, though, is the volatility of hydrogen."

It was obvious the Rotary Club thought Summer was rambling. Even though she had given them some wonderful SCIDAT, Blaine and Tracey were ready for their local expert to get to the point.

"But what about the moon?" Tracey asked. "Why is the presence of hydrogen on the moon such an interesting thing?"

"Ahhh, yes!" Summer giggled as though they were not in the middle of a tense standoff. "Hydrogen is used in fertilizers, in oil refining, in welding, in nuclear fusion, and . . . as rocket fuel!" Summer stated the last part of her sentence with wide eyes and outstretched arms like everyone would suddenly understand how rocket fuel connected everything she had said thus far. And they did understand—sort of.

"Wait . . . so the . . . what?" Blaine stammered.

"Yes, exactly!" Summer responded. "At low temperature and high pressure, hydrogen gas becomes a liquid."

"Okay," Tracey jumped in. "So, if you take the . . . and the . . . then . . ."

"That's right, Tracey," the scientist confirmed. "There is so much water in the form of ice on the moon, especially near the lunar south pole, that it makes it a perfect place for a rocket fuel gas station!"

"That's what I said." Alexander wanted some credit. "If you split water into hydrogen and oxygen and liquify the constituents, you have rocket fuel."

"That's what I was going to say," Graham chimed in.

Everyone nodded politely, knowing that Graham, in fact, was not about to say that.

"Now the moon is significantly depleted of hydrogen compared to the earth," Summer continued deeper into her explanation. "However, hydrogen is constantly implanted into the moon's surface by solar winds and is highly concentrated in places like this where there are deep and dark craters and chasms. Its concentrations are in the range of 40 to 50 parts per mill—"

"Enough!" Alexander shouted, cutting the scientist off. "Like Graham and Belle said, none of this is important to us. But what is important to us? Sending off this missile! So that's exactly what we're going to do right now. After you five are . . . taken care of."

"Taken care of?" Tracey was afraid to ask but did anyway.

Graham brought clarification to his brother's statement by holding up another stick of dynamite.

"Yes, taken care of," Alexander said again as he laughed wickedly.

"Not if I can help it," the boy interrupted, holding up his smartphone.

"What? You're going to stop us with your cell phone?" Alexander asked, finishing the laugh he'd started.

"No!" Blaine said defiantly. "I'm going to stop you with the taser application on my cell phone!"

"Yeah!" Summer interjected. "We're gonna be the base to your acid and the acid to your base!"

"Huh?" Alexander was confused.

"That's right!" Summer said, ever-present smile still visible. "Acids are chemicals that dissolve in water and can neutralize a base. They are hydrogen-containing compounds that split up in water to give hydrogen ions. Weak acids taste sour. And then bases are chemicals that dissolve in water and can neutralize an acid. They are compounds that react with an acid to produce water and salt. Weak bases taste bitter. All that is to say we're going to neutralize you!"

"You're going to neutralize us?" Alexander asked.

"Uh huh," Summer answered assuredly.

"So you think this boy's cell phone and its tase-a-macallit can stand up against Graham and his stick of dynamite? Is that your plan?"

Summer was still nodding yes, but Blaine suddenly didn't feel so confident.

"Well, I mean, I thought that maybe if I . . . you know . . . threatened you guys with a taser . . . that maybe you would . . . you know . . . stop your plans of worldwide cell phone destruction," Blaine stammered.

Alexander threw back his head and laughed his most wickedly

confident laugh yet. "You thought you could stop us with this cell phone?"

"Not this cell phone," Summer said. "That cell phone."

The scientist pointed toward the missile. Everyone looked. There was Tracey, standing at its base, cell phone out, taser app open, ready to shock the would-be weapon into oblivion.

Chapter 4: Underground Siberian Science and Neon Joviality

Abundant Alkali

The Triple S command center erupted in wild applause. Summer Beach and her small team had done it. They had found the stolen lunar module. They had apprehended the culprits, but not only that, they had also stopped a dangerous missile from being launched. The victorious cheers sounded now from the Swiss agents not only because of the success of the mission but because *Ulysses-1*, which was carrying Summer, her crew, and the culprits, had safely reentered the Earth's atmosphere.

Captain Marolf folded his arms in satisfaction and smiled. If he was honest with himself, he would have to admit he had doubted her, but Summer Beach came through again. "Okay, people," he stated loudly for all his subordinates to hear, "that's enough celebration. Let's make sure we have agents on the ground in Alaska ready to take the three culprits into custody upon arrival."

The cheering in the room died down, but the mood was still victorious as the eager workers obeyed their captain's directive.

Tracey folded her arms in satisfaction and smiled. The shower of sparks had been astounding. It had taken all the courage she could muster, but when Blaine had unwittingly created a diversion by threatening with his phone's taser. Tracey knew she had to jump into action. Summer had helped, too, by sharing a monologue about acids and bases. This had given Tracey enough time to sneak away, open her own taser app, and press her phone to the base of the missile.

The Sassafras girl knew that for the good of the world, she had to stop the missile. For the good of communication, she had to activate her taser. So she had activated the taser, and the light show it had created had been tremendous.

Sparks had showered everywhere.

The missile was rendered inoperable.

The Rotary Club had wept in defeat.

For good measure, Ulysses S. Grant had also pulled out the flag the Slotes had planted for an associate at the site of a future lunar fueling station. The arctic ground squirrel was adamant that no friend of these three had any legitimate right to such an important part of the future of space travel.

When *Ulysses-1* safely arrived back in Alaska, they were greeted by a small army of black suit-wearing Triple S agents who were even now hauling the Rotary Club back to jail where they belonged.

Blaine joined Tracey at her side, folding his arms in satisfaction and smiling. "It's been a pretty good start to the study of chemistry, right?"

"Sure has been," Tracey agreed with a nod.

"I wonder where we'll go next," Blaine mused. "I wonder what topics we'll get to study."

"Well, let's see," Tracey said, pulling out the phone that had stopped the Rotary Club and saved the world. The girl began to open her LINLOC app to find the answers to Blaine's questions. Before the twins saw anything on the screen, they were interrupted by an animated and loud Summer Beach.

"Okay, old friend," she was saying with her phone up to her ear. "I wanted to call and tell you the good news! Uh huh, uh huh . . . okay, well, like I said, the Swiss Secret Service now has the Rotary Club in custody, so that's good . . . yes, that's right . . . correct. Triple S has also volunteered to get both the module and the rover from the moon back to the museum, but it may take awhile . . . uh huh . . . okay, friend. Talk with you next time! Bye!"

Summer hung up and offered an explanation without being asked for one, although the twins didn't mind. "That was Paul Sims! I gave him a ringy ding ding to let him know all the good news."

"I bet he was happy with how everything turned out," Tracey said.

"He sure was," Summer confirmed. "I'm so glad for his sake that the Rotary Club is no longer a threat and that the museum is getting back its priceless possessions."

The Sassafrases were glad too.

"Paul Sims, my old junior high classmate," Summer mused. "Such a nice guy."

Chapter 4: Underground Siberian Science...

He folded his arms in agonizing frustration, and a disturbing frown formed on his face as he ended the call with his old junior high classmate. Everything had fallen apart. Alexander, Graham, and Belle had been apprehended. The satellite-destroying missile had not been launched. But, worst of all, his claim for the first lunar fueling station had been removed. Sure, everyone still thought he was a nice guy. As far as he knew, the Slotes had not divulged his name. He was pretty sure he remained unconnected, but did that matter if he didn't have his claim? Did it matter if untold riches were no longer coming his way?

Paul slammed his fist down on his desk and let out an angry shout. All at once his office door burst open, and in stumbled the two museum security guards: Wiggles and Fidget.

"Everything okay, sir?" Wiggles, the male security guard asked, his pudgy, circular face full of alarm.

Paul's frown immediately disappeared and was replaced with a cordial smile. "Yes, Wiggles, everything is fine," the museum curator responded.

"But we heard a bump and then a yell," Fidget, Wiggles' short, round female counterpart countered, equally concerned. "You sure you're all right?"

"I'm fine, Fidget," Sims assured convincingly. "I bumped my knee on my desk; that's all."

This explanation seemed to help the security guards ease up a bit.

"Great news," Paul announced, now struggling to maintain

his false demeanor. "The stolen lunar module has been located, and it's back on its way here."

At this news, both Wiggles and Fidget pumped their fists excitedly and jumped as high as they could, which with their short legs was only about one inch. "That's great news, sir!" they happily exclaimed in high-pitched unison.

"Yes, it's great," Paul Sims responded like he was on their side. "Really great."

"Siberia!" Tracey shouted as she looked at the information on the LINLOC app on her phone. "We're going back to Siberia!"

"Brrrrr, we're going back to Siberia," Blaine added, not quite as enthusiastically.

"Oh, yeah, brrrr," Tracey said, remembering how windy and frigid the place had been on their first visit there.

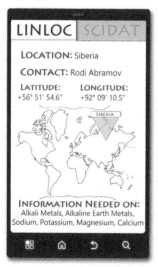

"What will you be studying?" Summer asked, full of spirit.

Tracey looked at her phone again. "Looks like we'll be studying alkali metals and alkaline earth metals, including sodium, potassium, magnesium, and calcium."

"All with a local expert named Rodi Abramov," Blaine finished the information for his sister.

"Oooohhhh, that sounds fun," Summer squeaked with a jump and a clap. "Looks like you're working right down, or should I say across, the periodic table!"

Cold location or not, the twins were always excited to be moving forward in their summer of science. They both began rummaging through their backpacks to find their helmets, harnesses, and three-ringed carabiners.

"Happy and maybe a little sappy," Summer sang. "It's time for us to say goodbye for now. Ulysses, REESE, and I will miss you two little cuties, but off you go. Your adventures will continue. Set those coordinates on the rings of your carabiners and zip, zip, zip away! Next to Siberia and then to all the amazing locations beyond!"

Blaine and Tracey donned their helmets, slipped on their harnesses, and turned the rings of their carabiners to the coordinates that would zip them to Siberia. As soon as the carabiners snapped shut, the twelve-year-olds were pulled up a few feet into the air, as they connected to invisible lines. They waved goodbye to Summer, Ulysses, and REESE, and then after a seven-second wait, they disappeared from Alaska, heading at the speed of light toward the study of alkali and alkaline earth metals. Swirls of light spun around them as they zipped, and then just as soon as it had begun, their zip-lining ended with a slight jerk.

As the Sassafras twins waited for their sight and strength to return, they wondered where they would land in Siberia this time around. Last time, they had landed on the back platform of a train—that had been a crazy adventure. Blaine and Tracey had traversed the length of the train, all while being chased by a crazed mad scientist, so they could help the immobilized conductor stop the speeding train before it crashed.

Blaine blinked his eyes repeatedly as his sight returned. Tracey stretched her arms out as she regained strength. They could see they had not landed on the back platform of a train, but they had ended up once more on a moving vehicle. This time around, it looked to be a . . .

"Dump truck? Did we land in a dump truck?" Blaine asked as he attempted to stand on the shaky pile of rocks.

"Yep, looks like it, bro," Tracey replied as she grabbed the rusty metal wall and peeked over.

Blaine eventually managed to get to the wall as well, gaining a view for himself. Sure enough, they were in the bed of a large dump truck, rumbling quickly down a steeply graded road. As the twins now took in a 360-degree view of their new location, they saw there wasn't only one road, and they weren't in the only dump truck. There were scores and scores of dump trucks, excavators, dozers, graders, backhoes, and more all driving and maneuvering around on a massive network of narrow, rocky roads. These roads intertwined and wound around, leading into a gargantuan hole in the earth. Clanks from the machinery rang out consistently and eerily. Clouds of dust and puffs of smoke rose as the landscape was disturbed. Everything was chipping and chugging, screeching and scraping, dragging and driving, down into the ominous, yawning hole in the ground. It was as if the land were a whirlpool made of rock and dust. The Sassafras twins felt like their truck was similar to a boat, a boat helplessly swirling. They were being sucked down into the dark, gaping center of an earthen whirlpool.

Blaine and Tracey looked at each other, not afraid yet, but slowly feeling like they were getting to that point.

"I feel like we're getting swallowed by a monster eating noodles," Blaine chirped.

"A monster eating noodles?" Tracey didn't quite get her brother's metaphor, but she got the sentiment of it. However, the Sassafras girl was choosing to reject the pessimism that was trying to creep in, opting for optimism instead. "Well, yeah, I guess the opening looks a little monstrous, and all of the intersecting roads kind of look like noodles, but doesn't everything seem sort of organized? Maybe we're supposed to be headed down into this big hole or cave or whatever. I bet that's where our local expert is."

Blaine nodded, thinking his sister was probably right, but fear was still an option for him as their truck continued down the precarious road directly toward the hole. All at once, they exited the daylight and entered into darkness. They had disappeared into the center of the "whirlpool." They had been eaten by the "monster."

The dump truck rumbled forward in what at first felt like complete darkness, but as their eyes adjusted, the twins could see dim electric lights hanging overhead. The underground tunnel had curved walls and ceilings that were fairly wide and high. The tunnel looked to be made of solid rock.

The twins looked forward and saw they were in a long corridor. However, there was light at the end of the tunnel—bright light, in fact—bright, flashing neon light. Blaine and Tracey looked at each other again in the current dimness.

"Where are we going?" They asked each other with just a look. Dark, dusty wind whipped around the pair as they bounced in the bed of the forward moving dump truck. The light grew closer. The end of the corridor drew near. Eventually they exited the tunnel, spilling out into a large cavity of a room. Sure enough, the dome-shaped room was filled with bright, flashing neon light, nowhere close to as bright as the sunshine but welcome, nonetheless.

Whoever was driving the dump truck suddenly slammed on the brakes, sending the Sassafrases careening forward toward the front of the truck's bed. They each landed, stunned, with a bump and a thud without pain. The truck's engine shut off, and they heard the driver's door swing open and slam shut. Immediately following, the passenger side did the same. Heavy, fast-paced footsteps echoed, sounding like they were made by work boots.

The stomping came to a stop rather quickly and gave way to shouting. "Vhat in the vorld do you two think you're doing?" an angry male Russian voice rang out.

"Vhat are ve doing?" a happy female Russian voice responded

with a laugh. "Vhy, ve are doing science and joviality! That's vhat ve are doing!"

Blaine and Tracey slowly stood in their hidden spot in the dump truck's bed.

"Yes, science and joviality," the female voice continued. "That's vhat ve Abramovs are known for, and that's vhat ve have been hired by Turgenev Mining Company to do! Ve are change agents, and ve are here to launch operation S and J!"

As the Sassafras twins got their eyes up over the brim of the front end of the truck bed and the truck's cab, they could see four people. Two huge, dusty, square-shaped, miner-looking types and two clean-cut shorter, office-looking types. Blaine and Tracey also could now see where all the neon light was coming from. There was a rather large stage set up here in this dome-shaped, underground room, complete with flashing lights of different colors situated at its back and front, and some even hung overhead. The twins saw that the tunnel they had come from wasn't the only entrance or exit. Rather, there were several larger tunnels leading to and from the room.

"Operation J and S? Science? Joviality?" the bigger of the bigs questioned, taking a threatening step closer to the two shorter individuals. "Ve are a mining company! Ve are here to mine for alkali metals and alkaline earth metals, not to be scientific or jovial!"

"That is true of the past but not the future," the small Russian woman answered with bright, unintimidated eyes. "Your CEO, Nestor Turgenev, has hired my brother and I, Rodi and Dina Abramov, to change the culture of this company!"

"Change the culture?" the big miner retorted, his tone still tinged with anger and frustration.

The woman named Dina nodded with a smile, but now it was her brother Rodi who responded, "Yes, my sister is in charge of the joviality part, and I'm in charge of the science part. I'm going to start teaching voluntary classes about all the science that goes into mining, with a focus on chemistry. For instance, you just mentioned both alkali and alkaline earth metals. I'm sure you know how to mine these metals, but do you know the science behind what you're mining?"

Both big miners made faces like they utterly and completely didn't care. This did not cause Rodi to stop.

"The six alkali metals include lithium, rubidium, cesium, francium, sodium, and potassium. They are extremely reactive metals that are soft and shiny but change color as soon as they hit the air. They are so reactive because they vant to bond vith other elements so they can get rid of the one electron that sits in the outer shell. As you go down the group of alkali metals on the periodic table, the more reactive they get. So for instance, cesium is much more reactive than lithium."

"Ve don't care!" the bigger miner grunted angrily.

Rodi still did not stop. "Lithium is the lightest metal on the periodic table. It has many uses from batteries to light-veight metal alloys for aircraft to absorbing carbon dioxide from the air that astronauts breathe. Rubidium has such a low melting point that it vill melt in your hand, and rubidium nitrate, a compound including rubidium, gives a purple color to fireworks. Cesium is so reactive that it explodes in vater, yet it is used to keep clocks accurate. Francium is the rarest natural element on earth. It has no practical use because it is so rare and because it decays so quickly."

The slightly smaller of the two big miners had a sudden look of understanding on his face. "Hey, Trof, that's probably vhy the boss man never has us mining for francium. It would be a big vaste of time. This science stuff kind of makes sense."

"No, Taras!" the bigger miner named Trof shouted toward the other miner. "I'll tell you vhat's a vaste of time. It's these two, talking all this nonsense and setting up this silly stage in our main rock chamber!"

Shiny Sodium and Purply Potassium

"Guys, doesn't knowing the science bring more purpose to vhat you're doing down here?" Dina proposed with a smile.

Trof looked like he was about to respond with another burst of fury, but Dina spoke again first. "Go ahead, Rodi. Tell them all about two of the most common alkali metals: sodium and potassium."

Rodi Abramov immediately obliged. "Sodium is a soft, silvery metal that is so light it can float on vater. The symbol for sodium is Na because the element is named after soda, which is *natrium* in Latin. Sodium's atomic number is 11, and its atomic mass is 23.000. It reacts quickly with chlorine to form sodium chlorides, also known as table salt. This sodium salt is one of the only rocks we humans eat. It can be mined as rock salt." The twins noticed that several bands of rock suddenly began to glow. This must be part of the joviality in the presentation that Dina was responsible for.

The twins grinned, and Rodi nodded before continuing, "Sodium can also be produced by the evaporation of sea vater.

Humans have just under nine ounces of sodium chloride in their bodies, vhich helps transmit nerve signals around the body. Because ve sveat out salt, ve need to constantly replace the sodium chloride through our diet. However, vhen the pure metal touches vater, it bursts into flames." At this, the lights changed so that it looked like the highlighted rocks were bursting to flames. The twins gasped in wonder.

Meanwhile, Trof was getting more and more frustrated as Rodi shared the scientific information. In contrast, Taras was getting more and more interested. "Vow, Trof, this is amazing! Rock and metal you can eat! Ve dig for sodium right here in this mine!"

Rodi continued before Trof could respond to his fellow miner in any way. "Potassium has an atomic number is 19, and its atomic mass is 39.098. The symbol for potassium is K because the element is named after potash, which is *kalium* in Latin. Potassium is a soft metal that burns with a lilac-colored flame vhen it hits vater, and it turns black in the open air." The lights on the wall moved to another section of the rock wall and changed from purple to black and back to purple again.

ELEMENT: Potassium
GROUP: Alkali Metal
INFORMATION LEARNED:
Potassium is a soft metal that burns with a lilac-colored flame when it hits water, and it turns black in the open air.

The twins' smiles widened as Rodi kept sharing, "Potassium is essential to life because it helps maintain the health of our cells and blood vessels. This element also vorks with sodium to conduct electrical signals around the body for muscle contraction. Humans can't make potassium, so ve have to get it through our diet. It is also necessary for plants, so it is often used as fertilizer." The lights on the wall faded from purple to green.

Taras grinned at the change. Not only was he interested in the information, but he was invested enough to ask, "So you said potassium vorks vith sodium to conduct electrical signals around the body. Does that mean all these metals and stuff can combine and mix together to do different things?"

Rodi nodded and answered, "A mixture is a combination of two or more elements that are not chemically bonded together. For example, air is a mixture of different gases. Seavater is a mixture of vater and salts. Soil is a mixture of different solids. All mixtures can be separated into their compounds using techniques like decantation, filtration, chromatography, evaporation, distillation, and centrifugation. Then ve have solutions. A solution is a type of mixture that consists of a solid substance called a solute. Vhen dissolved in a liquid, it's called a solvent. If the solid dissolves easily in the solvent, it is said to be insoluble. Soluble solutions can typically be separated by chromatography, evaporation, or distillation." As Rodi talked, the lights turned from green to a slowly rotating rainbow of colors mixing and swirling around on the rock wall. It was exciting to watch!

"Okay," Taras nodded his head in understanding. He seemed to be drinking in the information. "But what abou—"

"Stop!" Trof interrupted, his anger again boiling over. "You stop asking questions," he shouted at his counterpart and stuck a hand in Taras's face, literally pushing the man away.

"And you!" he yelled, taking a step closer to Rodi Abramov. "Stop talking! I don't vant to hear any more of this science!"

"But isn't it nice to better understand some of the science behind your job?" Dina asked, still seemingly unintimidated by the imposing man. "To know how metals and minerals vork and vhat they are used for? To know vhy your occupation as miners is so important? Oh, and vhat about the joviality part? Ve haven't even broached that yet."

With absolutely no trace of joviality, Trof shouted, "No! Ve don't need to know the science, and ve vant nothing to do vith any kind of joviality!"

"But Trof, maybe—" Taras tried to say, but he was immediately interrupted.

"No, Taras, no. Ve don't need it! Get back in the truck. You and I are going straight to the boss's office, and ve are going to put in a complaint! I don't like the direction this company is taking. Ve've alvays done mining a certain vay, and there's no need to change that now!"

Taras reluctantly complied and made his way back to the passenger side of the truck. Trof, too, started back toward the dump truck, but their movement was arrested as Dina continued talking, "Your boss is the very one who hired us to be the change agents of the culture here at Turgenev Mining Co. Yes, Nester Turgenev himself vants more knowledge and more heart here. Vhy continue on mindlessly chipping and digging away for bits of rock full of alkali and alkaline earth metals? Vhy exist day to day in a drab world devoid of excitement or color?"

The energetic woman reached into a box that lay next to her and pulled out a rainbow of neatly folded neon clothing. She took a second to look over what she'd grabbed, and then tossed something bright orange to Taras and something bright pink to Trof. The big miners each caught what had been thrown their way, letting the clothing unfurl and holding what was now revealed up in front of them.

"Jumpsuits?" Trof growled angrily. "Bright neon jumpsuits?"

Dina smiled. "Yes! It's time to replace all your dusty earth tones vith some color!"

"There's no vay I will ever put this on," Trof barked and immediately dropped his jumpsuit on the ground.

"Ve'll see about that," Dina said confidently, still smiling. "And for some additional joviality, ve are hoping that every Turgenev employee vill prepare a song or dance for tonight's concert!"

This caused Trof to clinch and grind his teeth. He lifted a thick, pointing finger to issue an imposing threat. "You Abramovs need to leave. And you need to take your science and your joviality vith you. If you don't, you vill be sorry!"

The big man hopped into the driver's seat of his truck and slammed the door shut. Taras followed in the passenger's seat, but without a slam, and still carrying his new orange jumpsuit. Trof cranked the engine to life. Then, with a belch of black smoke and creaking of tires, he whipped the big machine around to face the same tunnel it had entered through. The Sassafras twins had been a little anxious about first entering this tunnel from the outside. Now they were even more nervous about exiting it from this side, especially with such an angry driver behind the wheel.

Before the angry miner stepped on the gas to exit the big rock chamber, he hand cranked his window down and through a snarling laugh said, "Hey, Abramovs, got a present for you!"

Blaine and Tracey felt a new rumbling sensation as something like metal gears could be heard cranking to life. Then, all at once, the bed of the dump truck tilted upward. As it did, its back gate swung open, and the pile of rocks slid out of the truck. The twelve-year-olds reached out, grasping for something to hang onto, but both were unsuccessful. The pile of sliding rocks suddenly became a mode of transportation. With the bed of the dump truck now up at a 45-degree angle, Trof pressed down the gas, making the truck lurch forward. The pile of rocks, with Blaine and Tracey sitting on top of it, slid completely out of the truck's bed, landing in a heap on the floor of the large room. Never taking his foot off the gas, Trof drove the big vehicle out of the room without pause.

The rock chamber was suddenly quiet. In the dump truck's absence, all that was left was the Abramov's neon blinking lights, a box of brightly colored jumpsuits, and two kids sitting on a rock pile. The Sassafrases had expected to eventually meet their local expert but not like this exactly. The Abramovs, in comparison, had not expected to meet Blaine and Tracey, and their faces showed it.

Both twins raised their hands and wiggled their fingers in an attempt at a friendly greeting. Through sheepish grins, they eeked out, "Hello, there."

Finally, everything was set. Everything was in place, including his confidence. He stood tall and strong in his Dark Cape Suit, perched on his white pedestal overlooking his immaculate, underground science lab.

The scores of scientists who worked for him were absent. They were taking a break, a break he had given them, a well-deserved break because they had finished. They had successfully finished both of the groundbreaking tasks he'd commissioned them to do.

He smiled behind the tinted visor of the Dark Cape helmet as he looked out before him. To his right were one hundred Dark Cape suits, standing upright in perfect rows. They looked exactly like the original one he was currently wearing, and they all had the same capabilities. They could become invisible. They could make items vanish. And, if needed, they were space-worthy.

To his left was a new and improved Forget-O-Nator. It was shiny and sleek, rectangular in shape, and as large as a mobile home in size. It was impossible to escape from once inside. It could hold up to twenty people instead of just one. Best of all, it could accomplish its main purpose of wiping away a subject's memory in only one second.

The smile behind the helmet remained as the wearer grew more contemplative. He had let himself become side-tracked in the past. Whether it had been fear or overthinking or bad planning or even infatuation . . . ugh . . . Adrianna Archer.

However, that was all in the past. He stood confident, resolute, and laser-focused on his sole purpose, which was to exact revenge on the one who had taken the eyebrows from his face. Cecil Sassafras would finally pay for what he had done way back in that junior high chemistry classroom.

Thaddaeus let out a deep, confident laugh to go with his smile. It wouldn't be only Cecil who paid, either. It would be everything and everyone that Cecil loved. He would destroy Cecil Sassafras's entire existence. There was absolutely no way any of those Sassafrases, or Summer, or those rodent lab assistants, or that robot sidekick would be a match for what he now saw before him.

One hundred Dark Capes.

A Forget-O-Nator as big as a mobile home.

These would finally stop the Sassafrases and their summer of learning.

Thaddaeus ripped off his helmet, raised his arms, and let his now-wicked laughter fill his lab. Vengeance was about to be unleashed.

THE SASSAFRAS SCIENCE ADVENTURES

Chapter 5: Subterranean Dance-off— Dust versus Neon

Extravagant Earth Metals

Blaine wanted to be a break-dancer. It was something he'd never even told Tracey. But if there was going to be a talent show and concert tonight on the stage in the mine. And if he was invited to be part of it, Blaine was going to use the opportunity to showcase his love for the art of break dancing. He just needed to figure out how to talk Tracey into beatboxing for him.

Tracey was smiling, too, but it wasn't because she had an idea for a hidden talent. It was because she and Blaine had befriended the Abramovs. Even with such a strange first meeting—the twins had literally been dumped out of the back of a truck—Rodi and Dina Abramov had gladly welcomed the Sassafrases into all that was going on down in the big rock chamber.

First, the change agents had given the twins their own

jumpsuits. Blaine's was neon yellow, and Tracey's was neon green. Then, the Abramovs had shown the twelve-year-olds around the stage and invited them to perform later if they wanted to. When they found out that Blaine and Tracey had come to learn about science, the Abramovs—especially Rodi—had come to life.

Rodi was even now starting to share some information about alkaline earth metals. "All six alkaline earth metals, including beryllium, magnesium, calcium, strontium, barium, and radium, are good conductors of heat and electricity. But only magnesium and calcium are essential to life. These alkaline metals are a little less reactive than the alkali metals next to them on the periodic table because they have two electrons in their outer shells. Even so, they combine easily with oxygen to form many of the minerals found in the Earth's crust. On their own, the alkaline metals are shiny, silvery-gray, and lightveight." The lights on the rock wall turned white and appeared to shimmer, giving the appearance of a wall covered with shiny, grey metal.

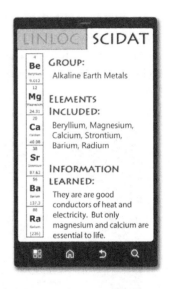

"So are those the main things that are mined down here?" Tracey asked. "Alkaline earth metals and the alkali metals you talked about earlier?"

"Yes, in this particular mine, that's the case," Rodi confirmed with a nod. "However, Turgonev Mining Company has operations going all over Siberia, and they mine for many other things as vell."

The Sassafrases had been inside a mine before earlier in the summer while studying geology in Australia with Jackie R. Wagon. That diamond mine hadn't been nearly as big or as organized as this place. The twins were impressed.

"So, what do each of the alkaline earth metals do?" Blaine asked. "What's their significance?"

"Good question, Blaine," Rodi said and immediately began to answer. "I'll start vith beryllium. Beryllium is the key element in the mineral beryl. It gives gemstones such as emeralds, aquamarine, and morganite their color. Then ve have strontium. This alkaline earth metal burns red and is vhat ve use in road flares. It is toxic in high levels. However, small amounts of it are used in toothpaste."

This information brought a wry smile to Blaine's face as he moved his tongue over his pearly whites, wondering if he had any strontium floating around anywhere in his mouth.

"Barium is the alkaline earth metal that gives some fireworks their green color," Rodi continued. "It is also used in glassmaking and in X-rays because a compound containing barium glows under X-ray light. Radium is another alkaline earth metal that vas vonce thought of as a miracle metal because it gave off heat and light, but ve now know that it is radioactive and can cause cancer. Next is magnesium. Magnesium is—"

"Crazy rad!" Rodi Abramov was suddenly interrupted by a new energetic voice in the rock chamber. "Crazy rad good!"

Instant looks of recognition formed on the Sassafrases' faces. They knew this phrase, and they knew this voice. The twins turned from their local expert and his sister to see a large flatbed truck driving into the chamber from one of the tunnels. On the bed of the truck was a whole group of people with guitars and a drum set. One of the people was a young woman with hair that was dyed neon green to match her neon green outfit.

"Sveta? Sveta Corvette?" Tracey exclaimed like it was a question. But the Sassafras girl knew that voice was from the friend she and Blaine had made last time they were in Siberia.

"Tracey? Tracey Sassafras?" Sveta responded with a tone that matched Tracey's. "And Blaine too? You guys are still in Siberia? I thought you had just up and disappeared."

"Well, we did disappear, but . . ."

"Good to see you two again!" the Russian teenager welcomed as she jumped off the back of the now parked truck. "Vhat are you doing down here in Turgenev mine?"

"Well, right now we're learning about alkaline earth metals from Rodi Abramov here," Blaine spoke up and gestured toward their local expert.

Rodi and Dina smiled.

"Velcome, Sveta!" the male Abramov greeted. "So glad you and your band made it."

"Band?" Tracey asked.

"Yes," Dina happily exclaimed. "Sveta and the Spark Plugs! They're the best punk rock band in all of Russia, in my humble opinion. They are the marquee band for our concert of talent tonight. Sveta and the Spark Plugs know how to bring the joviality!"

Sveta brushed the compliment aside with gratefulness. "It's our pleasure to come here and perform. Ve are thankful for any chance ve can get to spread our positive, uplifting tunes and crazy rad vibes all across the motherland."

The other members of the band, all of whom were male, nodded. They, too, jumped from the back of the truck.

"So, vhat do you think?" Dina asked the band and then pointed toward the stage. "Vill this vork?"

"Oh, yeah, it'll vork," Sveta answered with gusto. "It's a perfect setup down here underground with amazing acoustics and all these sick lights. It's gonna be crazy rad!"

"Crazy rad good," Blaine and Tracey declared in unison.

Volume 7: Chemistry

It was time for the break to be over. It was time for his scores of scientists to get back to work. He barked orders into a microphone implanted in his helmet, which was wirelessly connected to speakers all around his underground facility.

"All hands on deck! Every able-bodied scientist must report now to the main laboratory! I repeat, everyone must report immediately to lab A-1. Operation vengeance is a go! Again, I say green light for operation vengeance!"

Thaddaeus tilted his head back and cackled into the helmet's microphone, causing every room and corridor of the underground laboratory to be filled with his wicked laughter. This was the beginning of the end for Cecil Sassafras.

"Fa-la-la-la-la! La-fa-fa-fa-fa!" the red-headed man sang happily as he twirled about, his messy lab coat floating up around him and his feet barely touching the sidewalk.

Cecil was on his way home from the supermarket, where he'd bought supplies for the romantic table he was setting up for Summer Beach. More than likely, he wouldn't see her for a few more days, probably about the same time Train and Blaisey finished up their study about chemistry. However, it didn't hurt to be punctual and overly prepared. He wanted the table to be looking splendirifically perfect when Summer, the love of his life, showed up.

"Zippity yoo ya! Zippity yay! Howdy oh hootie, what a

fantabulous day!" Cecil sang and twirled.

"Hello, Cecil!" Old Man Grusher greeted from his porch across the street. Mr. Grusher was sitting in his rocker next to his snoozing black miniature poodle, otherwise known as the Guardian Beast.

"Hello, Mr Grusher!" Cecil greeted, somehow managing a wave, even though his arms were full of supplies.

"Well, hello there, Cecil." The scientist heard a salutation coming from his left. "Don't you look giddy and as light as a feather on this fine day."

Cecil turned with a smile to see his elderly next-door neighbor. "Hello, Mrs. Pascapali! Yes, oh yessity yes, it is a fine day indeed! I'm in love! I'm in love! And I'm going home to prepare a table for my sweet Summer Thyme!"

"Well, isn't that nice," Mrs. Pascapali responded with a kindly nod.

Cecil got to the front of his house, skipped through the yard, and jumped completely over the front steps, landing firmly on his front porch. "Gravity time," he announced, full of cheer. Immediately, the trapdoor on his porch opened, and down he went, supplies in hand, on the smooth slide leading to his basement. It was quite possible Cecil Sassafras had never been as excited about starting a project. Operation Love Thyme was now underway!

Down in the main rock chamber of Turgenev mine, Operation S and J was well underway. Sveta and the Spark Plugs had all their equipment and instruments set up. Their sound was checked and ready to go. The rock wall lights had dimmed, and the neon lights were flashing on the large stage. It was cleared and waiting for any and all acts of talent that were scheduled to take place in a bout an hour. However, the thing that impressed the Sassafras twins the most was the fact that Dina Abramov had actually talked a large percentage of the miners into donning the bright neon jumpsuits.

The place felt almost like an anthill overflowing with ants that were purple, blue, green, yellow, orange, and pink. Even now the rock chamber was alive with rainbow-colored energy as miners moved to and fro. Some were on foot, and some were driving or riding vehicles. Some were practicing their acts of talent, and some were planning on only watching. But all of them were excited for the joviality to begin!

His host of servile scientists began to pour into the main laboratory from every door and corridor that connected to this place. They looked almost like ants wearing white lab coats pouring into an ant nest comprised of only sleek surfaces.

He remained perched confidently on his pedestal as he watched them move to and fro. He wouldn't say they were excited, but they surely seemed motivated. He didn't know if it was caused by duty or fear.

As he watched his minions scurrying around with purpose, he allowed himself to stand on his white pedestal and reminisce all the way back to the time and place where he'd lost his eyebrows. He could see it in his mind's eye almost as clearly as when it had happened. It was the junior high chemistry lab, and Mr. Womberfraggle was standing at the front of the classroom giving instructions with Cecil Sassafras and Summer Beech at a table to his right. Paul Sims and that Chinese exchange student, Yang Bo, were at a table to his left. He stood alone at his table because his normal lab partner, a kid named Hodge, was out sick. He couldn't quite remember the topic they were studying in class that day, probably because he almost always copied Cecil's work, unbeknownst to Cecil, of course.

He did, however, remember it was the first time Mr. Womberfraggle had ever let the class fire up the Bunsen burners. A Bunsen burner was a small gas burner with a single open flame used for experiments and such. They were supposed to be completely safe to use.

At least that's what Mr. Womberfraggle had said . . .

He shook the memory from his mind and focused his attention back to the lab. He was pleased with the pace at which they were attacking the tasks of completing final preparations on the Dark Cape suits and the final preparations for the Forget-O-Nator. They were getting everything connected to the specially designed three-ringed carabiners, ready to launch them to do his bidding. If all went according to plan, they would be able to make that launch in about an hour.

With the 'J' of Operation S and J on hyperdrive, the Sassafras twins were left wondering a little about the 'S' part. They had their neon jumpsuits on. They were excited about being at their first Sveta and the Spark Plugs concert. And, Blaine was still planning to ask his sister to beatbox for him while he awed the crowd of miners with his break-dancing skills. But what about the science behind the mining operation?

Magnesium and Calcium Mash-up

What about the chemistry in all these activities? Hadn't Rodi begun to talk about magnesium a little earlier? Both twelve-year-olds were interested to hear and learn more about the alkaline metals.

"Hey, Mr. Abramov," Tracey called to the local expert as she and Blaine pushed brooms across the stage for one last sweep. "Didn't you start to say something about magnesium earlier? Blaine and I would love to hear more about that."

Rodi laughed with a kind smile. "You don't have to call me Mr. Abramov, Tracey. Rodi vorks just fine. And yes, I did," Rodi confirmed. "I did start to talk about magnesium. Vhat I was going to say is that magnesium is essential to life. There's more, but it's not a part of tonight's presentation. Do you vant to hear it?" Blaine and Tracey nodded.

"Great!" Rodi exclaimed before continuing, "It helps plants make their food, and it aids in more than 300 functions in the body, including supporting muscles and nerve function."

Blaine was as interested as his sister in the SCIDAT currently being shared, but being up on the stage was also piquing his interest in another subject: breakdancing. If he was going to wow the crowd later, he really needed to ask Tracey if she was interested in beatboxing for him.

"The symbol for magnesium is Mg. Its atomic number is 12, and its atomic mass is 24.305. This element is the third-most abundant element in seavater," Rodi Abramov continued. "It is also part of the metal alloy in materials used to build airplanes and cars. And vhen magnesium is burned,

LINLOC SCIDAT

12
Mg
Magnesium
24.31

ELEMENT: Magnesium
GROUP: Alkaline Earth Metal
INFORMATION LEARNED:
Magnesium is the third-most abundant element in seawater. It is an essential element to life.

it burns vith an intensely vhite flame."

Blaine heard what Rodi was saying, and he was committing it to memory so he could enter it into the SCIDAT app later, but he was also trying to sidle up next to his broom-pushing twin so he could ask her his all-important question. Tracey, either intentionally or unintentionally, kept sweeping in a direction away from him.

"Calcium is another alkaline metal mined by Turgenev Mining Co.," Rodi said, going on with his speech about the scientific data. "Like magnesium, calcium is essential to human life. It is a part of vhat gives our teeth and bones their strength. Calcium is sometimes referred to as the 'scaffolder' element because its effect is often to hold things together. It can be found in marble, limestone, chalk, rocks, shells, cement, and even in the very bones in our bodies."

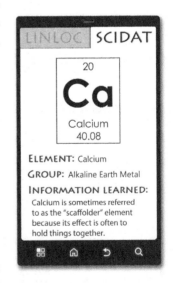

Blaine did a quick turn of the broom as he reached the end of the stage and now found himself sweeping directly toward his sister. "Now's the time," Blaine thought. "Time to talk Trace into beatboxing." However, as he got close enough to speak to her, Rodi interrupted him with more information about calcium.

"Calcium vill dissolve in vater vhich is then considered hard. Vhen the vater evaporates, the calcium is left behind, forming limescale. The symbol for calcium is Ca. Its atomic number is 20, and its atomic mass is 40.078."

"That's so cool!" Tracey said in response to the SCIDAT. "Chemistry is so fun to think about! All these elements make up pretty much everything we can see, and even things we can't see. And to think that we can actually dig down into the ground and find such important elements is fascinating. It makes this whole mining operation all the more impressive!"

Rodi nodded in agreement, and Blaine agreed too, but his pending request was still at the forefront of his mind. He made another sweeping turn in attempt to go toward his sister, but in the process, he misjudged the edge of the stage and went tumbling off with broom in hand, request unasked. The boy landed in a slightly embarrassed but uninjured heap.

"Vatch your step there, Blaine," Dina Abramov said, walking up with a smile. "You don't vant to break a leg quite yet!"

This brought chuckles from both Abramovs and one Sassafras.

Thaddaeus bent down, cringing as the next part of the memory of that infamous day played in his mind.

His pencil, for some reason, rolled off the table, so he bent over to pick it up off the floor. At the precise moment he got his head to table level, his Bunsen burner exploded. The flames slapped his face with a burst of heat and immediately burned both his eyebrows off. The classroom filled with laughter as he stood there alone, the sole victim of the explosion. Then, to add to his shame, Cecil had tackled him, saying something about being sorry before stomping on him. Thaddaeus managed to rip himself away from Cecil, got to his feet again, and darted out of the room.

"Grrr!" Thaddaeus growled out loud. Even now, he freshly felt the weight of the hurt, the pain, and the shame of that day.

"It's long overdue, Cecil," he growled, his voice dripping

with bitterness. "Vengeance is finally headed your way. I will make you feel the same hurt, pain, and shame that you made me feel that day. I will destroy you and what you love, including those science-learning twins!"

It was time. The stage was set. Everything was in place. Science had been learned. Now it was time for a lot more joviality! Dina Abramov grabbed a microphone off a stand and walked out to center stage.

"Good evening, Turgenev Mining Co.!"

"Good evening!" the crowd of neon-clad miners responded in jubilation.

"Are you ready for some joviality?"

"Yes!"

"Okay, our first act tonight is four miners who are going to sing a barber shop quartet-style song about calcium!"

Applause rang from the crowd as the four miners Dina had just mentioned walked onto the stage, looking nervous but excited.

"Here they are," Dina said happily. "Let's cheer them on!"

Cheer the crowd did, right up to the moment the quartet opened their mouths to sing. Blaine and Tracey, who were standing to the side of the stage, dropped their mouths open in amazement as soon as they heard the first note of the acapella song. These Russian miners were fabulous singers!

The crowd, which included the Sassafras twins, listened intently as the four men sang a perfectly harmonized song about the mining of calcium. Blaine, particularly, was enjoying the performance and was still hoping that he too could amaze the crowd later with his break-dancing skills. However, he still hadn't gotten the chance to ask Tracey if she would beatbox for him. Standing next to her now, he figured this was as good a chance as any.

Blaine leaned toward his sister and prepared to ask his all-important question, but before he could get any part of the request out of his mouth, he was interrupted by a terrible rumbling noise. Blaine frowned as he thought that didn't sound like part of the quartet. He looked back toward the stage.

The alarming sound was not coming from the stage. It was coming from one of the tunnels. The singing miners abruptly stopped their song as all eyes in the rock chamber looked toward the source of the rumbling. A huge, monstrous machine, one that looked like a mechanical dinosaur, rolled into the room. It looked as though it had a big, wide-open mouth with the top jaw made of sharp, spinning metal teeth and the bottom jaw made of some kind of straight-edged scraper.

"A continuous miner!" a miner wearing bright orange shouted.

"A continuous miner?" the Sassafrases wondered, having never heard of anything called that before.

"That's right. A continuous miner," a deep, surly voice confirmed as a now familiar character stepped out from behind the gargantuan mining vehicle.

It was Trof, and he was quickly joined by Taras, who was holding some kind of large, food tray-sized remote control-looking thing.

"It's not just any continuous miner," Trof bragged. "It's a remote-controlled, Russian-engineered continuous miner! Most of these machines vorldvide can only mine coal and other soft materials, but this one is strong and sturdy enough to mine anything! It can cut right through cobalt, copper, iron, nickel, zinc, gold, alkali metals, alkaline earth metals, and even a rock chamber full of joviality!"

"Vhat?" Dina asked from the stage as she picked a microphone up. "You vouldn't! You vouldn't doze through this stage and this crowd of fellow miners."

"I vould, and I vill," Trof answered defiantly. "If you don't immediately pack up all your science, joviality, and neon, I vill. Or should I say ve vill."

As Trof said the word "ve," a large constituency of frowning, dusty, drab-colored miners emerged from the tunnel and positioned themselves next to and behind the big man. They were a threatening-looking bunch, all carrying something, whether a shovel, pickaxe, or sledge.

"Vhy such anger? Vhy such disdain?" Dina asked. "All of this force and violence because your CEO hired us to teach some science behind the things you're mining? Because he wants us to inject a little color and joviality into the operations?"

"There vas nothing wrong vith how ve vere running things before." Trof grunted. "I liked things the vay thy vere."

Dina looked like she had a lot more to say but was too flustered to get any of it out. Rodi also looked shocked. The quartet of miners who had been singing stood frozen in stunned neon silence. Neither Blaine nor Tracey knew what to do or say.

The nerve-racking encounter had suddenly turned into a silent standoff. Not a miner from either side moved a muscle. The wall of neon faced off intensely against the wall of dust-ridden earth tones.

Who was going to make a move first? Would the science and joviality continue? Or would Trof and his crew drive that crazy-looking machine forward to destroy?

The Sassafrases' internal questions were answered by a single note. If Blaine and Tracey were right, it was a D-note played on

Volume 7: Chemistry

the strings of an electric guitar. All heads turned toward the stage, where Sveta Corvette had emerged with her neon green guitar in hand. The rocker let the note hang in the air for a few long seconds, and then she put her fingers to the strings again in a steady punk rock strumming pattern. The music was fairly quiet at first, but as Sveta continued, her strumming got heavier, and the music got louder.

All at once, her band joined her, which added more guitars and a drumbeat to the mix. Sveta leaned forward and, with a curled-up mouth, began to sing. "Crazy rad! Crazy rad! Crazy rad good! Crazy rad! Crazy rad! Crazy rad good! Good and happy vibes! Positivity I'm giving, loving words for living!"

As the punk rocker sang, all the miners dressed in neon began to move. At first it was a tapping of feet here and a head bobbing there. Then, slowly but surely it turned into dancing. It wasn't a discombobulated anything goes type of dancing, but it was on beat and organized dancing.

"Crazy rad! Crazy rad! Crazy rad good! Crazy rad! Crazy rad! Crazy rad good!" Sveta sang on. "Positively uplifting! Good and happy vibes! Positivity I'm giving, loving words for living!"

As the neon-clad miners happily continued dancing, the dust-covered miners began to move as well. However, the vibes their movements were putting out were not happy. They banged the blunt ends of their tools on the ground in rhythm.

At first the pace of the pounding was fairly slow and simple, but then the angry miners began to speed up the banging as their rhythms became more complex, almost like some kind of surly stomp routine.

Trof's menacing smile confirmed it was now clearly the drab miners versus the neon miners. The two groups faced each other—dust versus color. Neither line made advances, but both refused to relent.

Blaine and Tracey looked at each other. Were they in the middle of a dance-off?

"Operation" felt like too small of a word. Maybe "army" was better. Yes, this wasn't just an operation of vengeance. This was an army of vengeance.

Thaddaeus Wazeezy's confidence was at an apex as he stood on his white pedestal and looked out over his lab. The 100 Dark Cape suits were now manned as the scientists had put on each and every one of them. Each was equipped with harnesses and specially designed three-ringed carabiners, ready for invisible zip-line travel. The extra-large Forget-O-Nator was also prepped and ready for light speed transport. It had a custom harness wrapped around it, complete with its own three-ringed carabiner. To Thaddaeus's knowledge, this would be the largest item ever to travel on the invisible zip lines.

He was positive it was going to work. It was all going to work. After all this time, from that fateful day in the junior high classroom until now, he finally had a plan that was going to work.

Cecil Sassafras wouldn't know what hit him. That niece and nephew of Cecil's wouldn't be able to skirt it or stop it. Neither Summer nor that prairie dog nor that arctic ground squirrel nor that talking robot would be able to prevent what was about to happen.

This operation was going to work. The army of vengeance was about to zip out of the underground Siberian laboratory and annihilate the Sassafrases, starting with those science-learning twins. Everything he had tried this summer so far had failed, but this would not. Thaddaeus Wazeezy was sure of it.

As was becoming habit for him, the Man With No Eyebrows tilted back his head and let out a deep, wicked, guttural laugh. All that was left to do now was find out where in the world those twins were, calibrate each of the carabiners of this dark army of vengeance, and then go to that location.

Both lines were holding.

Both lines were dancing.

The neon side was using happy steps. The dusty side was using sad stomps.

All the while, Sveta and the Spark Plugs rocked on. "Crazy rad! Crazy rad! Crazy rad good! Crazy rad! Crazy rad! Crazy rad good! Positively uplifting! Good and happy vibes! Positivity I'm giving, loving words for living!"

Blaine and Tracey were not dancing or rocking out to the music. Both of them were feeling the weight of the situation. Yes, everyone was dancing, but the fact remained that they were in the middle of a stand-off. Would science and joviality prevail? Or would Trof, Taras, and the old way win out?

Currently, the Sassafras twins were looking at the faces of Trof and Taras, trying to read their expressions. Trof looked like he was getting angrier and was about to boil over. Taras, in contrast, was smiling and seemed to actually be enjoying both the dancing and the music. He was still holding the large remote control as he stomped.

All at once, Trof let out a loud, angry yell and grabbed the controller out of Taras's hands. He jammed his thick fingers onto the buttons it held, causing the continuous miner machine to crank back to life. This brought an abrupt end to the dancing but not to the music. The intrepid Sveta Corvette continued to belt out her optimistic lyrics and passionately strum at the strings of her guitar, even as Trof used the remote to guide the large mining vehicle directly toward the stage she and her band were on.

Chapter 6: Oh Iceland, Oh Iceland
Three Transition Metals

"What?" Thaddaeus shouted at the scientist who had presented the information to him. "How can that be? You're telling me those twins are here in Siberia?"

The scientist nodded nervously in confirmation, afraid of his furious boss. "Yes, sir, but not just here in Siberia. They're here in the lab."

"That's not possible!" Thaddaeus argued. "If they were here somewhere in my lab, we should be aware of their presence!"

"I'm just telling you what the data says, sir," the scientist said in a shaky voice. "It says Blaine and Tracey Sassafras are here."

Trof shouted in a loud, angry voice as he drove the continuous miner straight toward the neon flashing stage. He wasn't shouting actual words, only sounds, but they were clearly communicating his intentions to crush any and all science and joviality.

Sveta continued to sing, as bold now as she had been the day she'd faced off against Yuroslav Bogdanovich. However, bold or not, the twins could tell she was about to get smashed. Her courage would be no match for the monstrous machine that was barreling down on her and her band.

As the situation unfolded, Blaine and Tracey were still studying the faces of Trof and Taras. Although Trof's face was bent on destruction, Taras's was not. It was determined, and that determination now turned into action as Taras wrestled the large remote out of his counterpart's hands to regain control.

"Ve can't hurt anybody, Trof! And ve shouldn't destroy anything!" Taras shouted out over the rumbling of the machine and the loud lyrics of the punk rock song.

"It's time things change around here. It's time to allow science and maybe a little joviality to come in," Taras announced as he effectively steered the continuous miner away from the stage and Sveta and the Spark Plugs.

Unconvinced and still full of rage, Trof pounced on Taras and fought like a rabid animal to regain control of the remote. As the two large miners fought over the controller, its buttons were pushed and prodded in a way that led the still-churning vehicle straight toward one of the rock chamber's walls. Rather quickly, the continuous miner hit the wall with great force, immediately digging out a sizable hole.

As Trof and Taras continued fighting, the sharp churning teeth of the machine's top jaw cut through the rock wall like it was paper-mache. The powerful scraper of the machine's bottom jaw sliced through the stone obstruction like it was soft butter.

"Crazy rad! Crazy rad! Crazy rad good! Crazy rad! Crazy rad! Crazy rad good!" Sveta continued to belt as Trof and Taras battled. "Positively uplifting! Good and happy vibes! Positively I'm giving loving words for living!"

Neither one of the big miners seemed to be gaining an upper hand as they wrestled for the remote control. "Maybe that was a good thing," the Sassafrases thought. As the fighting continued between the miners, the continuous miner completely disappeared into the new tunnel it was digging. It was no longer a threat to anyone here in the rock chamber.

Thaddaeus let go of the scientist he'd been choking as a new sound suddenly reached his ears. "What is that sound?" he asked out loud to no one in particular. "Where is that rumbling sound coming from?"

The sound quickly morphed from just a rumbling noise to actual rumbling. Thaddaeus looked around in alarm. His whole laboratory was shaking. All at once, to his eyebrow-less horror, a mechanical monster burst through the wall and into the lab. Debris exploded around him. Lights flickered on and off. White lab coat-clad and Dark Cape-suited scientists scattered in fear. Thaddaeus, however, stood frozen in shock.

What was happening? What was this thing? The rolling machine truly did look like a monster with a menacing-looking jaw that was wide open and ready to devour everything in his laboratory.

The machine first crushed his white pedestal, which he was luckily not currently standing on. Then it blasted through a row of high-resolution monitors with sparks and smoke. Taking an abrupt turn like it had a mind of its own, it destroyed a large beaker storage

THE SASSAFRAS SCIENCE ADVENTURES

unit, causing shattered glass to spray in all directions. Then, to Thaddaeus's horror, the mechanical monster swiveled and barreled straight for them, its powerful jaws chomping and churning.

In sheer panic, the scientists inside the suits began fumbling around with the three-ringed carabiners, trying to get the longitude and latitude settings turned to coordinates before they were crushed and consumed by the threatening monster. The Man With No Eyebrows screamed as the machine drove ahead, not because he was concerned about the well-being of his scientists but because his scientists were escaping one by one, zipping off to places unknown to him. He was losing his army designed for vengeance not to the machine but to invisible zip lines. One by one they disappeared, unharmed by the rumbling machine and now free from him. Then, to crush his plans for vengeance against Cecil Sassafras even further, the horrible vehicle turned and collided with great force directly into the new and improved Forget-O-Nator, smashing it up like it was a simple tin can.

Other than the place along the wall where the tunnel had been dug, nothing had been smashed or destroyed. Neon lights still flashed. Sveta and the Spark Plugs still stood on the stage. Everything was intact—everything, that was, except for Trof's anger. The big miner had finally relented. He had given up his fight for the remote. He had stopped screaming and shouting, and at this moment, he looked to be at complete peace.

Trof's dust-colored entourage of miners had stopped their stomping and were gathering around him. Taras was patting his buddy on the back, and it looked like Trof was about to say something.

THE SASSAFRAS SCIENCE ADVENTURES

"I'm sorry," the previously surly miner apologized sincerely. "I'm sorry for the vay I acted and for the things I said. I realize now it is time for some change around here. It's time for some science and some joviality. It's time for crazy rad, crazy rad good."

The Abramovs nodded, accepting the apology. The miners, both neon- and drab-colored alike, released a collective sigh. Sveta Corvette smiled and took the apology as her cue. The punk rocker started the Spark Plugs again, and the underground cavern was filled with positively uplifting sound.

Whatever the opposite of "positive" and "uplifting" was, that's what Thaddaeus was feeling right now. His lab had been completely destroyed. The horrible machine that had exploded into his lab lay dormant now but not until after it had laid waste to absolutely every corner of his underground laboratory. What was he supposed to do now?

Blaine let out a long sigh. His dream of performing an awe-inspiring break-dancing routine had not come to fruition. The joviality had died down, and all the miners had returned to work. The Sassafras twins sat alone in a corner of the large rock chamber. "Oh, well," the boy thought, "at least we learned some crazy rad SCIDAT about alkali and alkaline metals. Plus we got to see Sveta Corvette again. So it's all good."

"Okay, it's all good," Tracey's voice cut off Blaine's inner

Chapter 6: Oh Iceland, Oh Iceland

monologue. "All the information we learned is entered into the SCIDAT app along with some great pictures from the Archive app. Now it's time to zip to our next location! Let's open our LINLOC apps!"

Blaine forgot all about his lost break-dancing opportunity as he joined his sister in the excitement of looking up where they'd be zipping off to next.

"Iceland!" Tracey exclaimed. "We're going to Iceland, longitude 19° 0' 5.6448" W, latitude 63° 25' 27.588" N, where we'll be studying the topics of transition metals, gold, zinc, and iron!"

"And our local expert's name is . . ." Blaine started but then paused because the name he was about to read seemed a little strange to him. ". . . Harland the Wise. Harland the Wise? Is that right?"

Tracey looked at the name listed on her screen then shrugged. "Harland the Wise it is. Let's zip!"

Shattered glass crunched under his black boots as he took a few slow steps forward before stopping again. Everything was destroyed. His lab was a complete disaster. Every last one of the Dark Cape suits was gone, having zipped off to unknown destinations on invisible zip lines.

To add insult to injury, the scientists who had not been inside

Dark Cape suits had also abandoned him. They had exited through the new hole in the wall that had been created by the destructive machine. None of them had even said goodbye. In fact, they had all seemed happy to go.

The Man With No Eyebrows let out a long, forlorn sigh. Here he was, all alone again.

Through swirls of wonderful light, they zipped and swooshed, enjoying every second of this exhilarating mode of transportation all the way up to the moment the zipping stopped with the customary jerk. Upon landing, Blaine and Tracey patiently waited for their sight and strength to return. When they did, the twins saw they had landed on . . . a tree stump. Yes, it was a large, round tree stump in the middle of a small clearing surrounded by forest. It was flat and polished, almost like a tabletop, and it was wider than the twins were long.

Blaine was lying on his back looking at the tall trees towering around them. Tracey was on her stomach counting the many rings of their landing stump.

"Blaine, this tree was, like, hundreds and hundreds of years old when it was cut down!" Blaine flipped over to his stomach as Tracey turned to her back. "Wow, you're right, Trace. This thing's old. I wonder why we landed here."

Tracey was about to take a guess when she was interrupted by a calm voice coming from the edge of the forest.

"And two shall rest upon The Hewn, one the sun and one the moon."

"Huh?" the twins mused and instinctively turned toward

the voice. It was a tall blonde-headed woman draped in a woolen cloak, revealing only her hands and head. Her kind face was even paler than her hair.

"My name is Ingrid the Hospitable," the woman informed as she approached the twins, her blue eyes sparkling like the pristine waters of a glacier-kissed fjord. "Welcome to The Hewn. We've been waiting for you."

"The Hewn?" Tracey asked.

"We've?" Blaine asked.

The woman smiled, revealing perfect teeth that shone even paler than her skin. "This clearing in the forest, with this ancient wooden table at its center, is called 'The Hewn.' And we, the Kunningskapur, have been waiting for your arrival for quite some time."

Now the Sassafras twins asked together, "The Kunningskapur?"

Ingrid the Hospitable smiled again. "Yes, the Kunningskapur," she confirmed. "We are a guild of adventurers, a fellowship of heroes, a company that seeks the three metals."

This last statement again prompted questions in the twins. Before they could make any more inquiries, two more tall, cloaked individuals emerged from the forest. Both were men. Both were heavily bearded. One had bushy red hair, and the other had waves of almost yellow hair. The red-headed one was sporting a scowl and carrying a large axe. The yellow-headed one had a magnanimous look about him and had a bow and quiver of arrows strapped to his back.

Ingrid held her hand out toward the two as they stepped up to the table and introduced them. "This is Magnus the Brave," she introduced the redhead. "And this is Harland the Wise," she named the yellow-headed man.

Being an expert at introductions, at least in his own mind, Blaine spoke up for himself and for his sister. "Hello, thou friends of us," the boy puffed out his chest. "Verily, verily, I am Blaine, Blaine the Handsome. And this is my sister Tracey, Tracey the . . . Tracey the . . . Tracey the Plucky."

Tracey's face scrunched in a funny way as her brother introduced her. Blaine couldn't tell if it was in amazement or annoyance.

"No!" Magnus the Brave suddenly shouted as he swung his axe into a nearby fallen log. Splinters exploded as his voice rang out, "You are not handsome! You are not plucky! You are the sun and the moon! You must be!"

Blaine's puffed chest deflated. Tracey's scrunched face expanded into shock. Ingrid the Hospitable, however, maintained her calm demeanor as she reached over and put a gentle hand on Magnus the Brave's shoulder.

"Dear Magnus, let us jump neither to haste nor vehemence. Rather, let us welcome these visitors to our land with the open arms of hospitality, and let us give them ample time and explanation."

Magnus looked like he wanted to split another log, but he chose to yield to his more compassionate counterpart.

Even though Magnus's outburst and swinging of the axe had scared him, Blaine was able to get a little air back into his chest. He managed to ask another question. "So you guys are looking for, like, three metals or something?"

This time it was Harland the Wise who answered, his voice as kind as Ingrid's but deeper. "Yes, it is three metals we seek, all of which are transition metals."

"Transition metals?" Blaine asked.

"Yes," Harland the Wise confirmed. "As of now, 38 transition metals can be found in the middle of the periodic table as part of the d-block. All these metals have high melting points, with the exception of mercury, which turns to liquid at room temperature. Elementals and compounds can exist in three main states on earth:

solid, liquid, and gas. Solids have tightly packed molecules with fixed shape and volume. Liquids have widely spaced molecules with a fixed volume. Gases have independently moving molecules with no fixed shape or volume. There is also a fourth state of matter called plasma. This state occurs when matter becomes an electrical-conducting medium. Things like lightning, welding arcs, and the auroras, like the ones we can see here in Iceland, are all examples of plasma. Plasma is created by heating gas to such a high temperature that it becomes ionized."

Ingrid the Hospitable nodded gently and smiled kindly as Harland shared.

Not Magnus. The redhead was huffing, puffing, and looking extremely perturbed.

"For the most part, these transition metals are shiny and hard. They are also useful, including iron, copper, gold, silver, and chromium. Many of these elements are excellent conductors of heat and electricity," Harland the Wise continued fluidly, despite his counterpart's attitude. "Some of these transition metals, such as platinum, iridium, and gold, are known as precious metals because they are rare or difficult to find, rendering them very valuable. Also, some bond with other elements to form important compounds, such as alloys. Alloys are usually a combination of two or more metals that result in a stronger metallic compound, one that is typically stronger or more resistant to corrosion."

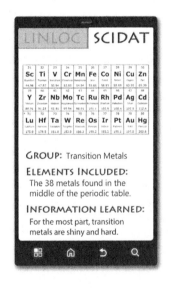

GROUP: Transition Metals

ELEMENTS INCLUDED: The 38 metals found in the middle of the periodic table.

INFORMATION LEARNED: For the most part, transition metals are shiny and hard.

Magnus the Brave's face was now as red as his hair. The man looked like he was about to explode. It was obvious he had something he wanted to say.

Harland continued, nonetheless. "Transition metals are typically grey in color when they are in their purest form. The main exceptions to this are gold and copper, which are often used to make jewelry. Even so, the transition metals can form compounds that are quite colorful. In fact, some gemstones, fireworks, and even paints get their color from traces of transition metal compounds. Speaking of gold—"

"Oh, c'mon!" Magnus shouted, interrupting Harland. He pulled his axe out of the fallen log it was in and swung it powerfully again, finding another nearby log to implant it in. "Enough with science! Let's get to the quest! Who cares about the details of these metals? I wanna know if these two are the ones of whom the prophecy speaks!"

Magnus's outburst was again met with the calm hand of Ingrid on his shoulder. She looked directly at him with her pristine blue eyes and repeated exactly what she'd said earlier without using any words.

Fearless Gold

Harland the Wise did not seem surprised or flustered that Magnus had interrupted him. And Magnus calmed down at the unspoken suggestion of Ingrid's hand.

The twins' big, blonde-headed local expert continued giving clear and precise information. "As I was saying, gold is one of two transition metals that is not a gray metal. Instead, pure gold has a yellow hue. Gold is also rare, which makes it a precious metal. This soft metal can be easily polished and formed into a number of different shapes. Gold is often found in jewelry, electronic equipment and crowns on teeth. Gold is also used as money in the form of gold bullion, which is how banks store gold. When you add palladium, another transition metal, to gold, the color is lightened, turning it to white gold. When you add copper to gold, the color reddens, turning it to rose gold."

"Oh, c'mon," Magnus burst out again. "Harland, you can be so long-winded! Wrap it up already! You said, 'gold is often found,' so let's go find it. It has been hidden long enough! It has been talked about long enough. Let's go find it!"

Harland the Wise nodded in agreement with his red-headed friend. When the local expert spoke again, he started with the statement Magnus had highlighted.

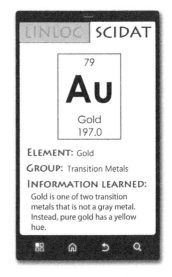

"Gold is often found in flakes or nuggets lying on the ground or in the dirt," the yellow-haired man continued. "It can also be found in geological veins or as tiny particles in quartz rock underground. Gold found in dirt can be easily separated by gravity and a bit of water. Gold is much heavier than the dirt and gravel found with it. If washed properly, water can wash away the dirt particles and leave the gold particles behind." Harland the Wise paused for a breath.

Blaine and Tracey nodded, encouraging the man to continue. "Gold found in rock, in contrast, can be extracted with chemicals. The gold-bearing ore, typically a type of quartz, that has been mined out of the ground is washed or soaked in sodium cyanide, which attaches to the gold and removes it from the ore. Then carbon particles are added, and the gold attaches to those. Another caustic bath removes the gold from the carbon, which can be used again. Finally, an electric current is based through the solution, and the gold is collected. Gold can also be extracted with the use of mercury by forming an amalgam, or mercury alloy. This alloy can be further refined and purified into usable gold."

Harland paused to take a breath. Magnus inhaled quickly and prepared to let out a bursting angry exhale, but before he could, Harland spoke again.

"The purity of gold is measured in carats. Twenty-four-carat gold is the purest. Alloys, or gold mixed with other elements, are usually 22, 18, 14, or 9 carats. Gold's atomic number is 79, its atomic mass is 197.0, and the symbol on the periodic table for gold is AU, which comes from the Latin word for gold, *aurium*. I say all this about gold because it is one of the three metals we seek. The other two are zinc and iron. So let me now tell you all about zinc. Zinc is—"

"No! No! No!" Magnus could stand it no longer. "No more scientific information!"

He shouted as he took up his axe. "We must find out if these two are the sun and the moon, the breath and the petal, the fulfillment of the prophecy, and we must find out right now!"

Now both Ingrid and Harland put their hands on the fiery man's shoulder to calm him. Knowing something needed to give, Tracey spoke in a sudden burst of pluckiness.

"No, no, it's okay. Magnus the Brave needs his answers," Tracey soothed as she stood on the stump to look toward the axe-wielding man. "What exactly are you talking about? What's the prophecy you speak of? How could my brother and I be the sun and the moon and whatever else?"

The fire in Magnus's eyes remained as he answered Tracey, but a civility that had been absent up to this point suddenly joined that fire. "We, the Kunningskapur, have been waiting for generations for the arrival of the sun and the moon. Today, the two of you blew in like chaff on the wind, appearing out of nowhere, which begs the question: are you the two that were prophesied about? If you aren't, then you should leave. But if you are, then we can finally start our quest for the three metals!"

Blaine stood on the stump looking as confused as ever. "I'm not going to lie to you, Magnus," the boy said plainly. "That explanation didn't help at all."

Any hint of civility faded immediately from the redhead's expression, and his grip tightened on the hilt of his axe.

Now Tracey's hand was the one that was placed on a shoulder—the shoulder of her brother. She shot Blaine a look that begged him not to say any more. Then, trying to recapture the civility that had been gained, she looked to Magnus and said calmly, "Actually, that response was helpful. Can you tell us more about this prophecy? Where did it come from?"

"Gunhild," Magnus grunted. "And it's as much poetry as it is prophecy, but we hold to it and always have!"

Blaine was still confused. Tracey was still trying to be helpful. And Harland was still oozing knowledge. He stepped in and began an expounded explanation.

"In 951 A.D. an Icelandic poet named Gunhild the Eloquent wrote a poem titled 'Oh Iceland, Oh Iceland.' In her poem she wrote about a grand treasure hidden and spread out in this land of ours. It was a treasure consisting of three metals. She also added a stanza about two that would come and prove their mettle. It is widely believed that the treasure cannot and should not be found without the presence of these two."

"Long ago, members of the Kunningskapur identified the location of the first parcel of the treasure. However, that spot is continually guarded by the family of Stin. The Stin were original settlers of these hallowed shores. They are a proud and stalwart Icelandic family. Like us, they desire that the treasure be found. However, over the years, they have boldly refused to let anyone, the Kunningskapur included, start the quest to find the three metals until those referenced in Gunhild's poem, the 'sun and the moon,' showed up."

Ingrid the Hospitable now gracefully glided in and recited the ancient poem in her placid voice.

Oh Iceland, Oh Iceland
Land of beauty and riches vast
Where farmers grow and fishers cast
Where mountains rise and sea doth foam
Lay down your arms and call it home

Oh Incipience, Oh Incipience
The longboats came o'er waves did crest
Hath Viking symbols on their chests
Set soles in sand on forlorn shore
Did find their home forevermore

Oh travail, oh travail
Must sew to bloom and sweat to reap
Must stack the blocks for protective keep
They worked the land and begged the sky
Wise they did live, brave they did die

Oh mystery, Oh mystery
Ice of glaciers ne'er be melting
Heat of volcanoes e'er be smelting
Within thy bosom, oh ancient land
Hides a treasure, parceled yet grand

Oh treasure, oh treasure
Zinc and iron and lastly gold
Whom shall seek, alas, whom shall hold
A band shall form that whilst ne'er settle
Shall set their hearts on ye ole three metals

Oh intimation, oh intimation
Ode to the village, hail to the bastion
Trepid yet wise, ask thee thy question
Black sand its bed, long years its rest
Up near the glow hides the last chest

THE SASSAFRAS SCIENCE ADVENTURES

> *Oh prophecy, oh prophecy*
> *And two shall rest upon the hewn*
> *One the sun and one the moon*
> *One a breath and one a petal*
> *Though they be chaff, shall prove their mettle*
>
> *Oh Aluram, oh Aluram*
> *Soldiers of fortune, take warning, take heed*
> *Draw ye the line between want and need*
> *Aye to hallow were the first on shore*
> *May this be Iceland forevermore.*

The eloquence of the ancient words rendered the small group speechless for a few lingering moments. Tracey was the first to say something. "What a beautiful poem," the girl said sincerely. "But wait; hold up."

Blaine began a question with the same amount of sincerity as his sister but lacking her couth. "So you guys think we're the two this poem was talking about because you found us in this clearing laying on this old stump?"

"The Hewn," Magnus corrected.

"Yeah, yeah, the Hewn. That's right," Blaine responded. "But we came here to learn about these metals, not to go treasure hunting. Although actually that really does sound like a blast, you know, because I'm always game for some hunting of treasure. But I mean, how can my sister and I be these two that were written about so long ago? How can we be the sun and the moon? How can we be a breath and a petal? I mean, not to slam the poem or anything, but isn't being the sun and the moon plus being a breath and a petal kind of an oxymoron? And what about being chaff plus proving our mettle? Isn't that also an oxy . . ."

"Moron," Tracey wanted to say but somehow managed to just think as she elbowed her brother in the ribs, urging him to stop. She quickly voiced the next question so that Blaine wouldn't.

"So when the three of you call yourselves the Kunningskapur, what you're saying in effect is that you're the band that has formed that won't settle until you find the treasure, right? Like from the poem?"

"That's right," Magnus growled in pride. "And we carry on a long line of Kunningskapur tradition. Many a member wanted to behold the sun and the moon in their lifetime but breathed their last before that happened. This is our hope too. So the question remains: are the two of you the sun and the moon? Are you a breath and a petal?"

"Well, I guess we did kind of blow in like chaff; didn't we?" Blaine chuckled. "And we landed on this stump."

"The Hewn," Magnus corrected.

"Oh, yeah, The Hewn," Blaine remembered. "So if we are the sun and the moon, and we join your band to go on this treasure hunt or whatever, could we call our group something besides the Kunningskapur?"

Tracey looked at her brother, aghast. Was he trying to stay on Magnus the Brave's bad side?

"I don't know; maybe we can call our crew here something a little less old-fashioned and a little more catchy or crazy rad?" Blaine continued, socially unaware. "I mean, we are looking for precious metals, right? So maybe we can call ourselves the 'Fellowship of the Bling'?"

Magnus again tightened his grip on the hilt of his axe and looked like he was attempting to sift through internal anger to form an external response. However, before the ruddy man could get any words out of his mouth, another gruff voice rang out in the clearing.

"Well, if it isn't the Kunningskapur! You didn't tell me of your plans to come to The Hewn today. And what do we have here? Have the sun and the moon finally arrived?"

Another huge Icelandic man emerged from the trees. He

too was built brawny and was hairy and bearded with midnight-black hair. The man was sporting an ornery-looking expression on a cruel-looking face. He was wielding a sword that was longer than the twins were tall.

Neither Magnus nor Harland nor Ingrid entertained the imposing man with a response.

Instead, the three carefully pulled the Sassafrases down off the top of the stump, while maintaining intense eye contact with this new character.

The black-haired man took slow steps toward the five at the stump, grinning as he approached. The Kunningskapur and the Sassafrases remained stationary, barely breathing. Then, all at once, the intimidating man lifted his sword up over his head and let out a huge roar as he sprinted straight toward the five.

As quick as a whip, Magnus picked up both Blaine and Tracey and bolted out of the clearing and into the trees, matched in speed by both Harland and Ingrid.

"Who is that guy?" Blaine asked as he bounced on Magnus's shoulder, being carried like a sack of potatoes.

"Oh, we didn't tell you about him?" Harland responded. "That's Dagfinn. Dagfinn the Wicked."

Chapter 7: The Three Metals Quest
Acquiring Zinc

How Magnus the Brave was able to carry both of them over his shoulder while at the same time keeping his axe in hand, the Sassafras twins didn't know, but what they did know was that they felt safe and secure in his grip. Not only was Magnus successfully carrying them, but he was also moving at tremendous speed through the forest, zipping around trees and other foliage with dexterous agility. He wasn't about to let this Dagfinn the Wicked guy catch them. They could still hear the grunts of their pursuer, but the volume of his huffs was fading as their group of five outran his party of one.

After several minutes of sprinting, the three Icelanders and two science learners spilled out of the forest into a space that was wide open with rolling, grassy hills that led straight down to a vast navy-blue ocean. Magnus quickly plopped Blaine and Tracey down off his shoulder.

The red-headed man then addressed his fellows, "Ingrid! Harland! You must now take the sun and the moon to the village of Stin. Make haste, and don't look back! I shall go back into the forest to face the wicked one. If I don't return, carry on without me!"

Ingrid the Hospitable and Harland the Wise responded by taking the twins by their hands and leading them quickly away. Magnus the Brave turned to the forest and rushed in without pause. As Blaine and Tracey were being pulled away, they heard Magnus shouting. His shout was immediately matched by a terrible yell from Dagfinn. Then the violent clanking of metal rang out, as axe met a sword.

The twins now understood why Magnus the Brave was named as he was. They only hoped he was the one winning the battle they could clearly hear but which the thick forest was cloaking from their eyes.

The hospitable one and the wise one moved at a swift pace as they ran down and away from the forest, over every soft rise and fall of the landscape, pulling the Sassafrases along with them all the while. Eventually the four got to the shoreline, where the grass changed to dark, coarse sand. It crunched under their feet as they continued to move hastily along—the green, rolling hills to their right and the vast, dark ocean to their left.

The group continued running on and on and on. Just when the twins thought they couldn't run any more, they caught a glimpse of something ahead. A village? Both twelve-year-olds wondered as they huffed and puffed.

"Behold, the renowned fishing village of Stin," Ingrid somehow informed in her normal, calm voice as they charged on.

As the four reached the edge of the village, Ingrid and Harland finally slowed their pace and released their grasp on the twins' hands. The village wasn't large, maybe only a dozen buildings or so, but it was well established. The twins could see by the moss-covered stones and the weathered wooden boards that the structures were built from that this seaside village had been here for a long time.

A chest-high stone wall encircled the village with only one gap in it that the Sassafrases could see. At that gap sat an old man on a wooden chair, his face stoic and wrinkled. The man had long silver hair flowing down from an old, oilskin bucket hat. He was dressed like a cold-weathered fisherman in rugged, hand-stitched leather clothing all the way down to his boots. In his left hand he held a large, gnarly metal hook. In his right hand, a vintage wooden fishing pole.

Ingrid and Harold walked right up to the man and stopped directly in front of his chair. At first, it seemed as if the man didn't realize anyone had approached him. However, after a few long seconds, acknowledgment came in the form of a lifted head and intense eye contact.

"I see the Kunningskapur have returned to the village of Stin," the man said in an elderly yet strong voice.

"We have," Ingrid nodded and calmly beckoned toward the Sassafras twins. "This time we have brought with us the sun and the moon."

The old man's intense eye contact shifted from Ingrid and Harland to Blaine and Tracey. The twins gulped. They could feel themselves being sized up. They didn't know how many prospective suns and moons had been presented over the hundreds of years since the prophecy, but it felt like an extremely important moment. They were not convinced they were the sun and the moon, but evidently that didn't matter. All that mattered was what this rugged and weathered fisherman thought. He was the judge, the jury, and the gatekeeper of this treasure quest.

Without breaking eye contact with the twins, the old man successfully tied the hook in his left hand to the line of the fishing pole in his right hand. He stood slowly. Surprisingly, although he was somewhat hunched, he stood taller than Ingrid and even Harland. Finally he broke off his gaze with the Sassafrases, but right before he did, they were pretty sure they saw a slight glimmer in his eyes. He turned and made his way through the gap in the stone wall and beckoned the four to follow.

The twins looked toward their cloaked friends as if to ask if this was a good thing or not, but neither Ingrid's nor Harland's expressions lent any answers. The group of four followed the old son of Stin down a worn path through a smattering of moss-covered cottages. Then they went past a row of wooden A-frame fish racks full of fish hanging to dry. The Sassafrases scrunched their noses at the strong fish smell. Next, they made their way to a small, leaning wooden building with a single door held shut by an old, rusty metal lock. The aged fisherman grabbed ahold of his fishing hook and used it to quickly open the lock.

"Must not be anything important in here," Blaine thought as he surveyed the shabby building and the pickable lock. But as soon as the creaking door swung open, he saw that he was wrong. Right now, on the ground in the center of the room in front of them, sat a large treasure chest.

"Within thy bosom, oh ancient land, hides a treasure, parceled yet grand," the son of Stin recited, his intense gaze having returned.

Blaine and Tracey immediately recognized he was quoting part of the old poem written by Gunhild the Eloquent, which Ingrid had recited earlier at The Hewn.

"Zinc and iron and lastly gold," the fisherman continued. "Whom shall seek, alas whom shall hold? A band shall form that whilst ne'er settle, shall set their hearts on ye ole three metals."

The old man finished the stanza and let the poetic words fall into the silence of the moment. Tracey was speechless. Ingrid and Harland looked as though they were waiting for an important verdict. Even Blaine was holding his tongue and waiting for whatever would come next.

"Honorable members of the Kunningskapur," the son of Stin said to the hospitable one and the wise one. "Today the long-awaited prophecy has been fulfilled. For you have brought with you the sun and the moon. Therefore, you may start your quest for the three metals."

The old man leaned down and opened the chest, revealing a heaping pile of silvery-colored coins. The silence was filled with gasps of delight. A charming smile formed on the fisherman's wrinkled face as the four treasure hunters carefully ran their fingers across the mound of beautiful, inviolable coins.

"Zinc," Harland the Wise said with delight. "These coins are made of zinc."

"The first metal listed in the poem," Tracey exclaimed.

The yellow-haired man nodded. "With an atomic number of 30 and an atomic mass of 65.39, zinc has the symbol of Zn on the periodic table." The local expert shared SCIDAT with excitement in his eyes as he continued to gently rummage through the coins.

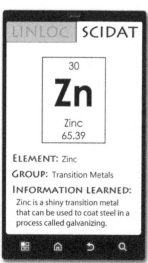

"Zinc is often found alongside lead, and sometimes copper, gold, or silver, in sulfide ores. It is a shiny transition metal that is known for its protective abilities. It can be used to coat steel in a process called galvanizing. Galvanizing stops water and oxygen from causing the steel to rust. Did you know that rusting is an example of a special type of reaction called a redox reaction?"

Blaine and Tracey shook their heads no.

"Redox reactions involve two reactions that always occur together—oxidation and reduction. Both of these reactions involve the movement of electrons in molecules and atoms. An oxidation reaction happens when a molecule or an atom has a loss of electrons. A reduction reaction happens when a molecule or an atom has a gain of electrons. Combustion, photosynthesis, rusting, and respiration are all examples of redox reactions." The old son of Stin smiled, obviously seeming to enjoy the scientific information as much as the twins were.

"Zinc is used in all kinds of things," Harland continued. "It is used in pyrotechnics to create a smoke effect. It can be mixed with carbon to make batteries that can power flashlights, toys, and other small electronics. It can easily mix with other metals, forming useful alloys like brass. A compound of zinc is used in sunscreen to prevent harmful UV rays from the sun from damaging skin. And finally, zinc is also considered an essential element for many processes in the body."

Blaine and Tracey were enjoying the treasure trove of zinc coins, but they were even happier for their friends from Iceland, who had been waiting for this moment for generations. How exhilarating this must be for them. They were also thinking about the interesting old gatekeeper they had met: the son of Stin. How long had he been sitting in that chair at the gap in the wall? How many times had he turned treasure hunters away because they were missing the sun and the moon?

"Whom shall seek, alas, whom shall hold?" The old fisherman quoted the line from Gunhild's poem again, this time with less mystery and more joy. "It is you, honorable members of the Kunningskapur; it is you. Alas, you hold this treasure in your hands even now."

"However, this is just the first of the parceled treasure," he said in a way that brought everyone's attention back to his gaze. "The time has come for the sun and the moon to prove their mettle. You must move from the village of Stin up to yonder misty chasm where you will find the two bastions. It is there you will find yourselves at the threshold of the next parcel of treasure. But be warned; take alarum; missteps and wrong choices could lead to your end."

This warning from the old fisherman wiped the smiles off the twins' faces and put gulps in their throats. They weren't sure they wanted the opportunity to prove their mettle.

"The two bastions are identical, and they guard the entry points of two bridges," the man continued. "The bridges are also identical, and they span the length of the misty chasm. When stepped on, one bridge will surely hold, and one bridge will surely fall. Stationed in the two bastions are two bridge keepers. You are allowed to ask one of the bridge keepers only one question, one single question of your choosing. One of the bridge keepers will surely tell the truth, whereas the other will surely lie."

The old man paused for a few long moments to let all of what he'd said sink in. Then he addressed the four with stern encouragement, "Be trepid yet wise and ask thee thy question."

The Sassafras twins gulped again. They weren't sure about wisdom, but trepidation wasn't going to be a problem.

"To move forward in your quest for the three metals, you must have empty hands, but full hearts and minds," the son of Stin added. "Leave this chest of zinc here, and bring the other parcels of treasure back to this spot. Go now. I implore you! Press on. Succeed in your quest. And do it for the glory of Iceland. Aye to hallow!"

"Aye to hallow!" Harland and Ingrid responded in unison.

Harland the Wise added, "Ode to the village!"

To which the fisherman replied, "Hail to the bastion!"

Blaine and Tracey weakly followed the three Icelanders from the small treasure shed, through the village, back out of the gap in the stone wall. They waved goodbye to the son of Stin and followed the hospitable one and the wise one around the outside of the stone wall to the other side of the village to a rocky trailhead. The twelve-year-olds weren't paying much attention to where they were going because their thoughts were being bogged down by the weight that now rested on their shoulders. They were considered to be the sun and the moon, the two prophesied about in Icelandic lore, the two who were supposed to come and "prove their mettle," the ones who should be wise and help find this wonderful treasure. How in the world were they supposed to do all that?

"You weren't thinking about going on without me; were you?" A booming voice suddenly brought the twins' attention back to the here and now. It was Magnus the Brave. He was approaching with head held high and battle axe still in hand, yet he also now had a pronounced limp.

"Are you okay, brave one?" Ingrid asked. "Have you vanquished our enemy? Does Dagfinn the Wicked still pose a threat?"

Magnus the Brave gave a small chuckle as a preface to his response and then said, "Vanquish may be a strong word, but I did rough him up a bit, as he did me. Alas, I presume I got him good enough to buy us at least a little bit of time."

The red-headed man motioned toward Blaine and Tracey. "Where do we stand on our quest? Are these two really the sun and the moon?"

"Indeed they are, brave one," Ingrid replied with a smile. "Because of their presence, the son of Stin allowed us passage into the village, where we were shown the first parcel of treasure—the first of three metals—a chest full of zinc coins."

Magnus's bushy, red eyebrows rose up on his forehead, fully interested and partially impressed.

"Now we make our way toward the second parcel of treasure,"

Harland the Wise said. "Up and onward to the bastions at the misty chasm, the threshold for the second metal, where a timeless riddle awaits."

Magnus the Brave nodded and took his place in line as the group of five resumed their way up the rocky trail. The higher they climbed, the darker the sky seemed to get. The navy-blue ocean was still visible down below them to their left, but it now looked far away, like a distant spot on a map. The grassy, green hills that had been to their right were now nowhere to be seen, as rocks monopolized the terrain. What they walked over was sharp and gray.

As they climbed the trail, Blaine mused out loud about the situation. "Okay, so I get that there is a big chasm with cliffs and stuff with a couple bridges going across, because of course you need a bridge to cross a chasm. But what's up with everything being in pairs? I mean, why do there have to be two bridges that look alike and two bridge keepers and two bastions? And on a side note, I don't know what a bastion is. But it's like two, two, and two, and then when it gets to the important part—the question—it's only one? Really? We can only ask one question of one of the keeper guys? I mean, if one of those bridges is going to fall, I think we should get more than one question."

"The son of Stin is stern, yet in his sternness, he is dependable," Ingrid the Hospitable informed. "We can trust that the riddle at the misty chasm works exactly as he says it does."

"Okay, okay, I get that," Blaine continued. "So if that's the case, what question should we ask the guy, and which of the guys do we ask? Because even if we can think up the perfect question, but then we ask the liar guy, everything is kaput."

Blaine was right, Tracey thought. This riddle did seem almost impossible.

"The obvious question to ask is, 'Which bridge will get us safely across the chasm?'" Tracey spoke, a dash more articulate than her brother.

"If we ask this question of the truth-telling bridge keeper, then no problem, but if we ask the lying bridge keeper, then we have a big problem," Blaine nodded and added, "a big, deep, painful problem."

"If the two bridges look the same, and there's no way to tell which bridge keeper is the truth teller," Tracey continued. "Then at first glance, the riddle seems unsolvable."

"Maybe there's another way across the chasm," Blaine postulated, "like a hanging vine we can swing on or some hidden handholds and footholds we can use to climb across. Or maybe there's another way to get around the chasm altogether."

Harland the Wise shook his head before saying out loud, "The bastions and the bridges are located exactly where they are by design. They are a threshold for the next parcel of treasure. If there is another way around the misty chasm, it will serve as neither pathway nor threshold to the second metal."

Both the twins had many more thoughts on the matter. Blaine was about to voiced his thoughts, but he was interrupted by the sight in front of them. The group of five had reached the top of the rocky trail, and they stood facing the misty chasm. It was aptly named because the gorge had clouds of mist slowly rising and rolling out of it almost like a giant, oblong cauldron. Any sight of the ocean had long since disappeared, and the chasm stretched as far as the eye could see in either direction. Even though they weren't at its edge, it was apparent that the misty chasm was both hopelessly wide and impossibly deep.

To add to the ominousness of the chasm, two bridge keepers stood about 20 yards apart from each other. They were old men, hooded and cloaked. They were holding tall, gnarly, wooden staffs in their hands, making no movement except for the men's long white beards blowing slightly sideways in the misty wind. Each stood in front of small, stone, fort-like buildings that served as the entry points to the two expansive bridges.

Inquisitive Iron

"These stone forts must be bastions," the twins thought. Their thoughts and eyes turned to the bridges that the bastions were guarding. The two bridges were not made of stone, and they did not look to be sturdily built at all. Instead, the bridges sagged across the wide chasm. They were made only of rickety wooden planks and knotted, frayed rope. To the Sassafrases, it looked like neither of the bridges could be used to safely cross over. So even if they could somehow identify which bridge keeper was the liar and which was the truth teller, how were they supposed to trust their lives to either of these dilapidated bridges? Both twelve-year-olds shuddered at the thought of it and again pondered how much easier it was to feel trepidation than to have wisdom.

Blaine again verbally processed their situation out loud. "Okay. The question. The question. The question to ask. Well, wait, maybe the question should start with a nice greeting like, 'Hello, sir,' or "Mister honorable bridge guy keeper man.' No, that's probably too much. What about walking up and saying, 'Sup, bro?' No, no, no, that's not formal enough."

Blaine paused, closed his eyes, and let out sigh before continuing, "Okay, let's forget about the greeting right now, or maybe stick with a nice 'hello,' and get back to what the question should be. 'Hello, what bridge should we take?' Nope, that wouldn't work because we might accidentally pick the liar. 'Hello, are you the liar?' Nope, that wouldn't work because the liar would say no and the truth teller would also say no and we can't tell them apart. Okay, how about 'Hello, is the other bridge keeper the liar?' Oh, man, at first that kind of seems like it works, but again the liar would lie, and even if we figured out who was who, we still wouldn't know which bridge to cross. Golly gee, we need more than one question. Okay, wait, how about this: 'Hello, can—'"

"How about this?" Magnus the Brave interrupted, having grown weary of Blaine's monologue. "How about I pick you up right now and—

Ingrid the Hospitable again put a gentle hand on Magnus the Brave's shoulder. "One a breath and one a petal, though they be chaff, shall prove their mettle," she said, graciously quoting the prophetic line from the ancient poem.

A look of understanding replaced the look of irritation on the brave one's face.

Simultaneously, a look of understanding formed on Harland the Wise's face. However, he was thinking about a different stanza of the poem altogether:

> *Oh intimation, oh intimation,*
> *Ode to the village, hail to the bastion,*
> *Trepid yet wise, ask thee thy question.*

Immediately, Blaine could see by Harland's expression that the man knew what question to ask. The Sassafras boy smiled and looked toward his sister, wanting her to know that the wise one had figured it all out. It was then that Blaine saw that Tracey had solved the riddle as well. It was as clear as day on her face that his sister knew the correct question to ask.

However, before any questions were directed toward either of the bridge keepers, a loud, angry shout rang out in the dark, foggy air behind the treasure hunters. The Kunningskapur and the Sassafrases turned to see a scowling, black-haired figure emerge from the rocks at the top of the trail. Dagfinn the Wicked was back.

Magnus the Brave immediately jumped into action, gripping his axe tightly and limping straight toward the intimidating newcomer. Even with the limp, he reached the wicked one within seconds in a fiery ball of red hair and grunts. Dagfinn brushed Magnus aside with a substantial blow to the back of the brave one's head using the hilt of his sword. As Magnus fell to the ground stunned, Dagfinn roared fiercely and ran straight toward the remaining four.

Now Harland the Wise rose in one fluid movement. The yellow-headed Icelander grabbed the bow from his back and an arrow from his quiver, nocking the arrow in place and taking aim at the approaching villain.

"Swick!" the arrow sounded as it shot out from the bow.

"Clink!" Dagfinn's sword sounded as it knocked Harland's arrow harmlessly out of mid-air.

Swick! Swick! Two more arrows were released in succession.

Clink, clank. Both were knocked to the ground.

Dagfinn the Wicked raced forward and reached the spot where Blaine, Tracey, Ingrid, and Harland were standing. The Sassafrases were shocked by his proximity. He seemed even bigger now that he was this close to them.

"I want the treasure," Dagfinn spat out through clenched, grimy, black-outlined teeth. "You silly members of the Kunningskapur can use these two children to help you find it, but when you do, I want it. I want it for myself. It's mine. It's all mine."

As imposing and scary as the angry man's threat was, the twins felt encouraged that evidently Dagfinn wasn't aware they'd already found a parcel of the treasure in the village of Stin.

"Well, you know," Blaine spoke up, "the treasure is supposed to be for all of Iceland, not just for one person. Don't you remember the line from the poem? The one that says, 'Soldiers of fortune, take warning, take heed. Draw ye the line between want and need.'"

Dagfinn the Wicked looked at Blaine aghast. Had this small child had the audacity to rebuke him? A dark indignation formed and deepened on the wicked one's face. He raised his sword as though he wanted to crush Blaine with it.

However, Harland the Wise was not about to let that happen. His arrows had missed, but his hands and arms did not. With a powerful punch, the wise one was able to knock the sword out of the wicked one's hand. Then, in a lightning-fast move, Harland slid around behind Dagfinn and put him in a headlock, and although Dagfinn was bigger than Harland, it was immediately apparent the headlock was solid and vice-grip like. Still, Dagfinn the Wicked was squirming and thrashing around. It was only a matter of time before the wicked one escaped.

Blaine turned toward Tracey, grabbed her by the shoulders, and looked directly into her eyes. "Tracey, I know you know what question to ask. I saw it on your face earlier. Now is the time. Go ask the question, Tracey. Go!"

Worry replaced certainty on the girl's face. "What if I get it wrong, Blaine? If I ask the wrong question, the bridge will collapse. We'll fall into the chasm."

Blaine looked even deeper into his sister's eyes. "I trust you, Tracey. I trust you."

Ingrid the Hospitable, who was paying close attention to them, nodded in encouragement. Tracey took a deep breath and turned from Ingrid and her brother to face the misty chasm. She looked back and forth between the two bridge keepers several times. Neither of the old men had moved a muscle. Tracey locked eyes with the one on the right and made her way toward him.

Blaine took a deep breath. His sister had chosen a bridge keeper and had settled on a question. This thing was about to go down—hopefully not literally down. Tracey stepped directly in front of the old man and cleared her throat, hesitantly.

"C'mon Tracey. You can do it. I trust you," Blaine affirmed silently.

Ingrid stood, with an encouraging smile, next to Blaine. Harland held fast to the wiggling Dagfinn. Magnus picked his injured body up off the ground, listening for the question Tracey was going to ask.

The Sassafras girl cleared her throat one more time and asked the old bridge keeper, "Which bridge will the other bridge keeper tell me will fall?"

The old man remained stoic and frozen for a few agonizing seconds more. Then, he slowly lifted his wooden staff and pointed over toward the other bridge keeper's bridge.

Tracey swiveled back toward her people with a wry smile and a dubious shrug of the shoulders. "I guess that's the bridge we should take," she said. "The one he's pointing toward."

Harland the Wise looked at Tracey with a profoundly proud smile on his face, a look that confirmed to all—the Sassafras girl had indeed chosen the correct question to ask.

Suddenly, Dagfinn the Wicked arched his back, roared, and broke free from Harland the Wise's grip. The huge man grabbed the sword off the ground. However, before the hulking man could take one swing of the sword or shout even one syllable of a threat, the bridge keeper near Tracey swung his staff and knocked Dagfinn out cold with a single blow. The old man brought the staff back to his side and returned to his expressionless, motionless stance as though nothing had happened.

The Sassafras twins' jaws dropped in awe. The three members of the Kunningskapur stood as if in salute.

"Hail to the bastion," Harland the Wise stated respectfully.

"Hail to the bastion," his four companions repeated.

"And now let us go to the bridge," Ingrid motioned. "Let us not tarry at this threshold, but let us cross it."

The hospitable one then led the way toward the bridge to the left. The Kunningskapur all seemed confident that Tracey had identified the correct bridge with her question.

Blaine was certain his sister had figured it out. He trusted her. Tracey, however, was having doubts. What if she had asked the wrong question?

Mist from the chasm swirled around them as they reached the bastion at the precipice's edge. The bridge keeper stationed here, like his counterpoint, remained statue like and did nothing to stop the group of five from entering the small stone building that served as the entryway to the bridge. Ingrid walked first, then the men, and last, Tracey entered the bastion.

The structure was only about the size of a large elevator, and they passed through it quickly, ready to set foot on the bridge. Without pause, the hospitable one stepped out and put all her weight on the first plank. Tracey sucked in a nervous breath. The plank . . . held. Ingrid continued out further onto the precarious-looking bridge with the three men in step behind her. The bridge squeaked, bounced, and shook a bit in rhythm with their steps, but it was holding.

Tracey exhaled the breath she had sucked in and took her first step out onto the bridge. Even as her foot hit the first plank, she could see down past her shoe through the large gaps in the bridge, down into the seemingly endless depth of the chasm. Tracey shivered and brought her gaze back up horizontally.

"How about no more looking into the chasm and instead just crossing the bridge," the girl said to herself. That's exactly what Tracey proceeded to do, and with every step, there was less anxiety and more surety—the correct question had been asked.

Upon safe arrival to the other side, the group could see that their path forward was going to drop down, sloping away from the imposing gorge. All five glanced toward the bridge they had crossed and the bastion who stood on the other side of the chasm. They bid it all farewell and made their way down the rocky, wide path.

The Sassafras twins had assumed the second parcel of treasure was going to be waiting for them in a clear spot once they crossed the bridge, but it hadn't been. So the troop's treasure hunting continued.

Soon, they could see the navy-blue ocean to their left. As they got closer, they saw that where the ocean met the land, there was lots of black sand. It was obvious their pathway was leading them straight toward the black beach. In little time they were there.

The black sand was shiny and fine and compressed softly under their footsteps. Directly in front of the group lay something Blaine and Tracey had never seen before, but somehow the sight seemed expected and familiar. Maybe it was because of the "Oh Iceland, Oh Iceland" poem.

"Are those longboats?" Blaine asked.

"Yes, they are," Harland the Wise confirmed. "Two beached, ancient longboats. And look at the center of them. There lies a chest."

Harland was right. Half buried in the black sand, in between the two boats, was a large, wooden chest that looked much like the one they'd found in the village of Stin. Magnus the Brave, who hadn't been present for the first parcel, was the first to reach the second chest.

The big, red-headed man dropped to his knees in front of the box and immediately opened its lid.

"Iron!" The Brave One bellowed in glee. "A chest full of iron! And look, it's the ancient, hand-forged iron weapons of our ancestors!"

As the other four reached the spot, they saw that Magnus was correct. It was a chest full of antique Viking weapons. There were arrowheads, spear tips, axe heads, assorted blades, and so much more. It was a trove the twins were sure must have great historical significance and therefore more than likely priceless.

"'Lay down your arms, and call it home,'" Blaine quoted a

line he remembered from Gunhild the Eloquent's poem.

"And it looks like that's exactly what they did," Tracey concluded.

Harland the Wise nodded in agreement and shared about the science behind the iron treasure they'd found. "The symbol on the periodic table for iron is Fe, which comes from the Latin word, *ferrum*. Iron has an atomic number of 26, an atomic mass of 55.85 and is mainly found in hematite and magnetite, which are quite abundant. In fact, about 90 percent of metal that is refined is iron, making it probably the single most important transition metal in modern society. However, iron working began more than 3,000 years ago when people learned how to separate iron by heating its ores with charcoal. As the technique developed, iron replaced brass in tools and weapons, like in this treasure of ancient weapons we see now before us."

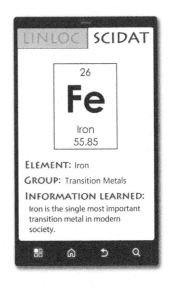

This time around, Magnus didn't seem to be bothered at all by the scientific information Harland was giving. Maybe that was because he believed Blaine and Tracey to be the sun and the moon. Or maybe it was the fact that he was literally holding part of the treasure in his hands.

"Iron's crystalline structure is strong when heated," Harland the Wise continued, "because the space between the grains shrinks further in the heat, making it even stronger. Iron mixed with carbon creates steel. Steel is the most important metal in the world. Steel can be cast, formed, or welded into many different forms to create everything from paper clips to the framework for skyscrapers.

Additionally, iron is one of the few transition metals that is ferromagnetic, meaning its elements have magnetic properties. This means that it has the ability to attract or repel other metals."

Harland admired some of the ancient iron arrowheads before continuing. "The same metal that was used to form these arrowheads is at the core of the Earth. There is actually iron in our red blood cells as well, which makes it possible for the cells to carry oxygen. So not only is iron a transition metal that is extremely useful, but it is also essential to life."

Looking at the treasure in front of them, on this unique and beautiful beach, and thinking back to the chest full of zinc coins they'd found in the quaint and picturesque village of Stin, the Sassafras twins could see why Gunhild the Eloquent's poem began with, "Land of beauty and riches vast."

This wasn't even everything. There was still one parcel of treasure to be found.

As if she were thinking along the same lines, Ingrid the Hospitable quoted the line most befitting of the illuminating poem for the current place in their venture: "Up near the glow hides the last chest." The snowy white woman pointed her finger into the distance, causing the entire fellowship to cast their gaze beyond the beach and up into the hills.

There, up in the foggy Icelandic landscape, stood an actively smelting volcano.

Chapter 8: The Masaki-Do Dojo
Kihuping Lanthanides

"So that's called what?" Blaine asked again.

"*Alfhòl*," Ingrid repeated graciously. "They are small homes and buildings that have been built for, or quite possibly by, Huldufòlk."

Blaine's face scrunched in skepticism as the troop of five hiked past the small structure nestled into the hillside. Ingrid the Hospitable had already explained that Huldufòlk were legendary, elf-like creatures that were said to live in the most rural locations in Iceland. Tracey, too, was finding it hard to believe that actual elves had constructed this small abode they were passing now. It wasn't the first one they'd passed. There had been several more lower on the hill and now as they continued to hike closer to the glow of the smelting volcano, the twins could see more of these *alfhòles*. They were colorful and intricately built structures with doors and windows and roofs. Some even had little fenced-in yards with things like tiny gardens and mailboxes.

"C'mon," Blaine scoffed. "You guys don't believe that elves built all these little places; do you?"

Magnus the Brave looked at the Sassafras boy and growled. "I like it better when you're the sun than when you're the breath."

Blaine gulped, slightly intimidated, but at this point he knew that although Magnus remained gruff with him, the axe-wielding man actually liked him.

"There are stories of the Huldufölk carrying off large scores of game like wild rams and reindeer," Magnus scoffed back at Blaine, defending the legend. "It's also been told that the Huldufölk help to protect our hallowed shores and have fended off many a threatening foe."

Blaine was about to shoot another comment to the brave one, but he was stopped by a look from his sister that said both don't you dare and let's focus on finding the third parcel of treasure. Blaine the Breath held his tongue, and the five treasure hunters continued their hike through the *alfhòl* toward the glow. It turned out to be a rather short jaunt because, before the group hiked, there it was, the third chest, sitting right next to the most elaborately designed *alfhòl* they'd seen yet.

The three members of the Kunningskapur looked at each other with big, satisfied smiles. They had done it. They had found all the parcels of treasure. They'd found the first, second, and now third metal. Blaine and Tracey, the sun and the moon, smiled along with them. They were beyond happy that after so many years and so many generations, this great Icelandic treasure had finally been found.

With the hot glow of the volcano above them, the group of five inviolably approached the chest. Ingrid the Hospitable was the first to set a hand on the chest, and with that hand she opened the lid. Immediately it was confirmed: this was the treasure chest full of shiny gold! Awe and wonder outlined the eyes of everyone in the fellowship.

Magnus the Brave, sounding more like a giddy, innocent child than an axe-wielding tough guy, said, "Ha ha ha, we've found it! We've found the grand treasure of this land. After all this time, we've found it! Now we can give it back to Iceland."

"That's right," Harland the Wise agreed. "With joy in our hearts, let us give it back to Iceland! Let us take up this chest of gold and also the chest of iron we left back by the longboats, and let us cheerfully haul them back to the village of Stin to be joined with the first chest of zinc. This parceled treasure will now be united. It will be the pride and joy of Iceland!"

The whole fellowship agreed as if with one heart. However, before they could take up the chest, a loud, angry roar sounded from down the hill behind them. Before they turned to see, they already knew from whence the roar came. Relentless as he was, Dagfinn the Wicked had somehow made it across the misty chasm to continue his pursuit.

"Ah ha! You've found it! You lovely little measly members of the Kunningskapur have actually found it," the black-haired man shouted as he ran at them with his gargantuan sword. "And now it's mine, all mine!"

This time it was Tracey, the moon and the petal, that reminded the wicked one of the last stanza of Gunhild the Eloquent's poem.

Soldiers of fortune!
Take warning, take heed,
Draw ye the line between want and need!
Aye to hallow were the first on shore!
May this be Iceland forevermore!

"Aye to hallow!" Tracey's four companions echoed in ardent conviction as they took a defensive stance.

"Aye to nothing!" Dagfinn the Wicked growled in defiance, close enough to do damage with his sword. Immediately, a series of things happened so fast they were virtually unbelievable. A pitter-patter, clink-clank, pitter-patter sounded from behind them. Instinctively, the treasure hunters swiveled in response only to see that more gold had somehow been piled on top of the already heaping mound in the chest. Next, a pitter-patter, oof, drag sounded from behind them. They swiveled again to see that Dagfinn the Wicked was . . . gone.

The big, surly man was nowhere to be seen. He had disappeared without a trace.

Sometime later, Blaine and Tracey Sassafras were also preparing to disappear without a trace. They didn't think the Kunningskapur would mind. After all Gunhild the Eloquent's poem did say of the sun and moon, 'Though they be chaff shall prove their mettle.' The twins hoped they had proven their mettle. Now it was time to be like chaff and blow out of this wonderfully mysterious and beautiful place just as they had blown in.

The two twelve-year-olds had all the SCIDAT data and pictures about transition metals entered into their phones. They had their helmets and harnesses on, and they were about to open up the LINLOC applications and zip to the next location.

As they sat outside the village of Stin, against the stone wall, they still had some questions. Sure, they'd found all the parceled treasure and had successfully hauled it back to the village of Stin, but what in the world had happened to Dagfinn? Had Huldufólk actually knocked him out and carried him off in a matter of seconds?

And, sure, everything had worked out at the misty chasm, but was one of those bridge keepers really a liar, and would one of those bridges really have fallen? There were these questions and more, but they would have to linger in the twins' minds because now it was time to zip to . . .

"Japan," Tracey explained as she read the information on

the LINLOC app. "Longitude 141° 0' 19.1" E, latitude 37° 25' 6.6" N. We will be studying the topics of lanthanides and actinides, along with neodymium and uranium."

"All with a local expert by the name of Sensei Masaki," Blaine added. "Hmmmm, Sensei Masaki. Another interesting name for a local expert."

"All right, bro, let's calibrate and zip!" Tracey exhorted as she grabbed her three-ringed carabiner. Blaine joined her, and within a matter of moments, the two were dangling in the air with their harnesses and carabiners attached to the invisible lines that would take them to Japan.

Swoosh! The two science learners shot off at breakneck speed through wonderful whirls and splendid swirls of beautiful light. Upon reaching their destination, they landed with a jerk, their carabiners automatically unclipping from the invisible lines. Their bodies slumped over, devoid of sight and strength. The Sassafrases couldn't see or feel a thing, that was, until they felt themselves being . . . punched? Or were they being kicked? Either way, they didn't like it, so when their strength fully returned, they knew they were either going to need to fight back against whatever was assaulting them or take up a defensive stance.

Tracey chose the latter and stood with both her arms in front of her, crossed over each other in a sort of x-shape. Blaine chose the former and hopped to his feet with flailing arms and legs, looking more like he was dancing on a red ant pile than doing any kind of fighting.

"Whoa, whoa, okay, okay, settle down, friends," the twins heard a voice with an American accent say.

THE SASSAFRAS SCIENCE ADVENTURES

The invisible zip-line travelers' eyesight had returned. They were able to see the voice belonged to a boy who looked to be about their age. He had sunshine-colored blonde hair, bright happy eyes, and a smile that was kind and friendly. He was wearing a white gi with a black belt to complete his martial arts uniform. Even though he looked so kind and nice, the Sassafrases were pretty sure he'd been the one who had been simultaneously punching and kicking the two of them.

"You guys are superb at the art of stealth, but you should work on your kumite," he said, still smiling.

"Kumite?" Tracey asked.

"Yeah, kumite," the boy responded. "You know, the light sparring we do to practice our kihon and katas."

The twins were dumbfounded. Not only did they not know what kumite, kihon, or kata meant, but their minds were reeling with questions. They thought at every new location they were supposed to land as closely to their local expert as possible without being detected. Had this boy seen them land and appear out of nowhere? Was he Sensei Masaki, their local expert?

"That was light sparring?" Blaine chuckled and rubbed his shoulder in a spot where he'd been punched or kicked, trying to take his thoughts back to what the boy had just said.

The boy responded with a chuckle of his own, stepped forward, and put his arms around Blaine and Tracey like they'd been friends forever. "Oh, man, we never know what Sensei Masaki is going to surprise us with; am I right?" he asked with a smile. "I love that he had you two drop in on me while I was practicing my kata. That kind of thing will keep me on my toes and make me a better ninja."

"You're a ninja?" Tracey asked.

"Well, yeah," the boy responded like his statement shouldn't have been shocking. "We all are. Look around."

For the first time since their arrival, the Sassafras twins brought their eyes up from the spot they'd landed in and let their gazes take in their full surroundings. They were inside a large karate dojo. They had landed on a mat near the back of the dojo, but it was just one of many mats where students were practicing moves and sparring with each other. By the twins' estimation, there were nearly 50 students here, all teenagers, all wearing white karate uniforms. They all looked to be of Asian descent, all, that is, except for the blonde-haired student Blaine and Tracey were standing next to.

Although it was a building designed to train fighters, it was also a breathtakingly beautiful place. The windows and sliding doors were designed in a traditional style with wood-framed latticework housing horizontal, rectangular panes made from translucent white paper that let the perfect amount of calming soft light in. There were large, framed, traditional Japanese paintings evenly spaced along the exterior walls. Also spaced perfectly around the dojo were scrolls with Japanese characters inked on them in exquisite calligraphy. Another thing the twins noticed was that there was melodious flute music drifting through the building from some unseen spot.

"Pretty sweet place, huh?" the boy said, bringing the twins' eyes back to him.

Both Sassafrases nodded.

"I feel lucky to be a part of this dojo," he said sincerely. "I was the first non-Japanese student Sensei Masaki has ever invited to be a member here at Masaki-do."

"Wow, what a great honor," Tracey said.

The boy nodded.

The Sassafras twins both exhaled in a peaceful way, looking around the amazing dojo once more. It was then the two realized their presence had been noticed by several more of the students.

Four teenagers approached them—two boys and two girls. One of the girls was abnormally tall. The other girl was of normal height and size but had a fierce set of eyes that seemed to be transfixed in a gaze toward them. One boy was short and small, whereas the other was square, solid, and built like a tank.

"*Konnichiwa*," the blonde-headed boy greeted in Japanese and bowed as the four kids approached.

The four responded with bows and greetings of their own, sort of. The girl with intense eyes did a sort of grunt and a half bow, while keeping her eyes locked on the Sassafrases. The tank-like boy bowed but didn't say anything. The smaller boy spoke and bowed but did both quickly, and the tall girl did both as well, but she did hers slower than the rest.

Blaine and Tracey stood awkwardly for a few long moments, not knowing if more pleasantries were going to be exchanged, if they were about to do some more "light" sparring, or what was supposed to happen.

All of a sudden, the blonde-headed boy exploded into a joyful introduction, "These four are my best friends here at Masaki-do!"

At this, the approaching people seemed to lighten up a bit with the exception of the staring-eyes girl. The boy motioned to her first and said, "Meet Hageshi Tora, or in English, Fierce Tiger. She's not afraid of anything."

Next, he motioned toward the tallest of the bunch. "Meet Chiteki Kirin, or Intelligent Giraffe. Her proverbial mind can outsmart anyone. Next, we have Attosuru Tonbo, or Overpowering Dragonfly," he said, referring to the short boy. "He's probably the most determined person I've ever met. Last but not least is Sairento Sai." He gestured toward the last boy. "Silent Rhino. He's completely mute, but he's also the strongest ninja in the entire dojo."

The twins bowed and smiled, saying, "*Konnichiwa*," hoping

this was proper etiquette.

"And what's your name?" Tracey asked the blonde-headed boy.

"Haipa Yagi," he answered.

"Super cool," Blaine said, bobbing his head. "What does that mean? Something like Mighty Lion, Stealthy Wolverine, Soaring Falcon, or something like that?"

"Hyper Goat," the boy answered with a smile.

Blaine gulped. "Excuse me?"

"Hyper Goat," the boy repeated. "Haipa Yagi—Hyper Goat."

"Huh," Blaine responded, again bobbing his head, trying to pretend like he loved the boy's ninja name. Tracey could tell the boy didn't care if Blaine liked his name or not. Somehow this non-Japanese boy had found his place here at this dojo.

"Outside of the dojo, my name is Seth Everett Prue, or Seth E. Prue," he said. "My parents work for an NGO here in Japan. They moved here from America when I was only two. I've grown up here, and I've adopted Japanese culture as my own. I absolutely love everything about it! To my delight and honor, Sensi Masaki and the students here have accepted me as one of their own."

Both twins smiled and nodded, thinking this was pretty cool.

"And what about you guys?" Seth E. Prue, the Hyper Goat, asked. "Who are you?"

"We are Blaine and Tracey Sassafras," Blaine responded. "I'm Blaine; she's Tracey. We're twins, but I'm older by five minutes and fourteen seconds." The last part received an eye roll from Tracey. "We're actually here in Japan because we want to learn—"

"Masaki-do! *Konnichiwa!*"

Blaine was suddenly interrupted by an elderly yet strong

voice. All at once, every student in the dojo snapped to attention, bowed, and responded as if in one unified voice. "*Konnichiwa,* Sensei!"

The Sassafras twins attempted to be unified in their bowing and greeting, but they were unsuccessful. Standing straight after the bow, Blaine and Tracey saw the strong voice had come from a smallish, wrinkled old man who'd entered the dojo and stood front and center with the absolute attention of everyone in front of him. He was bald apart from a few whisps of long, white hair flowing from above his ears. He also had a long rather narrow white beard and mustache. The old man was wearing a black gi, and although he was wrinkled and of smaller stature, he still looked strong and solid from their vantage point at the back of the dojo.

"Sensei Masaki?" Blaine leaned toward Seth and whispered to ask.

The boy gave a small affirmative nod without breaking his focus on the sensei.

"Masaki-Do! What is our motto?" Sensei Masaki asked.

The students responded in one unified voice. "Knowledge in a disciplined mind. Power in a restrained fist!"

Sensei smiled, nodded, and continued, "Today before I give you any instructions, we will talk about lanthanides."

"Does he always start practice with some scientific information?" Blaine asked, still whispering in Seth's direction.

Another wordless affirmative nod came from the Hyper Goat, who was not currently acting hyper. Rather, he was trying to stand at attention to honor his sensei.

"Does he alw—" Blaine started to ask Seth another question but was jabbed firmly in the ribs by his sister, who was silently imploring him to stop and stand at attention like everyone else.

"Lanthanides and the actinides below them are in a special

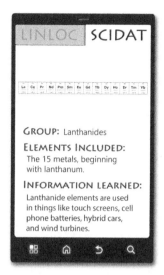

GROUP: Lanthanides
ELEMENTS INCLUDED: The 15 metals, beginning with lanthanum.
INFORMATION LEARNED: Lanthanide elements are used in things like touch screens, cell phone batteries, hybrid cars, and wind turbines.

place on the periodic table," Sensei Masaki continued. "Typically, they are shown below the main table because if all the elements were kept in a line, the periodic table would be too long. So below the main table is where we find the lanthanides, or lanthanoids. They are a group of 15 naturally occurring heavy but soft metals. Their grouping is named after the first element in the group: lanthanum. These elements are called rare earth metals, not because they are especially rare but because they were discovered later because they are typically found with other compounds, making them tricky to separate. It took more than 100 years for scientists to figure out how to purify lanthanum.

As Sensei Masaki spoke, the twins glanced over to all the martial arts students in the room. All stood at attention. All seemed to be taking in this scientific information. Evidently, it was customary for the teacher to start his classes like this.

"In modern times," Sensei Masaki continued with every ear listening and every eye watching, "lanthanide elements are used in things like touch screens, cell phone batteries, hybrid cars, and wind turbines. The lanthanides europium and terbium are included in the ink of some currencies, like the Euro, because these elements glow under UV light. Europium glows red, and terbium glows green. The lanthanide lutetium is found in space rocks. Scientists often disagree as to whether this element is a transition metal or a lanthanide because it has properties of both."

As the sensei spoke, he delivered the information in a clear and deliberate way like he'd been an instructor for a long time and he not only loved what he was talking about but also knew what he was talking about. It was still a little weird to the Sassafrases to see an elderly Japanese sensei talking about science instead of martial arts.

"Several of the lanthanide elements have interesting magnetic properties," the old man continued. "Remember that magnetism is an invisible force that attracts different kinds of metals, especially iron and steel. Materials that put out this force are described as magnetic. Magnets typically have a north and south pole. If you have two magnets, the north pole of the one magnet will be attracted to the south pole of the other magnet because the different poles attract each other, whereas the same poles repel each other. The lanthanide, praseodymium can generate a magnetic field that cools things down. Scientists use it to recreate the coldest environments in the laboratory. Gadolinium is not magnetic at room temperature, but when you cool it below freezing, its magnetic properties appear. When samarium is mixed with cobalt, it creates a magnet that is 10,000 times more powerful than an iron magnet."

"Whoa, that's sick," Blaine exclaimed in amazement, accidentally whispering out loud again.

Tracey closed her eyes in embarrassment. However, either the sensei didn't hear Blaine's whisper, or he chose to ignore it. "Probably the latter," Tracey thought. After all, he was an instructor of ninjas.

"Several of these lanthanides with interesting magnetic properties have been used to power high-speed trains—even high-speed maglev trains, several of which we have right here in Japan." There was a short pause from the sensei, then he said, "This is where I will transition from science to a dire situation at hand."

Although every student was already paying attention, it became undivided attention at this statement.

Neodymium Ninja Magnets

"The A.B.G. Nuclear Power Plant has been hijacked," Sensei Masaki stated. "A rich, power-hungry businessman named Hayato Doi stormed the facility a week ago with an army of evil ninjas known as the Jaken. He expelled all the workers from the plant with the exception of one. Doi is now holding Natsuki Saito hostage somewhere in the facility. She is A.B.G.'s CEO. Hayato Doi has been known in the past to be interested in nuclear energy, and although the A.B.G. plant exists to use nuclear power to create sustainable and clean energy, the fear is that Doi wants to use nuclear power for nefarious purposes. Several ninja dojos have already tried to enter the power plant, rescue Ms. Saito, and supplant Doi. All have failed. It is now up to us in Masaki-do. Are you willing to take up this task?"

Immediately, in complete unison, every student in the dojo snapped their hands down to their sides, bowed toward the sensei, and answered, "Yes, Sensei!"

"Hayato Doi is blinded somewhat by his need for power, but he is smart," the old instructor continued. "Hiring the Jaken as mercenary ninjas has proven to be effective, not only to get in to take control of the plant but also to maintain control. It has also been discovered that Doi is using some kind of powerful magnets to defend himself and the facility as a whole. None of the other dojos were able to figure out exactly how, but we must. We must get past the Jaken, and we must get past whatever magnetism is in place. Masaki-do! Are you still willing to take up this task?"

"Yes, Sensei!" was the resounding response again.

"Then suit up!" Sensei Masaki instructed.

Instantly, the dojo split in half with the girls going to a locker room to the left, and the boys going to a locker room to the right.

"What's happening?" Blaine asked as he was pulled to the

right alongside Sairento Sai, Attosuru Tonbo, and Haipa Yagi.

"It's time to don our *shinobi shozoku*," Hyper Goat answered in delight.

"Huh?" Blaine questioned.

Seth clarified, "Our fighting uniforms."

A few moments later the students reconvened, and now Masaki-do, in its entirety, was wearing black. From head to toe, every individual had transformed from white-gi-wearing karate students to black-clothed ninjas. Hands and eyes were the only parts left unveiled. Blaine made eye contact with Tracey and shrugged. For some reason, although they were not ninjas, current karate students, or even jiujitsu experts like their Uncle Cecil, the Sassafrases had both been given the black *shinobi shozuku* of a ninja and instructed to put it on.

"I guess we are now a part of this little rescue effort," Blaine whispered to Tracey.

"But Blaine, we don't have the martial arts skills to sneak into a nuclear power plant or fight other ninjas or whatever else they have to do!"

"Ah, it's all right, Trace, we'll find our way," Blaine reassured.

"Find our way? Blaine, this is cra—"

"Attention, Masaki-do!" Sensei's strong voice cut off Tracey's sentence.

"Yes, Sensei!" came the unified response; the twins even joined in this time.

"Before we go over our rescue plan, we must first learn about a lanthanide metal that we may encounter—neodymium," Sensi Masaki said, still standing front and center.

All students stood statue like, ready for instructions or scientific information or whatever their esteemed sensei had for them.

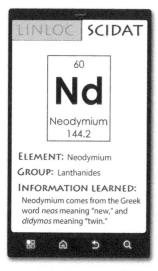

"The symbol for neodymium is Nd. Its atomic number is 60, and its atomic mass is 144.2. Neodymium comes from the Greek word *neos* meaning "new," and *didymos* meaning "twin." This is because when it was first discovered, scientists thought it was a part of another element called didymium, which at the time was considered to be the twin of lanthanum. However, more than 40 years later, didymium was found to be a combination of praseodymium and neodymium."

"Did you hear that, Tracey?" Blaine said, not able to stop himself from whispering when he should have been keeping silent and standing at attention. "Neodymium is the new twin metal. Maybe we can be the neodymium ninjas!"

Knowing Blaine could see only her eyes, Tracey responded to his suggestion with an annoyed scowl. The Hyper Goat, however, responded to Blaine's suggestion with a silent chuckle.

"Neodymium can be used to help scientists determine the age of certain rocks," Sensei Masaki continued. "It has also been used as a catalyst in the chemical industry. In its pure form, neodymium oxidizes quickly in the air. Therefore, pure neodymium has to be either coated or stored in oil. Neodymium is found in everyday products like earbuds, computer hard drives, cell phones, protective goggles, wind turbines, and it is used to hold dentures together. The reason we must learn about it now is because the A.B.G. nuclear power plant has been used to store large amounts of neodymium. And we know neodymium can be used to create powerful magnets, magnets that can help to power trains and electric cars. As a permanent magnet, neodymium can pick up 1,000 times its weight. We don't know exactly what kind of magnets Hayato Doi and the Jaken are using at the hijacked power plant, but we know they have been effective in thwarting the rescue attempts of the other dojos. Maybe they are using neodymium. Maybe they are using samarium mixed with cobalt. Or maybe they are using something altogether different. Whatever the case, the magnetism they've created will be formidable. That said, Masaki-do, are you still willing to take up this task?"

"Yes, Sensei!"

Sensei Masaki smiled slightly, proud of his students and their stalwart response. His smile was set in a face full of focused determination. "Then let us now go over the rescue plan in detail," the old instructor stated as he turned, took a couple steps toward the wall, then reached up and touched the bottom left corner of the traditional Japanese painting hanging there.

Immediately, the entire painting rotated, revealing what had been its backside. However, it was not the backside of a painting. It was a large monitor—a screen as big as the painting had been. Blaine was about to make a comment about how cool he thought this was, but Tracey's eyes shot him an intense glance telling him not to speak. Sensei Masaki tapped at the screen, and it illuminated with color, showing what looked to the Sassafrases like blueprints.

"This is the layout of the A.B.G. nuclear power plant in its entirety from a bird's eye view," the instructor informed. "As you can see, it is a large facility, which provides Hayato plenty of places to hide Natsuki Saito. However, I have an idea of where I think she probably is, which I'll share with you all in a moment. Also, you can see here that the power plant is located on an island, meaning the only way to get to it is either by boat or by helicopter. We will go by boat."

The Sassafras twins gulped. Tracey had already known how daunting this task was going to be, but it was now hitting Blaine. He thought to himself, "A rescue mission probably under cover of night where we ride boats to a mysterious island and have to fight evil ninjas? Maybe I'm not as ready for this as I thought I was."

The twins glanced to their left, where the girls stood and to their right, where the boys were, to study the eyes of their peers. Not a hint of fear could be seen in the eyes of Hageshi Tora, Chiteki Kirin, Sairento Sai, Attosuru Tonbo, or Haipa Yagi. They were ready for the task at hand.

"As you can see by the blueprints, the plant is completely surrounded by a tall wall," Sensei Masaki showed by pointing at the screen. "All other dojos have started their rescue attempts by scaling these walls. Our point of entry, however, is going to be different. We are going to go in beneath the wall. We are going to go in underwater."

Blaine gasped out loud. He didn't mean to. In his shock he just couldn't hold it in. This time it was Hageshi Tora, the Fierce Tiger, who glared at Blaine. The Sassafras boy gulped again. Her intense eyes were way more intense than his sister's.

"The facility is shaped like a giant triangle," the sensei continued in spite of the gasp he'd heard. "At the three points of the triangle there are large buildings built into the wall called screenhouses. Although the screenhouses are built out of reinforced concrete and provide no gap in the walls, they do provide gaps under the walls. They are called screenhouses because inside they have large screens that stop debris from circulating into the power plant's water system. The screenhouses also have powerful water pumps that bring in large amounts of water from the outside through intake canals and into the facility's cooling tower basins. We will enter through these intake canals."

As Sensei Masaki explained the plan, he pointed out the buildings he was talking about on the blueprint map. "I suspect that right here, at the center of the plant, is where Hayato Doi is holding Ms. Saito. This small triangle-shaped building is A.B.G's command central and main office. To get there, we must move from the cooling towers, through both the turbine and the reactor buildings, and then around the containment dome where the nuclear reactor is housed. If we reach command central alive, and Natsuki Saito is indeed being held there, then we will extract her, backtrack through the buildings, and exit the facility this time by going over the wall."

Blaine was tempted to gasp again, but he held it in.

"None of the ninjas from any other dojos who previously attempted this mission returned," Sensei Masaki continued gravely. "So, we know the threat of Hayato Doi and the Jaken is real. We just don't know the specifics of these threats. We don't know what kinds of magnetic traps the wicked mind of Doi has conceived. We don't know how many of the Jaken we'll come up against or where they will be hiding. That said, Masaki-do, are you still willing to take up this task?"

"Yes, Sensei!"

Masaki again smiled a proud, determined smile. "It is settled then. After dusk we will ride the high-speed maglov train topside to the pier, where we will ride ferries to the island. As always, practice the art of stealth. Not one set of eyes should see us. We will strive to complete this mission without receiving any recognition or glory. Remember, if at all possible, the ninja will attain victory without a war. Knowledge in a disciplined mind, power in a restrained fist!"

"Yes, Sensei!"

The teacher paused, then asked. "Is the mission clear?"

"Yes, Sensei!" came the unified response.

"Then armor up!" Sensei Masaki directed.

Immediately the room split in two again, but this time it wasn't the girls going one way and the boys going the other. And nobody was going to the locker room. This time the student ninjas headed to the traditional Japanese paintings on either side wall of the dojo and tapped on them. Like the painting had flipped over for Sensei Masaki revealing a monitor, all the paintings now flipped over for his students. Rather than monitors being revealed, however, it was caches of traditional ninja weapons.

    Blaine gasped again, and this time, instead of scowling, Tracey gasped with him. This was crazy! There were swords, bo staffs, nunchucks, throwing stars, grappling hooks, triple-pronged daggers, blowguns, and more. Haipa Yagi, Sairento Sai, Attosuru Tonbo, Chiteki Washi, and Hageshi Tora raced to different openings and grabbed strategic weaponry. The twins stood where they were with their mouths open. Haipa Yagi quickly returned to the Sassafras spot with his hands full. He paused, looked each twin in the eyes, and handed them weapons—nunchucks for Blaine and throwing stars for Tracey.

    "Here you go, Blaine and Tracey," the Hyper Goat said. "Now it's official. You two are the Neodymium Ninjas."

Chapter 9: The Nuclear Rescue Mission
Actinide Bailout

"So you guys are really ninjas?" Tracey asked, still finding it hard to believe. "Not just karate students?"

The five Masaki-do members nodded.

"But you're teenagers like Blaine and I are about to be. How can you be ninjas?"

"Rock is more solid than water, yet continual surf can cut banks of stone," Chiteki Kirin, the Intelligent Giraffe, responded. The Overpowering Dragonfly and the Fierce Tiger grunted in agreement with her statement, while the Silent Rhino and the Hyper Goat bobbed their heads in affirmation. But the looks in both the twins' eyes gave away the fact that neither understood the proverb.

"What Giraffe is saying," Seth, the Hyper Goat, explained, "is that, although we are just teenagers, we have completely committed ourselves to our craft. And even if we have to practice a move a billion times before we perfect it, we will, and we have."

The Sassafras twins still didn't quite grasp the Giraffe's proverb, but they understood what the Goat was saying. The seven black-clad adolescents were currently sitting on top of a ferry that was taking them from the bustling city piers into dark water toward the mysterious island where the hijacked A.B.G. nuclear power plant was located. Along with all the other ninjas from Masaki-do, they had successfully made it from the dojo to the train station, where they had ridden on top of the magnetically powered high-speed maglev train somehow without being seen and without falling off. From the train station located near the waterfront, the large group of ninjas had moved through the busy nighttime marketplace at the piers, using mostly the tops of stalls and buildings. They had successfully reached the docks, where they had climbed on top of several different boats, again, all without being seen.

They were careful to make sure the boats they had boarded had routes that would take them near the island with the power plant. Blaine and Tracey had surprised themselves with the amount of stealth they had been able to muster during the journey, and they were glad they hadn't yet messed up the mission for their friends.

So here the Sassafrases were, sitting on top of a ferry, dressed like ninjas, on their way to a nuclear power plant for a dangerous rescue mission. There were passengers and crew riding below, but the sound of the waves and the loud chugging of the boat made any conversation up here on the topside permissible for the ninjas.

"What about all these weapons we're carrying?" Tracey asked, at the moment much more talkative than her brother. "Are we going to have to use these? Do we have the skills to fight the Jaken? Is there going to be some kind of battle?"

Attosuru Tonbo, the Overpowering Dragonfly, chuckled at Tracey's worry-filled questions.

"The first priority of the ninja is not to fight with fury but to succeed in silence," the short boy informed.

"So what you're saying is that first and foremost we need to practice the art of stealth," Tracey reasoned. "And confrontations should happen only if there are no other options."

"Exactly!" Hageshi Tora, the Fierce Tiger, answered, speaking for the first time since the Sassafrases had met her, although, even as she spoke, she maintained her intense glare.

"Huh," Blaine mused. "Maybe because of the movies and stuff, I guess I always thought ninjas were kind of like the bad guys."

"A common misconception," the Goat said. "Ninjas actually originated in Japan as farmers who were trying to protect their land and homes from corrupt higher castes. The farmers knew they couldn't win a war against the much stronger foe, but they could succeed if they perfected the art of stealth."

"But what about the Jaken?" Tracey asked. "They're ninjas, and they're bad, right?"

The Dragonfly nodded. "Many have taken the ninja way and twisted it to fit their own purposes. So it is with the Jaken."

"Even monkeys fall from trees," the Giraffe added.

Again, the twins didn't understand her meaning, but they were sure there was some wisdom in her words.

"What about the power plant?" Blaine asked, changing the subject a bit. "Why is it called A.B.G.? What does that stand for? Is it actually supposed to be the A.B.C. nuclear power plant?"

"No, it's supposed to be A.B.G.," the Hyper Goat said. "The letters stand for alpha, beta, and gamma."

"Alpha, beta, and gamma . . . why?" Blaine asked.

"It's very obvious," the Fierce Tiger said bluntly.

Blaine did not agree with the glaring girl. However, he did not dare voice his differing opinion with her at this juncture.

"These are the three types of radiation that can be emitted

from an atom," the Intelligent Giraffe chimed in, thankfully not speaking in the form of a proverb this time.

"Within the nucleus of an atom, there is a large amount of energy," she continued. "Some atoms with a large number of protons and neutrons in the nucleus are considered unstable. This means these atoms are more likely to release some of the nuclear energy from its nucleus as a particle, making the atom radioactive. And as I mentioned, the three types of radiation an atom can emit are alpha particles, beta particles, and gamma particles. Alpha particles comprise two protons and two neutrons. Beta particles are extremely high-energy electrons, and gamma particles are high-energy electromagnetic waves."

Chiteki Kirin finished her explanation, but Blaine still couldn't figure out how and why this made sense in regard to the nuclear power plant's name. The clueless look in his eyes gave it away, and the Tiger picked up on his confoundment immediately.

"You still don't get it?" the glaring girl asked, exasperated.

"Well, I . . . um . . ." Blaine stammered through an attempted answer.

"It's because in the nuclear power plant these particles are being used to produce power and clean energy," Hyper Goat explained further, bailing Blaine out. "If radiation is managed and used responsibly in a state-of-the-art facility like we're going to tonight, it can be beneficial."

Blaine finally nodded in actual understanding.

Tracey, however, had some more questions. "Beneficial maybe, but is it worth the risk? Know what I mean? Those kinds of particles and that kind of power being housed inside a building is kind of hazardous, isn't it?"

The Dragonfly chuckled again at Tracey's alarm and responded by saying, "It's like our motto."

"Huh?" Tracey wasn't tracking.

"Knowledge in a disciplined mind. Power in a restrained fist," the Giraffe quoted the Masaki-do motto for everyone.

Blaine nodded in understanding, and Tracey joined him. "Ah ha," both Sassafrases murmured.

"So like we are trained as ninjas to attain the highest of proficiencies in knowledge and power but to use neither with irresponsibility," the Hyper Goat explained. "The A.B.G. power plant has used the powerful particles and elements, but they have used them all responsibly."

"That's why we have to take down this Doi clown," the Fierce Tiger cut in. "Because he will wield the power in the plant irresponsibly."

"That is absolutely right," a new voice agreed.

All seven ninjas whipped their heads around to see that Sensei Masaki was sitting directly behind them.

"What did . . . how did . . . where did . . . ?" Blaine stammered through conjoined questions.

Sensei had not been on the ferry with them when they had first climbed to its top, and none of them had heard him arrive.

"How did he get here? How long has he been here?" the minds of the Sassafras twins asked. "Well, he is a legendary ninja after all, so it doesn't matter how or when he got here. He probably does this kind of thing all the time," they concluded.

"We must stop Hayato Doi before he uses the power he has hijacked irresponsibly," the old man stated.

"Yes, Sensei!" the seven responded instinctively.

"But first, before we get there, as we ride this ferry, let us talk about actinides—one of the groups of elements we might encounter."

"Yes, Sensei," came the response of seven students, excited and willing to learn anything their good instructor wanted to teach them.

"The actinides, or actinoids, are a group of 15 heavy metals," the sensei started. "They were named for the first element in the group: actinium. Actinium is so radioactive that it gives off a blue glow in the dark. Uranium and thorium are the only two actinides that occur naturally in large quantities. The rest of the actinides are present in miniscule quantities in nature, are created in a laboratory, or are found in nuclear reactors and particle accelerators. With the exception of uranium and thorium, all of the actinides were discovered within the last century and a half."

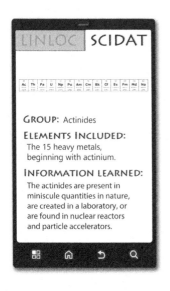

The twins were still a little jittery about this whole rescue mission thing, but being with the sensei, who was sharing scientific data, was calming to them. It was funny to the twelve-year-olds how science had gone from being the bane of their existence to a source of peace.

"Many of the actinides are radioactive," Sensei Masaki continued, "which means they easily break apart, releasing energy and potentially damaging particles. This is because their nuclei are heavy with 89-plus protons in them. They can also be extremely beneficial, as Haipa Yagi just explained. Currently, actinides are being used worldwide by astronauts, doctors, firefighters, engineers, and more. For instance, curium is used to provide power on space missions. Americium is used in smoke detectors and portable X-ray machines. Actinium is used in neutron soil probes. Thorium is used in making parts for aircraft and spacecraft. And plutonium was once used to power pacemakers. Now it is used in the nuclear industry in nuclear power plants just like the one we've just reached!"

"Wait, what did Sensei say?" the twins thought, a little shocked. They, along with the five others, turned from the instructor to look toward the open water. However, instead of open water they saw in front of them the dark outline of an island.

"Behold, the A.B.G. nuclear power plant," Sensei Masaki said. "From here, we swim."

His head was swimming. It had been confirmed that Alexander, Graham, and Belle Slote were back on Earth, heading to jail. Surely it was only a matter of time until the authorities pried his name out of one of the three siblings and connected him to the crimes that had been committed. It wasn't only the local authorities or the feds that were involved. It was Triple S: the Swiss Secret Service. Their prowess in fighting crime and tracking down bad guys was world renown. Surely, they would eventually find him and arrest him too.

The museum curator rubbed both of his temples with his index fingers. Why had he aligned himself with those three Slotes? They hadn't done anything right. They hadn't accomplished anything they'd set out to do. And most disappointingly by far, they hadn't helped make him richer.

"Ahhhh!" Paul Sims whisper-shouted in frustration, being careful not to be loud enough for Wiggles and Fidget, the two energetic museum security guards, to hear him in his office.

"It's all the Sassafras twins' fault," he gritted out through clenched teeth. "Everything was going fine until they showed up. And Summer and Cecil, my old junior high classmates, I wish I had never been reunited with them."

"Wait," Paul suddenly thought, like his brain had come up for air out of the pool of his swimming head. "Reunite, that's it! The Swiss Secret Service sees the Sassafrases as the good guys. I think Summer may even be officially connected to Triple S somehow. If I can reunite with Summer and Cecil and that niece and nephew of his, maybe the Triple S will see me as a good guy, too. And then even if my name does come up, there will be some doubt because of my alignment with the Sassafrases. Yes, that might work! Summer and the Sassafrases see me as a friend and a nice, responsible man. I'm sure of it."

Paul picked up his phone, clicked it on, and scrolled through his contact list. "Cecil Sassafras," he said when he found his old classmate's information. "1104 North Pecan Street," Paul Sims smiled. "I think maybe it's time for a visit to the old neighborhood."

Their swim through the dark water had been laborious and frigid, but they had made it to the island. No sound or light at all was coming from anywhere inside or outside the power plant. No Jaken or any trace of them had been spotted.

Blaine and Tracey, along with their sensei and fellow ninjas, were preparing to start the immeasurably harder phase of this rescue operation. They were going to go underwater and enter the plant through the intake canals. The Sassafras twins shivered as they sat on the large, water-caressed rocks that served as the shore of this island.

After approximately 10 yards of rocky shore, the solid cement wall of the nuclear power plant shot up into the night sky, high and wide, looking very much like an impenetrable fortress. It was hard for the twins to imagine the ninja dojos before them attempting to scale the walls to start their rescue efforts. Even here, where one of the giant screenhouses was built into the wall, providing a slight difference in the wall's texture, it still looked impossible. Really, though, it was even harder to imagine what they were on the verge of attempting. Surely, submerging into the dark water, holding their breath for a crazy long time, and making their way through the intake canals would be even harder than scaling these walls?

"Maybe so," thought the Sassafrases, but they had to trust their sensei's leadership. If the other over-the-wall rescue attempts had failed, maybe this under-the-wall attempt would succeed. Blaine and Tracey strained their eyes through the darkness to see Sensei Masaki. The only available light was being cast by the moon, and it wasn't offering much at all as it hit everything faintly, dimly, and ominously. They waited for the instructor's signal to make the next move.

There it was. Sensei silently made a motion with his hand. All the Masaki-do ninjas submerged without sound or splash. The Hyper Goat, the Intelligent Giraffe, the Overpowering Dragonfly, and the Fierce Tiger disappeared under the water right in front of the Sassafrases with the Fierce Tiger being the last to submerge. She did so with her eyes wide open, locked on the twins in an intense glare. Blaine and Tracey were glad she was on their side—she was crazy scary.

The science-learning brother and sister looked at each other with eyes that were trying to be determined. They took big deep breaths and dove under the black water. They stroked their arms and kicked their legs as powerfully as they could and swam to a depth of 10 feet, then 15, and then 20. It was at this ear-popping depth that they began to feel the suction of the intake canal. Five more feet down and both twins were pulled into the underwater tunnel by the force of the powerfully flowing water. Now, even if they wanted to, they couldn't turn back. They were no longer swimming or stroking or kicking. They were being pulled involuntarily, at breakneck speed, through the completely dark canal. It was terrifying, and it made the thought of scaling the wall outside seem like a cakewalk in comparison. At least this fast pace of underwater travel might mean they wouldn't have to hold their breath quite as long, which was good, because the twelve-year-olds' lungs were already screaming for air.

All at once, the Sassafrases' bodies slammed into what felt like a chain-link fence. "The screen of the screenhouse!" they both realized.

Now they needed to climb up the screen, and then they would be out of the water and inside the screenhouse building. The thought was exhilarating, but that exhilaration quickly evaporated as Blaine and Tracey both realized in horror that they couldn't move. The force of the water coming through the intake canal and rushing through the screen was keeping them hopelessly pinned in their current positions.

Blaine thrashed his arms and legs around, trying to get off the screen. Tracey grabbed the screen with her fingers and hands and tried desperately to pull herself up. Both were managing to move upward slightly, but it was going to be too little too late. The twins could hold their breath no longer.

Suddenly, Blaine felt a hand grab ahold of his *shinobi shozoku*. Tracey, too, felt someone grab her by her ninja garment. Both Sassafrases were pulled out of the dark water by powerful jerks.

Trapping Uranium

They opened their eyes to see Haipa Yagi, Sairento Sai, Attosuru Tonbo, and Chiteki Kirin looking at them with relief in their eyes. Even Hageshi Tora, the Fierce Tiger had a level of concern in her expression, which was a welcome surprise to the twins. It was the Silent Rhino who had pulled Blaine out of the water, and the Intelligent Giraffe had used her long, strong arms to nab Tracey. The twins wanted to express their thanks, but complete silence was the order of the mission. Without pause, the five actual ninjas turned and climbed up the screen. Blaine and Tracey took a deep breath of wonderful and welcome fresh air, and followed the others.

The inside of the big cement screenhouse was kind of like the inside a large grain silo. It was a tall, perfect circle, but instead of being filled with grain, this building had rushing water down below. The screen they were on led up to a catwalk above them. They were not the only seven here. Blaine and Tracey saw that Sensei Masaki was already on the catwalk. It looked like all the Masaki-do ninjas had made it through the intake canal and were here now, climbing above them. The Sassafras twins were the last to reach the top of the screen, and then it was a fairly easy transfer from the screen to the catwalk.

There was still no sign of the Jaken. Blaine and Tracey wondered if that would change soon. They followed this catwalk and exited the screenhouse through an arched, doorway-sized opening. The twins saw that the catwalk kept going and turned into a bridge. The bridge led to another tall, circular structure.

"That must be the cooling tower," Tracey thought as they crossed the bridge. Like the ninjas in front of them, the twins tried to keep their footsteps soft so as not to echo off the metal grate walkway. The two took in their surroundings as they crossed the catwalk bridge. They were inside the nuclear power plant complex.

Behind them was the screenhouse and the imposing wall. In front of them was the cooling tower with steam billowing from its top. Below, about 50 feet or so, were the dark, shadowy grounds of the mysterious plant. No light of any kind was shining. No movement could be detected. No human life seemed to be present.

The bridge they were on spanned the length of the two circular buildings. When it reached the cooling tower, it remained on the exterior of the cement building. There was no entryway into the cooling tower. Instead, the bridge turned into a staircase affixed to the tower, curving down and around and leading to the ground.

With Sensei Masaki leading the way and the Sassafras twins bringing up the rear, the stealthy group of ninjas continued to make their way deeper and deeper into the nuclear complex. After alighting from the staircase, they went through two more buildings. According to the sensei's earlier descriptive instructions, Blaine and Tracey assumed these were the turbine and reactor buildings, respectively. Both were filled with a massive tangle of pipes, and both had futuristic-looking equipment in them. Although the twins didn't know how this equipment worked, they were sure it was extremely expensive and important.

After sneaking quietly through these two buildings, the small, black-clad army made their way around a large building with a domed top. "This must be the containment dome, the Sassafrases' thought, "where the nuclear reactor is housed." They shuddered. Another chill went through their bodies as they looked around and still saw no trace of the supposedly evil ninjas called the Jaken. "Maybe Sensei Masaki had been misinformed. Maybe they had come to the wrong island or the wrong power plant. Maybe there had been no hijacking at all. And what about all the other ninjas from the other dojos who had supposedly tried to storm this place? Where were they? Not to mention the supposed threat of powerful magnetism." The twins' thoughts were suddenly cut off by the sound of something hitting the wall of the containment dome directly in front of them.

"Well. Lookie there," Blaine thought to himself, "a throwing star just implanted in the wall . . ."

"Ahhh!" the boy whisper-screamed the next second. A throwing star implanted in the wall!

What happened next was a blur of lightning-fast activity the Sassafrases were not ready for. The Jaken emerged out of every shadowy spot like fire ants out of an anthill and began an assault on Sensei Masaki and his students. These evil ninjas were also dressed in black *shinobi shozoku*, but theirs had streaks of red fabric criss-crossed around the sleeves and legs. Their faces were all covered with wicked-looking red masks. The Jaken were all head and shoulders taller than any of the ninjas of Masaki-do, with the exception of Chiteki Kirin, and they moved like they had a lifetime of ninja experience under their black belts.

Initially, the ninjas of Masaki-do might have been a little stunned by the sudden attack, but because of their courage and preparation, they quickly recovered and proved they were a force to be reckoned with. While Sensei Masaki and his ninjas skillfully engaged in hand-to-hand combat with the Jaken, Tracey fumbled for her throwing stars, dropping most of them on the ground. Blaine hit himself with his own nunchucks . . . repeatedly.

The formerly silent grounds of the nuclear power plant were now alive with the sounds of battle. Bo-staffs met triple-pronged daggers. Swords clanked against spinning nunchucks. Throwing stars and darts from blowguns whizzed through the air. It was mayhem.

Hageshi Tora fought like the fierce Tiger she was.

Attosuru Tonbo spun and dodged attempted Jaken blows like a hyperactive dragonfly.

Sairento Sai barrelled through the red-masked ninjas like they were bowling pins.

Chiteki Kirin used her height and strength to match the attacking foe blow for blow.

Haipa Yagi proved that he had indeed practiced his disciplines billions of times over as he battled with skill and agility.

Chief among them, however, was their teacher. Although short and old, Sensei Masaki was a martial art wonder to behold. With complete calm and precise movement, the elderly instructor seemed to be able to anticipate the Jakens' moves before they even made them. It looked like he could fend off a dozen of the evil ninjas with one pinky finger.

Even so, the Jaken were succeeding in pushing Masaki-do back, not back toward the containment dome, but deeper into the dark corridors of the power plant.

There were many more of the Jaken than there were of Masaki-do. Still the members of the intrepid dojo fought on skillfully and courageously. With everything around them happening so fast, the Sassafrases didn't have time to be scared. The twins were trying to react to whatever was right in front of them.

Tracey had picked up her throwing stars and she was chucking them as fast as she could at anything with red on it. Blaine had given himself a whelp with his nunchucks, but by this time, he had figured them out a bit better. He was actually succeeding in doling out some whelps to the Jaken. The two were starting to feel pretty good about themselves, that was, until a quartet of red-masked Jaken made a charge directly toward them with weapons in hand.

Tracey threw stars, but they all missed. Blaine spun his chucks like helicopter blades over his head with energy, even though he wasn't sure what it would accomplish. The four approaching Jaken left their feet as their charge turned into a pounce, spelling the end of the Sassafras twins. However, the last second before collision, Seth E. Prue—Haipa Yagi—the Hyper Goat, flew out of nowhere with a magnificent spinning kick that connected with three of the four Jaken, knocking them out cold and off their trajectory toward Blaine and Tracey. The fourth Jaken eluded Hyper Goat's kick and immediately countered with a powerful blow to Seth's midsection. It was a blow using a bladed weapon; the Hyper Goat looked at the twins with a sudden desperation in his eyes, and pointed at four more approaching Jaken.

"Go!" he implored the twelve-year-olds. The brave boy then fell into the shadows.

Tracey tried to stay and help their fallen hero. Blaine wanted to stay as well, but he forced himself to pull away, grabbing his sister's arm and pulling her away with him. Haipa Yagi had told them to go, so go they would. With tears in their eyes, the Sassafrases fled the area and joined the dwindling members the Masaki-do.

The tide had turned. The red-masked ninjas were obviously winning this ninja battle. Farther and farther the Masaki-do ninjas were pushed back, deeper into the nuclear complex. Eventually, they entered a long, metallic corridor, and that's when the strangest thing happened. The Jaken, every one of them, stopped fighting. The red-masked ninjas laid down their arms and backed away from the Masaki-do ninjas.

Blaine and Tracey looked around in confusion. What was happening? Tears still flowing because of the loss of their new friend, the twins looked for the other four friends. Were Attosuru Tonbo, Sairento Sai, Chiteki Kirin, and Hageshi Tora still with them? Did they know that Haipa Yagi had been lost? Did they know what was happening now? What about Sensei Masaki?

All at once, the Sassafrases saw what the Jaken were doing. They weren't calling a truce. They weren't backing away in retreat. They hadn't laid down their weapons to stop fighting. They were reaching into the shadows to grab bigger, strategically placed weapons.

The twins' minds instinctively asked, "What are they going to use these for?"

The question was immediately answered as one of the Jaken pulled the trigger and shot a sprawling net that hit a Masaki-do ninja who was standing to the twins' right. The ninja was immediately entangled and hopelessly pinned to the wall.

"Neodymium or samarium mixed with cobalt?" Blaine turned and asked his sister this seemingly random question at the most inopportune time.

"Huh?" Tracey responded.

Chapter 9: The Nuclear Rescue Mission

"The net," Blaine explained. "It's gotta be magnetic. That's why it pinned that guy against the metal wall. And they must be super strong magnets because, look, the guy can't even move. So what do you think? Is the net made out of neodymium, which can pick up a thousand times its weight? Or samarium mixed with cobalt, which is 10,000 times more powerful than an iron magnet?"

Tracey was impressed that her brother had figured all this out about the net so quickly and also that he had remembered the scientific facts about the magnetic elements, but was this the time to—

The Sassafras girl's thoughts were cut short by a barrage of shots fired from the net launchers. The Jaken were firing at will, sending magnetic nets flying in virtually every direction. The metal corridor was narrow; its walls were tall; and it provided no real source of cover so the only choice Masaki-do had was to run deeper into it. One by one, the teenage ninjas were being pinned to the metal walls ensnared by the indelible nets.

As the Sassafras twins fled, they saw that Sensei Masaki was indeed still present. They also saw the Tiger, Giraffe, Rhino, and Dragonfly still running free. They wished the Goat was here too.

Somehow the twins continued to elude and escape the threatening nets shot by the Jaken, but as they sprinted deeper into the corridor, a horror caught their eyes. They were passing ninjas who had already been pinned to the walls before they had gotten there. None of these ninjas were from Masaki-do, and they were all unconscious.

"The ninjas from the other dojos!" the twins realized, sharing the same thoughts. "They've all been trapped by magnetic nets in this corridor. And if this was their fate, what will happen to us? Will it be ours as well?"

Quickly their question was seemingly answered. Blaine and Tracey saw in terror that the corridor they were in was abruptly coming to a dead end. The Jaken had chased them straight into a trap! Greatly outnumbered, with well over half of their dojo fallen or magnetically trapped, the remaining ninjas of Masaki-do stopped and turned to face their red-masked foe.

Sensei Masaki silently stepped to the front of the remnant. Sairento Sai and Hageshi Tora stepped forward and stood to his left. Chiteki Kirin and Attosuru Tonbo stood to his right. The Neodymium Ninjas hung back a little, but they did make a stand, and they were willing to give their all.

The horde of Jaken reached the dead-end spot where the Masaki-do group was and came to a stop. They paused their launching of magnetic nets and faced the remaining members of the beaten-down dojo. Their facial expressions were hidden because of the masks, but their confidence and hubris were obvious in their eyes. They knew they were going to win.

Sensei Masaki slowly pulled his arms in front of his chest and put his open-palmed left hand over his right hand, which was clenched in a fist. "Knowledge in a disciplined mind. Power in a restrained fist," he reminded, as calm as a slight breeze on a summer day. He bowed toward the Jaken, but as he came up, he swung his open-palmed left hand straight up behind him and thrust his fist directly out to the front. He bent his knees and ankles, putting himself in what looked to the twins like a crouched attack stance.

For a long second, there was no sound or movement from anyone.

"Oh, snap, this is about to get real!" Tracey accidentally yelled out loud, sounding very much like her brother.

Then it happened. In the blink of an eye, the tables of the battle turned. The confidence and hubris of the Jaken were gone. They tried to point the launchers and pull the triggers, but it was too late. Sensei Masaki's fist had been completely unrestrained. The aftermath looked somewhat like a bomb had gone off, with Sensei standing in the middle of a completely unconscious army of

Jaken. The red ants had met the exterminator.

The Sassafrases stood dumbstruck with their mouths hanging open behind their ninja masks. The other members of the dojo stood still and silent as well. It was obvious they had never seen their sensi go full tilt before.

Chiteki Kirin broke the silence with another one of her proverbs. "Opposite poles attract, but the same poles repel."

"Wait a second, that's not just a proverb; that's science," the twins said.

"You're absolutely right," Sensei said to his student. "That's how the net launchers work. The nets and the launchers have the same magnetic pole, whereas the nets and walls of this corridor have the opposite pole."

"And more than likely," the Intelligent Giraffe continued, thinking and understanding the same as her teacher, "there is a way to reverse the pole of the launchers so we can use them to release all the ninjas who are stuck, both Masaki-do ninjas and the others."

"Exactly," the sensei responded. He addressed the others. "Masaki-do, will you work with Chiteki Kirin to use the launchers to free the trapped ninjas?"

"Yes, Sensei!"

"Very good," he responded proudly. Then he gestured toward Blaine and Tracey. "In the meantime, I will take these twin Neodymium Ninjas to command central to try and rescue the CEO from the madman."

"Huh?" the Sassafras twins responded. Again, their mouths were open behind their masks.

Instead of explaining, Sensei ran up the corridor, and instead of arguing, the twins followed him. It was much easier to run without the Jaken fighting or standing in the way. In no time, the trio found the triangular-shaped office at the center of the nuclear complex.

Without pause, and seemingly without effort, Sensei Masaki kicked the door wide open, revealing a decent-sized room outlined with a few windows and lots of metallic trim. Almost as if he'd been expecting their arrival, a tall, handsome, evil-looking man stood in the center of the room holding an equally tall, attractive, yet panicked-looking woman in a sort of headlock.

"Haiyato Doi?" the martial arts instructor asked.

The crazed man nodded and then asked, "Sensei Masaki?"

The sensei nodded.

"Natsuki Saito?" Blaine asked, gesturing toward the woman.

Now everyone nodded, like this was a given. No one asked the twins if they were the Neodymium Ninjas.

Sensei Masaki made a subtle move toward the two at the center of the room. The Sassafrases noticed it and had no doubt the sensei could rescue this poor woman with ease. However, when Natsuki noticed the sensei's move, she responded with a yelp.

"No! Don't come any closer! He has a detonator, and it's connected to a cache of uranium!"

Hayato Doi smiled in wicked conceit and revealed the detonator. "Yes, I do, and if you come any closer, I'll light this whole island up. You may have gotten past my Jaken, but you won't survive my uranium!"

Without arguing and without moving a muscle, the old instructor responded, "Uranium is symbolized on the periodic table by a U. Its atomic number is 92, and its atomic mass is 238.0. In a nuclear

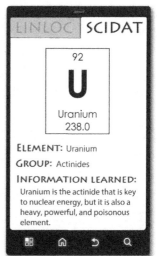

SCIDAT

92
U
Uranium
238.0

ELEMENT: Uranium
GROUP: Actinides
INFORMATION LEARNED:
Uranium is the actinide that is key to nuclear energy, but it is also a heavy, powerful, and poisonous element.

power plant, enriched uranium is split into two small nuclei and uranium-235. This releases a literal ton of nuclear energy. This energy heats water, producing steam. The steam rises and is used to turn turbines, which generate electrical energy. The steam then condenses and is recycled. Depleted uranium left over from the uranium enriching process has been used as tank armor, bullets, and ships' ballast."

"What's your point, old man?" Doi shouted, getting tired of the instructor's information. The twins wondered if maybe the sensei was stalling in preparation to make a move.

"My point is that uranium is the actinide that is key to nuclear energy, but it is also a heavy, powerful, and poisonous element," Masaki explained. "If you fire a neutron at a uranium atom, the nucleus splits to form uranium-235 and, as I said, releases a ton of energy. This releases several more neutrons that impact with several more uranium atoms, setting off a chain reaction. This chain reaction can be slowed down and controlled to produce clean nuclear energy, as Ms. Saito had been doing as the CEO of the A.B.G. power plant, or it can be uncontrolled, which could result in an explosion that could flatten an entire city."

Instead of being alarmed by this last bit of scientific information, it seemed to energize the crazy villain. "Exactly!" Doi shouted. "Why do you think I wanted to take over A.B.G.?"

The twins couldn't believe it. This Hayato Doi guy was absolutely mad. Sensei Masaki needed to do something fast!

However, before any heroic move could be made by the martial arts expert, something totally unexpected happened. A surviving Jaken ninja with a net launcher in his hand burst through the open doorway and discharged his weapon. Almost as if they were seeing it in slow motion, Blaine and Tracey watched as the magnetic net shot from the launcher and pinned their sensei securely to a section of the room's metal trim.

Chapter 10: Singapore's Merlion Fashion Extravaganza
Modeling Main Group Metals

Instead of shrinking back in fear, Blaine and Tracey stood bravely. They were aware they had no chance against a ninja wielding a net launcher and a madman wielding a uranium detonator. But they also knew they had to try to stop these two. With their sensei immobilized but watching, the Neodymium Ninjas put open-palmed left hands over fisted right hands and bowed toward Hayato Doi, who was still holding Natsuki Saito. Coming up from the bow, they recited the Masaki-do motto, "Knowledge in a disciplined mind. Power in a restrained fist."

They then moved their bodies exactly as they had seen the sensei do earlier in the metal corridor. In unison, the twins moved their left hands up behind them and their right hands straight out in front of their bodies in tight fists. They then bent both their knees and ankles, crouching into an attack position.

For a long second, there was no sound or movement from anyone.

"Oh, snap, this is about to get real!" Strangely enough, it was Sensei Masaki who had made the outburst this time. He was still inside his magnetized net on the wall.

Then it happened. However, it wasn't Blaine or Tracey who made a move. It wasn't the red-masked Jaken ninja shooting out another net. It wasn't the wicked Hayato Doi pushing the uranium detonator. It was an unexpected figure who came crashing through one of the office windows in a spray of shattered glass. It was Haipa Yagi, the Hyper Goat! He was alive!

In one fluid movement, the teenage expat ninja swiped the detonator away from Hayato Doi's hand and simultaneously freed

Natsuki Saito from Doi's grasp. He also somehow managed to jerk the net launcher free from the stunned, red-masked Jaken without another net firing. Blaine and Tracey, who were still frozen in the crouching attack stance, broke free from their statue-like poses and embraced their friend.

"Seth, we thought you were . . . we saw the . . . how did you . . ." Tracey stumbled through her words, trying to make sense of seeing Seth fall into the shadows earlier and seeing him now, alive and well. It didn't look like he had been wounded at all. The Hyper Goat opened his mouth to explain, but he was interrupted by the CEO of the A.B.G. nuclear powerplant.

"Thank you, young man. Thanks to all of you!" Natsuki Saito gushed in overflowing gratitude. "You have rescued me, but even more important than that, you have stopped Hayato Doi from carrying out any kind of destruction! Thank you! Thank you!"

Just then, four more ninjas burst into the office unexpectedly. They were holding magnetic net launchers, but none of them were wearing red masks. It was Chiteki Kirin, Attosuru Tonbo, Sairento Sai, and Hageshi Tora!

"Fall down seven times, get up eight," the Intelligent Giraffe spoke another proverb with a smile.

The Silent Rhino grunted and nodded in agreement.

The Overpowering Dragonfly added, "There is indeed a way to reverse the magnetism of these net launchers. We were able to free our fellow ninjas. We freed the ninjas from the other dojos as well."

"And now, Sensei," the Fierce Tiger said. "We will free you."

Hageshi Tora walked to where the esteemed instructor was and placed the magnet-shooting contraption up against the net. She pulled a lever on the bottom of the launcher. Immediately, the magnetic net disengaged from the metal wall. The intense female ninja then turned toward the twins and glared deeply. Blaine and Tracey gulped. Why was Hageshi Tora still so adverse toward them? Hayato Doi and the Jaken had been defeated. Natsuki Saito had been rescued. The A.B.G. nuclear power plant was in good hands. Couldn't this girl just be happy?

The Tiger walked straight up to the Sassafrases with the fiercest look in her eyes they had seen yet. For a long second, there was no sound or movement from anyone. Then, all at once, Hageshi Tora's face broke forth into a huge smile, and she wrapped the twins up in a hearty hug.

Several hours later, after some rest, food, and shared laughter with their ninja friends, Blaine and Tracey found their way to a secluded corner of the A.B.G. power plant to enter the SCIDAT data and pictures from this location into their smartphones. When that was done, they opened LINLOC to see where they would be zipping off to next.

"Singapore!" Blaine exclaimed. "Longitude 103°51'16.4"E, latitude 1°17'11.8"N."

"We'll get to study the topics of main group metals, aluminum, metalloids, and silicon with a local expert named Aishaanya," Tracey added.

The *shinobi shozokus* of the ninjas had been traded for the backpacks, helmets, and harnesses of globe-zipping science learners. Blaine and Tracey each calibrated their three-ringed carabiners to the coordinates and let them snap shut. Immediately, the carabiners connected to the invisible zip line that would take these two twelve-year-olds to

Singapore.

Approximately seven seconds later, the Sassafrases zipped off through swirls of light. They liked this much better than swirling through dark underwater canals. Their zip-lining quickly came to an end. The carabiner automatically unclipped from the lines, and down they fell.

Moments later, the twelve-year-olds sat up and took in their new surroundings. They had landed in the back of a van. By the looks of it, it was some kind of news van. There were several monitors on and running. There were all different kinds of cameras and camera equipment. There was even some signage, apparel, and other assorted equipment with "THE DROP" branded on it. Underneath "THE DROP" it said, "A NEWS NETWORK."

Tracey was about to ask her brother if he thought they should stay in the van or leave it when she was interrupted by the sound of their local expert being named on one of the monitors. "Here comes Aishaanya to the podium now, to answer questions about the alleged burglary," an unseen news anchor's voice announced.

A tall, exquisitely dressed woman walked confidently to a wooden podium littered with microphones. The podium was on a small stage surrounded by a crowd of reporters. The woman looked to be of Asian descent and was breathtakingly beautiful. Her long, wavy, brunette hair outlined her unblemished face and rested gracefully on the tops of her shoulders. Her eyes sparkled over her high cheekbones. Her confident, understated smile backed up her confident body language. She looked like she was about to open her mouth to speak, but before she could get a word out, she was interrupted by an eruption of questions from the anxious crowd.

"Aishaanya, is it true that your warehouse was robbed and ransacked?"

"Are you faking a robbery to get attention before the Merlion Fashion Extravaganza?"

"Can you give us a quote about the alleged infighting at Aishaanya Inc?"

"Was this burglary an inside job?"

"Do you think Tamina Threads had anything to do with this theft?"

"Are you worried about how this will affect your legacy?"

"How concerned should your investors be?"

"Aishaanya, have you, the queen of Sinapore fashion, fallen off your throne?"

Seemingly unshaken by any of the pointed questions, the twins' local expert gently raised her hand to quiet the crowd and responded in a calm, strong voice.

"I am not here today to address the possible burglary of Aishaanya Inc. I am here, however, to highlight tomorrow's Merlion Fashion Extravaganza. As you know, it is the tenth annual fashion show here in Singapore at the base of our beloved Merlion.

In decades past, cities like Paris, London, Milan, and New York were known as the leaders in the world of fashion. Our hope is that Singapore will also be known as one of these upper echelon cities, one that sets the trends, produces products ethically, and leads in fashion. We, as a Singaporean fashion community, have gained the knowledge, put the work in, and deserve to be recognized as leaders and torchbearers in the world of fashion."

"As all of you know, the Merlion's fish-like body represents Singapore's humble beginnings as a fishing village, and its lion head represents how Singapore has now become a power in all facets on the world's stage. So, too, we believe Singapore is a superpower in the world of fashion. We want tomorrow's Merlion Fashion Extravaganza to showcase this fact. Tomorrow's extravaganza is not about Aishaanya Inc, and neither should this news conference be. Let us take these opportunities to celebrate the entire Singaporean fashion community."

"Oh, c'mon, Aishaanya," one of the reporters blurted out, not satisfied with the fashion icon's judicious answer. "Tell us what happened at Aishaanya Inc. Did you get robbed or not?"

Maintaining her composure, the elegant woman behind the podium answered placidly. "Instead of talking about Aishaanya Inc., let me again highlight tomorrow's Merlion Fashion Extravaganza."

Even though the Sassafrases were watching the news conference on a video screen, they could tell the perturbed reporter was annoyed that his question wasn't getting answered. Yet, he held his tongue, as did the other reporters.

"As you know, every year there is a different theme for the extravaganza, and this year, the theme is the periodic table," Aishaanya continued. "This means every garment that comes down the runway must somehow include the periodic table itself or elements from the periodic table."

This information sent a murmur through the crowd; the twins couldn't tell if it was good or bad.

Aishaanya continued. "As has been reported before, to go along with my love and passion for fashion, I also have a love and passion for science. So this theme has been a complete joy for me to work with this year."

"What element are you going to incorporate into your runway line tomorrow?" a female reporter asked, finally redirecting a question away from the combative line of questioning.

Aishaanya's understated smile widened, revealing perfect teeth. "I'm not going to give any specifics," the fashionista responded. "But I will take this question as an opportunity to talk about science, possibly dropping a clue or two."

The reporter who had asked the question seemed satisfied with this answer. However, now there was a definite negative murmur coming from the other reporters in the crowd. They wanted headlines, not science.

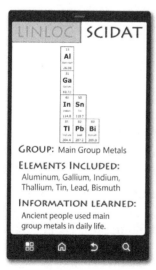

GROUP: Main Group Metals
ELEMENTS INCLUDED: Aluminum, Gallium, Indium, Thallium, Tin, Lead, Bismuth
INFORMATION LEARNED: Ancient people used main group metals in daily life.

Regardless, Aishaanya proceeded in giving scientific information, "I am looking forward to seeing all the creative ways my colleagues will incorporate the periodic table into their designs. Among other elements, I am hoping to see many of the different metals worked in. Let me now highlight the main group metals. The main group metals include elements from group 13, specifically aluminum, gallium, indium, and thallium, from group 14, including tin and lead, and from group 15, bismuth. These metals are post-transition, meaning they come after the block of transition metals on the periodic table. They are also sometimes referred to as ordinary metals, base metals, or poor metals. 'Poor' means they are typically softer than other metals, with low melting and boiling points, making them easy to shape. However, they are still relatively strong and are also capable of conducting electricity and heat."

The twins were impressed with the new local expert as they listened to her talk about the SCIDAT information from the monitors in the back of the news van. They were, however, wondering if, when, and how they were going to get to meet her in person.

"Maybe we'll see some Egyptian-themed garments tomorrow," Aishaanya continued. "As you know, many of the ancient people used main group metals in their daily lives. Ancient Egyptians used the main group metal, lead, as eyeliner in hopes that it would protect them against illness. Ancient Romans lined their pipes with lead, and the first printing press incorporated lead. Nowadays we know that lead is poisonous to humans. That said, all designers and stylists have been carefully instructed not to use any element from the periodic table that would be harmful or dangerous to themselves, the models, or the crowd."

"Is that what happened at Aishaanya, Inc.?" an angry reporter broke in. "Did harmful elements destroy your warehouse, studio, or office?"

Instead of the fashion expert responding to the outburst, a large man in a black suit with shoulders as wide as a building, a head and neck reminiscent of a hippo, and the facial features of a seasoned wrestler, took the podium. "Ms. Aishaanya will not be answering any more questions," he bellowed in a deep, authoritative, bass voice as low as the rumbling of a freight train. The group of impudent reporters tried to disregard the big man's matter-of-fact statement, firing off more questions. But he gently yet quickly ushered Aishaanya away from the podium and off the stage, making their inquiries obsolete.

The Sassafras twins exhaled and took note of what they'd witnessed on the monitors as well as the SCIDAT they'd heard.

Once again, Tracey was about to ask her brother if he thought they should stay in the van or leave it when she was interrupted by the sound of the two back doors being yanked open. The twelve-year-olds jerked their heads in that direction to see two people, a man and a woman, standing in front of them, both looking as shocked as the twins were suddenly feeling.

The man was holding a large, black camera equipment box on one shoulder and looked like an average joe. The woman, holding a microphone, looked anything but average with her heavy makeup and hairspray-assaulted bangs. Both were wearing long-sleeve T-shirts that said, "THE DROP."

The woman gathered herself quickly, lifted the microphone to her mouth, and speaking like she was on camera, said, "Hello, I'm Sadie Nichols with The Drop. And what, may I ask, are the two of you doing in our van?"

She shoved the microphone in front of the twins' faces. Tracey recoiled a bit, but Blaine leaned forward and tried to give an answer like he was actually on a live newscast. "Hello, Sadie, nice to meet you. Yes, we just came from Japan, and we are here now to learn about—"

"That's wonderful," Sadie Nichols interrupted Blaine without listening to his complete sentence. "From Japan to Singapore, no doubt to witness the tenth annual Merlion Fashion Extravaganza and also, quite possibly, to witness the downfall of Aishaanya, Inc."

Blaine shook his head. "No, no, that's not exactly—" he attempted to explain, but he was again interrupted by the eager news reporter.

"You heard it here first on THE DROP." Sadie pulled the microphone down and frantically turned toward her partner. "Okay, Grady, that's a wrap. Let's drop off the big equipment and grab the smaller camera. That way, we can be mobile! We've gotta see if we can catch Aishaanya in transit before she disappears somewhere inside one of her buildings!"

The equipment guy or cameraman or whatever he was, named Grady, rolled his eyes like his colleague was crazy yet he was used to it. However, he obeyed her directive by sliding the big equipment box off his shoulder, placing it in the van and grabbing a smallish camera. Off the two scampered on foot, leaving their van open and the Sassafrases without any more explanation or questions.

Bisaam's Aluminum Cans

"Tracey, did you see that?" Blaine exclaimed. "I might actually be on the news!"

"Blaine, there wasn't even a camera rolling."

"There wasn't?"

"No, and also I don't think that woman's microphone was hooked up to anything."

"It wasn't?"

"No, and look at how absent-minded those two were. They left us here in their van."

"They did?"

"C'mon, Blaine, snap out of it. You're not going to be on the news, but we can go meet our local expert."

"We can?"

"Yes! Let's get out of this van and follow Sadie and Grady! She said they were going to catch Aishaanya in transit."

Blaine shelved his dream of being on the news, and the siblings hopped out of the van. They courteously closed the two doors before sprinting after THE DROP reporters. As they ran, the twins found themselves in a modern, pristinely clean metropolis of a city. Instead of the skyscrapers being square and blocky, it was as if they were works of art, rising into the sky with color, interesting architecture, and daring angles. The roads and sidewalks looked brand-new and were filled with cars and people.

Many of the cars looked extremely expensive and were models the twins had never seen in real life. Most of the people were dressed smartly and walked with perfect posture like they were important or at least hoped to be.

The two twelve-year-olds wanted to be awed by all of this, but the most important thing to them right now was catching up with Sadie and Grady. They could see the two DROP reporters about a block up in front of them. The Sassafrases also saw the podium and small stage Aishaanya had been live telecasted from.

Because of traffic, a few stoplights and some unexpected jaunts, it took the twins longer than anticipated to catch Sadie and Grady, but they finally did. And when they did, they caught more than just Sadie and Grady. Blaine and Tracey saw they had in fact caught up with an entire group of reporters. Many of them the twins recognized from the video screens in the back of the van. It appeared that the reporters had caught Aishaanya.

The fashion icon had been cornered and surrounded on a small side street by the rowdy crowd of headline chasers, but she was not alone. The hulking man in the black suit who had stepped in to stop the news conference was here too, and he looked angry. He stood head and shoulders above everyone else. His muscles were flexed and visible, even from under his suit. His face was red and full of ire. Both his intimidating stance and his massive presence were helping to protect Aishaanya. However, the insatiable crowd was bombarding the beautiful woman with questions and were pressing in closer and closer.

Sadie and Grady, as goofy as they seemed to be, had managed to wiggle their way to the front of the crowd. They were trying to get some answers from Aishaanya. "Hello, I'm Sadie Nichols with THE DROP. Ms. Aishaanya, can you respond to the rumors that the line of elemental garments you were going to reveal at this year's extravaganza have gone missing?" Sadie followed the question by sticking her microphone in the fashionista's direction.

Behind her, Grady held his camera high above all the other heads and leaned in.

The large, black-suited man saw the two and swatted at them with his skillet-sized hand. He missed the microphone but connected with the camera, causing it to flip and point in the opposite direction.

"Ms. Aishaanya? Ms. Aishaanya?" Sadie Nichols relentlessly asked with her outstretched microphone. "Do you have a response to the rumors?"

Aishaanya's face didn't have any of the anger her bodyguard showed, but she did look concerned. "There could be some truth to the rumors," the beauty answered. "But rest assured, regardless of what you've heard, Aishaanya, Inc. will have a dazzling array of garments walking down the runway tomorrow."

"I'm Sadie Nichols, and you heard it here first on THE DROP," Sadie stated confidently, even though Grady's camera was no longer recording her.

The crowd of reporters had heard the fashion icon's response, and what they considered to be a juicy admission caused them to get even more rowdy. The cramped little side street turned into a pushing free-for-all with little concern for anyone's physical safety. In all the frenzy, Blaine and Tracey somehow got pushed from the back of the crowd toward the front. Before they knew it, they were accidentally shoved down, landing at the feet of the giant, angry man and the Asian fashion queen.

Thinking the Sassafrases were reporters, the fired-up, overprotective man grabbed the twins by their shirt collars and lifted them off the ground, one in each hand. He had a look in his eyes like he wanted to bash the two together. However, before he did anything rash, a gentle hand found its way to the man's shoulder and stopped him. It was Aishaanya, her warm mocha-colored eyes full of compassion.

"Brutus, stop. Put them down."

"But, Aishaanya, they charged at you. They want to harm you!"

"No, they don't, Brutus," the woman refuted with a kind smile. "Don't you know who these two are?"

"No. Should I?"

"Yes, Brutus, you should. This girl is a new model of mine, and the boy is your new trainee."

"What?"

"That's right, so why don't you go ahead and put them down, and let's get out of here."

The big man, whose name was evidently Brutus, set the twins down on the ground, looking thoroughly confused about who they actually were. What he was not confused about, however, was the "let's get out of here" part of Aishaanya's statement. Brutus spread his arms out wide and moved a whole section of reporters out of the way, almost like a human bulldozer. He then proved he had speed to match his strength as he swept Aishaanya and the twins away from the crowd, off the small street, and back out onto a main thoroughfare at a swift pace.

The riotous group of reporters chased them, but at the speed Brutus was going, the Sassafrases doubted the crazy crowd would catch them. They turned right from the big street onto a somewhat smaller street, where a long, white limousine was parked. Brutus ran to the luxury vehicle, yanked open the passenger door, and shooed Aishaanya and the twins quickly in. Once all three boarded, he shut the door behind them, and he himself got into the front passenger seat. Whoever the driver was immediately punched the accelerator. With a loud screech of the tires, off the white limousine went through the downtown streets of Singapore away from the bothersome question-mongers.

From where they were in the large, plush passenger section,

the twins could see through the little window into the cab. Brutus leaned over from the passenger seat toward the driver in frustration. "Where were you, man? You parked on the wrong street! We almost got . . ." but the rest of the conversation was muted as Aishaanya pushed a button to roll the partition window up.

Blaine and Tracey found themselves sitting in a limousine on a fine, black leather seat, directly across from the fashion queen of Singapore, or quite possibly the world. Even after running from the paparazzi, the woman's appearance remained perfect. Not a bead of sweat was on her brow. Her classy white pantsuit was pristine and without wrinkle. She sat upright with her legs elegantly crossed. The compassionate eyes the Sassafrases had seen from her earlier were looking at them now accompanied by a kind smile.

"My name is Aishaanya," the woman greeted. "So very nice to make your acquaintance. Who might the two of you be?"

"We are Blaine and Tracey Sassafras," Blaine answered, always eager to introduce the pair.

"Thanks for rescuing us from all those reporters," Tracey added. "Oh, and thanks too for rescuing us from Brutus by calling me a model and my brother a trainee."

"Yeah, that would be the day," Blaine chuckled. "You a model and me a bodyguard."

"Oh, but I was serious," Aishaanya said, smiling but not laughing.

"What?" the twelve-year-olds asked in unison.

"Yes, Tracey, I clearly see in you the poise and natural beauty it takes to be a world-class model." Tracey's face accurately portrayed the shock she was feeling.

"And Blaine, Brutus can always use a new trainee." Blaine didn't feel like Aishaanya's statement to him was a compliment; still, he chose to be flattered.

"This limo is taking us directly to Aishaanya Inc's main office," the fashionista informed. "I would like to invite both of you to join us. What do you think?"

Still in shock at being told she could be a model, Tracey stumbled through an attempted response. "Well, we . . . I mean. . . we could possibly ummm . . ."

"Yes! We'd love to!" Blaine cut in. "And in addition to joining your crew, we would love to hear anything you'd be willing to tell us about science, elements, the periodic table, and such."

Aishaanya smiled. "Well, it's official then. Welcome to Aishaanya, Inc. And, yes, of course I'd be more than happy to talk about science with you!"

Several minutes later, the stretch limousine pulled to a stop in front of one of the coolest-looking buildings the Sassafrases had seen yet. In addition to its tasteful color combinations and its interesting architectural features, it also was a "living building" with an array of potted plants worked into the exterior design of the building.

Brutus got out of the limo and opened the door for Aishaanya and her two new hires. The big man led the way to the front doors of the building where he used a key card to open them. As he held the door open for the three, he watched the two ladies walk in without batting an eye. But when Blaine walked by him, it was obvious he was sizing the boy up and was not impressed.

Once inside, the twins were again awed. They had expected a fashion designer's office to look like a boring fabric store or a mannequin storage space, but this place was awesome. It looked more like an exciting interactive museum. It wasn't only fashion that was being celebrated here. It was fashion, and science, and art, and even technology. There was music playing and bulbs lighting the modern workspace in beautiful ways. There were dozens of people scurrying around looking busy and mostly happy. Aishaanya greeted each person as though they were friends.

CHAPTER 10: SINGAPORE'S MERLION FASHION...

The Sassafras twins followed Aishaanya and Brutus as they walked up a polished wooden case of stairs that looked as though they were free-floating. At the top of the stairs there was a long half wall where a young intern stacked soda cans—a lot of soda cans. Even with all the diversity they had already seen in the office, the twins were confused as to what stacking cans had to do with anything in the office.

Aishaanya read the looks on the twelve-year-olds' faces, smiled, then explained. "This is Bisaam, one of my technology experts. He also happens to be a conceptual artist, and he is making a giant model of the periodic table out of aluminum cans."

"He is?" the twins responded.

"Yes, he is," Aishaanya confirmed. "He is doing it to celebrate the theme of this year's Merlion Fashion Extravaganza."

Bisaam nodded, smiled, and kept stacking cans.

"The periodic table can have several different visual representations," Aishaanya shared. "One periodic table is full of color, dividing elements into families, or categories, giving them names. Another has blocks of elements in different colors. And yet another periodic table has columns or groups in different colors. Add to that the differences in where and how the inner transition metals (the lanthanides and actinides) are shown, plus elements occasionally being added or renamed. Poor hydrogen doesn't seem to know what group it belongs to, same with selenium, which is sometimes a nonmetal and sometimes a metalloid. It can get confusing. The key is to remember that the periodic table is a way for us to visually show the relationships among the elements."

As the fashion boss spoke, the group took a few steps back from the half wall, and from this new vantage point, the Sassafrases could clearly see that the cans, stacked the way they were with different colored cans grouped together, did indeed look like a version of the periodic table.

"Like our human relationships, these elemental relationships can be defined, or shown, in different ways," Aishaanya continued. "Plus, as technology grows, our ability to define those relationships grows as well. As we experiment with the elements, we discover new things that help to shape the periodic table. So, although a newer periodic table may depict new elements, it also shows a deeper understanding of the relationships among the elements. This doesn't make the older version wrong; it's just a different snapshot of our understanding of the elements."

The Sassafras twins already knew that Aishaanya was smart, but even now as they listened to her talk about the periodic table and beheld of this company she'd created, they enhanced their thinking—this woman was a genius. She wasn't just playing dress-up. The Sassafrases were also impressed with Bisaam. How cool was it that he was creating a huge, 3-D periodic table with aluminum cans? By the looks of it, he was almost finished.

"What can you tell us about aluminum?" Blaine asked with a goofy smile. "Get it? What CAN . . . because Bisaam is stacking the . . ."

"Yeah, yeah, we get it, Blaine," Tracey cut her brother off, more than a little ashamed of her brother's lame joke.

Aishaanya smiled as she started sharing, "The symbol for aluminum is Al. Its atomic number is 13, and its atomic mass is 26.98. Aluminum is a silvery gray metal that is relatively light but also very strong. It has been used to make cans, foil, circuit boards, airplanes, and many of the machines that power the modern age. Aluminum is the third-most abundant element on Earth, but it is

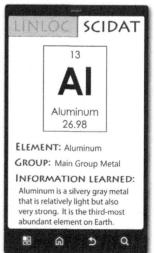

difficult to get because it is tightly bound in the mineral ore called bauxite. Because it takes so much energy to isolate, there is a high demand for recycled aluminum. Recycling aluminum takes 95% less energy to produce than removing the element from bauxite."

They looked at Bisaam. Only a few more cans remained, and then he would be finished with the periodic table he was creating. "What a cool piece of scientific art," Blaine and Tracey thought as their local expert continued with a few more facts about the current topic.

"Aluminum was once considered a noble metal like silver or gold. For instance, Napoleon had a whole set of cutlery and plates made of aluminum that he reserved for his most important guests. Also, aluminum oxide, a compound of aluminum, is the main component of both rubies and sapphires."

Suddenly, as Aishaanya finished, the front doors of the office swung violently open, barely hanging on to their hinges and slamming into the walls behind them. All the hustle and bustle in the office stopped. Every voice hushed. Every eye turned toward the front doors. Even the music on the speakers stopped playing.

Standing in the entrance was a tall, slender woman in a dark, jeweled dress with a dark arrogant smile. She was flanked by four men in suits and shades, all who were about the size and stature of Brutus.

"Tamina!" Aishaanya gasped from her post at the top of the stairs.

"Hello, Aishaanya," the woman named Tamina greeted smugly.

"How did you open the front doors? I thought we took your key card," Aishaanya asked, aghast.

"I had a spare," Tamina answered.

Tamina made her way to the staircase, her dark high heels clacking menacingly on the floor with every step. Her muscle-bound entourage followed her closely like a school of bloodthirsty sharks. The woman walked like a supermodel: sure, confident, and straight-backed. She took the bottom step and then the next, walking straight to where Aishaanya was standing.

The twins stood silent and tense. "Who is this Tamina woman?" they were thinking. Does she have bad intentions toward Aishaanya? Is Brutus going to do anything? The menacing group reached the top of the staircase, coming face-to-face with Aishaanya, Brutus, Bisaam, and the twins.

"You shouldn't have fired me, Aish," Tamina growled out with a smile that was not happy. She seemed to be seething.

"You were embezzling money, Tamina. You left me no choice."

"Oh, c'mon, Aish, you never proved that. But let's change the subject. The Merlion Fashion Extravaganza is tomorrow, and I heard through the grapevine that you have . . .misplaced . . . your entire runway line for the show."

Tamina slid past Aishaanya smugly as she said the word "misplaced." The twins' local expert followed the darkly dressed woman with her gaze, a look of accusation in her eyes, but she said nothing. Brutus, although visibly boiling, also remained silent and still.

Followed by her four henchmen, Tamina walked to the half wall where Bisaam had finished his conceptual masterpiece.

"I see you are still having your yes men make ridiculous and pointless pieces of art for you," she hissed like a snake. The skinny woman lifted up an arm with one finger pointing out. Locking eyes with Aishaanya in a death stare, she forcefully poked at one of the bottom cans of Bisaam's periodic table. Like a crumbling pile of dominoes, the entire piece of art fell, can by can.

"Oops," Tamina said through a wickedly sarcastic smile.

THE SASSAFRAS SCIENCE ADVENTURES

Chapter 11: Models and Mysteries
Observing Metals

Tamina and her goons had long since left. Tracey now found herself being prepped for the unexpected start of her modeling career by several attendants.

Aishaanya was sharing about metalloids as Tracey got ready. "Metalloids include the elements from groups 13, 14, 15, and 16. Boron is from group 13, silicon and germanium are from group 14, arsenic and antimony are from group 15, and tellurium and polonium are from group 16. These elements are also known as semi-metals because they look like metals and even have some metallic properties. They are often brittle and sometimes don't behave like metals typically do. Metalloids are known as semiconductors because they will conduct heat and electricity but not as well as a conductor."

Tracey understood and slightly nodded. She tried to stand as still as possible in her assigned spot as one of the women fussed with her hair, another measured her height with a paper tape measure, and yet another evaluated her jawline and cheekbones, poking around on the twelve-year-old's face with her index fingers.

"I threw around the idea of using metalloids in some of this year's extravaganza fashion line, but instead I went exclusively with gold as the featured element. Of course, that entire line is now missing," Aishaanya sighed. "Still, some of these metalloids are pretty interesting. For example, arsenic, from group 15, which can be found in apple seeds is actually a deadly chemical in large amounts."

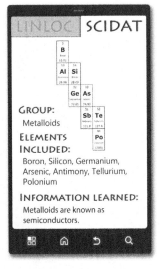

Tracey almost gasped at this information, but she held it in, trying to remain still.

"And borax, a compound of boron, was one of the items exported from Tibet and was traded along the Silk Road. The ancient Chinese would put boron in the glaze of their roof tiles as well as in their pottery and porcelain," Aishaanya added.

This information took Tracey's mind back to the time when the invisible zip lines afforded her the opportunity to travel in Sichuan, China, with her friend Tashi to a Tibetan village. Aishaanya sighed again, exasperation still clearly present.

"Tamina was such a good friend, almost like a sister," the fashion icon shared. "And she was such a good designer. In the beginning she had the most daring design ideas, but . . . she got lazy. Eventually, instead of coming up with her own stuff, she started stealing ideas from others, and not just ideas, but she was pretty much stealing everything: ideas, designs, materials, and, we suspect money, too. We never pressed charges, but I was forced to fire her. Instead of being sorry, Tamina decided to take the things she had stolen and use them to start her own design company here in Singapore. She is still bold and daring in a smug way, but I'm certain she's the one who stole my entire gold fashion line. I'm not sure how she did it, but I know she did."

Aishaanya let out one more long sigh full of more exasperation than all the other sighs before combined. She looked at Tracey like she considered her a friend. "I hope Brutus and your brother are successful in finding the missing line in time for tomorrow's Merlion Fashion Extravaganza. If not, I don't know what we're going to do. If they can prove Tamina's guilty, I guess that would be good too."

Tracey attempted to form an expression that communicated both agreement and empathy, but with a lady now assaulting her face with a makeup brush, she wasn't sure the sentiment was conveyed.

All at once, Aishaanya clapped quickly and stood a little straighter. "Okay, that's enough whining and complaining," the woman stated, looking more like the consummate professional Tracey knew she was. "It's time for me to leave you alone and get back to work. And, by the way, can I say that I was totally right about your poise and natural beauty, Tracey. Although you've only just begun your makeover, I can already see that you are going to be the most stunning model on the runway tonight."

Tracey's expression stayed the same, but her face flushed as red as a ripe tomato. She wanted to help her local expert, but the thought of walking down a runway with everyone watching her was terrifying.

THE SASSAFRAS SCIENCE ADVENTURES

Blaine raised an eyebrow and slightly bobbed his head, a sure and confident look on his face. The Sassafras boy wasn't positive his intended sentiment was making its way through to Brutus. The big man had not seemed impressed when Blaine let him know that he'd recently been on the winning side of an epic ninja battle. It was almost like Brutus would rather be out on this assignment alone, as opposed to having a twelve-year-old tagging along with him. The two of them were currently sitting in a dark sedan with dark tinted windows, parked in the middle of a sprawling industrial park.

"Hey, Brute," Blaine said from the passenger seat, "you know how Aishaanya said I'm your new trainee for security detail or to be a bodyguard or whatever?"

Brutus slowly turned his head toward the boy as he spoke, looking at him like every word was annoying.

"Well, to be honest, this doesn't seem like security detail or bodyguarding," Blaine continued. "This seems more like yes-man detective work; doesn't it? I mean, with me a professional ninja and you a 300-pound tank, shouldn't we be out there busting heads or something? You know, instead of all this slinking around?"

An immediate response was at Brutus's lips. He visibly held it in, took a deep breath, and formed a secondary response. "If Aishaanya wants us out here, out here is where we are going to be. Our goal is not to 'bust heads;' it's to find the missing fashion line."

"Oh, c'mon, Brutie! Shouldn't we—"

"Find the missing fashion line!" the big man cut off Blaine's wayward sentence, this time with emphasis. "And it's not Brutie or Brute. It's Brutus," the giant bodyguard clarified through clinched teeth.

He took another big breath, then lifted his hand and pointed to a warehouse a block away. "That unmarked building is Tamina's. My guess is that's where our stolen line can be found. We are going to wait until I'm sure it's clear, and then we're going to go check it out. That's the plan."

Blaine lifted his eyebrow, trying out his sure and confident look again. "Reading you loud and clear, Brutimus," the boy affirmed to the man who now had an angry face as red as a ripe tomato.

"Yes, that's right. It's Rosemary Rajan," the young woman confirmed that Tracey had gotten her name right.

The Sassafras girl had finished prepping for the evening's fashion show and was walking through the large garment hall at Aishaanya, Inc. with this bright young woman. Rosemary was in her early 20s, of Asian descent, and capable and smart, like everyone else Tracey had met here so far. She was one of Aishaanya's new and upcoming designers.

"I think it's so cool that Aishaanya picked you out on the street," Rosemary chatted with a kind smile as she and Tracey walked past rows and rows of assorted clothes and material on racks. "And can I also say I totally agree with her. You definitely have what it takes to be a top model."

Tracey's face flushed again.

"I'm also excited she assigned me to you for the rest of this afternoon," Rosemary continued. "I know our entire golden line for tonight's show is gone, but I think the line I've been working on has the potential to awe people if I can get it to the runway. I'm hoping you can try on some of the garments and prove the concept. If Aishaanya sees you in my line and likes it, maybe my stuff can make it to the runway for this evening's extravaganza."

Tracey could feel that her face was still red. She wondered if she would be in a perpetual flush the rest of the time she was here in Singapore. She wasn't sure what Aishaanya, Rosemary, and the others saw in her, but she was trying to believe it. Tracey had never viewed herself as any kind of model at all, but she did hope that she had some sort of beauty to offer the world, natural beauty that could maybe inspire someone.

The two ladies turned from the large hall into a large space filled with designers all hovering around either mannequins or live models. "The real question," Rosemary said to Tracey as she led the Sassafras girl to her assigned workspace, "is—are your brother and Brutus going to find the missing line? Or is Aishaanya going to deem one of our other fashion lines worthy? Either way, Aishaanya, Inc. must have something to present tonight at the Merlion Fashion Extravaganza."

Tracey didn't want Rosemary to know it, but part of her hoped that the boys would find the missing line. Then maybe she wouldn't have to walk down the runway.

"Oh, c'mon, Brute-to-the-max," Blaine chided impatiently. "Surely it's clear now. There hasn't been any movement at all around that warehouse the whole time we've been here!"

The big man's face seemed to be perpetually red as he interacted with the Sassafras boy. "I said we are going to wait until it's clea—"

"Oh, look, Brutastic!" Blaine interrupted the big man with a shout and a point at the warehouse. "There are some people coming out of the building! Does that mean it's clear? Can we go in now?"

Brutus studied the individuals coming out of the warehouse.

One was clearly the tall and slender Tamina. Four others looked to be the henchmen she had brought to Aishaanya Inc. earlier. The last goon who exited made sure the door was closed and locked behind them. No one was carrying anything, and they didn't seem to be in a hurry. Nor did they seem to suspect they were being watched. Brutus remained silent, and his eyes remained focused on the group until they disappeared around the other side of the warehouse.

"So, what do you say, Bru-ha-ha? Can we go in? Can we storm the warehouse?"

Without making eye contact with Blaine, the huge man let out a long sigh filled with unnoticed exasperation. He gave the slightest of nods and reached for his door handle. Taking his trainer's motions as a green light to go, Blaine smiled and reached for his door handle as well. He opened the door, and the Sassafras boy ran toward the warehouse steps ahead of Brutus.

"Yes, that's right. It's Bisaam," the young man confirmed, seeming impressed that Tracey had remembered his name. "Bisaam Sepat. And yes, I'm more than a conceptual artist, as you saw earlier with the can wall that is sadly no longer. I actually consider myself to be more of a technical artist, not in a gaming or computer sense, but in a conceptual sense, which I guess is why Aishaanya calls me a conceptual artist. I like to work technology into objects that you can touch and feel and use. I like to highlight both function and beauty."

Tracey wasn't sure she understood what Bisaam was saying. Rosemary Rajan, however, definitely understood because she nodded vigorously and added, "Bisaam is the best! That's why

I asked him to team up with me for this periodic table-themed fashion line."

The three were standing in Rajan's workspace, surrounded by multiple garments she had designed. Tracey was truly awed by Rosemary's creativity and skill. The young designer had the ability to use, shape, and combine different fabrics to create breathtaking works of art, art that also happened to be wearable. However, although the garments were impressive, Tracey wasn't sure how any of them represented the periodic table.

Tracey had had plenty of time to look around the large room at many of the other designers' workspaces. It was clear how most of them were working the periodic table into their designs. There were garments that looked metallic or had different kinds of metal attached to them somehow. There were garments with patterns that were designed to look like floating gasses. And there were many garments that looked like the actual periodic table in creative ways. Tracey liked Rosemary's fashion line the best, but she couldn't see the periodic table in any of it.

"Conductivity," Bisaam suddenly exclaimed.

"Huh?" Tracey responded, taken off guard.

"That was my idea as to how to work the periodic table into Rosemary's line."

Rosemary was nodding and smiling. Tracey was still confused.

"Conductivity is the ability of a material to conduct, or pass along, electricity or heat. Typically, metals are great conductors, whereas non-metals are not. Some conductors, like silicon and germanium, lie somewhere in between."

"But get this, Tracey," Rajan said excitedly. "Bisaam figured out how to make a conductive thread out of silicon."

Tracey wanted to understand, but she was still in the dark.

"It's actually a silicon compound," Bisaam declared. "Silicon on its own would be way too brittle."

Still nodding excitedly, Rosemary implored. "Tell her, Bisaam, tell Tracey about the wearable tech ideas we came up with!"

"Wearable tech?" Tracey asked.

"That's right," the conceptual artist nodded. "By using these conductive threads in the fabric used to make Rosemary's garments, we were able to produce an entire line of wearable tech for this year's Merlion Fashion Extravaganza."

"Wow! Really?" Tracey responded.

"Oh, yes," Bisaam answered as he stepped over and pulled a stunning dress off a rack. For instance, this is the GPS dress. The silicon-based conductive threads combined with the use of contact sensors allowed us to use haptic navigation in this dress."

"Haptic navigation?"

"Yes, enter a location in your smartphone or smartwatch; the dress will wirelessly connect. And as you walk, the haptic navigation and sensors in the dress will send a variation of small vibrations through the dress to communicate with you whether to turn right, turn left, or go straight or backward. The haptic technology can also sense obstacles in your path before you reach them. So, our hope is that dresses and clothes with this technology can be used not only by sighted people but also by the blind community."

Tracey's face showed the awe she was feeling. She still didn't completely understand how the technology worked, but this GPS dress was one of the coolest things she'd ever seen.

"Oh, and look, Tracey," Bisaam grabbed another article of clothing from an adjacent rack. "This is the Jump Higher Track Suit. It's ladies' athletic apparel that uses biomimicry. The shoulder and hip areas of the suit are equipped with small bird wing-inspired flaps that remain compressed while you are walking or running. Then, they open when you jump, creating a small amount of lift."

"Oh, oh, show her the camera dress next," Rosemary squealed before Tracey could even fully take in the coolness of the track suit.

"This one's called the Camera Dress," Bisaam shared as he grabbed another garment. "You can't tell by looking, but there are hundreds of tiny cameras spread all over this dress."

"There's no way," Tracey blurted.

"I know it's hard to believe," Bisaam agreed, holding the dress a little closer so Tracey could see it better. "But there are cameras that are small enough to attach to the end of the threads and then sewn in so that the cameras are spread all over this dress. The conductive silicone threads lead to the 0.99-millimeter cameras that have 0.66-millimeter sensors with image resolution of 850 pixels. This dress can take pictures and videos from all different angles as you're on the go."

Tracey again was shocked but once more she didn't have time to process everything before the next garment was introduced.

"This one is called the Smart Glove Smart Suit," Bisaam communicated, holding up the next outfit for the Sassafras girl to see. "It's a sharp-looking pantsuit equipped with matching gloves, which, of course, are made with conductive fibers and filled with contact sensors that track the movements of your hands and fingers. The suit and gloves allow you to do things remotely, like computer design, data entry, device control, 3-D object manipulation, gaming telepresence, and even create things like art and music."

"All right, Bisaam," Rosemary cut in with a smile. "Let me show Tracey the next one."

Bisaam obliged as Rajan stepped over and grabbed the most gorgeous dress Tracey had seen yet. "This one is my absolute favorite!" the young designer beamed. "This is the Chameleon Dress! It uses photonic manipulation as it reads the environment around you to creatively refract light and makes you virtually invisible!"

Tracey's mouth dropped open. "Invisible?" the girl asked.

Both Rosemary and Bisaam nodded happily in confirmation.

Silicone Trends

"Invisible, Blaine. I said invisible. Not invincible," Brutus whispered in exasperation to his unwelcome sidekick.

"So we're not going to try to be invincible as we bust into the warehouse?" Blaine asked, attempting to flex his bicep as he spoke.

"No!" Brutus reprimanded. "We are going to try to be invisible as we sneak into the warehouse."

"But Brutopia, we saw the whole group walking out, and they weren't carrying anything, so that's gotta mean the missing fashion line is inside with no one guarding it! C'mon, let's bust in and get it!"

"Sneak, not bust," Brutus ordered resolutely.

Blaine silently yielded to his trainer—at least momentarily. The two were already crouched near the locked door. Brutus slowly reached up and grabbed the substantial-looking padlock with his big bare hand. Blaine thought he was going to pick it. But instead, the gorilla-sized man pulled the padlock and broke it with his brute strength, making it look as easy as picking a piece of fruit from a tree.

Brutus slowly pulled the door open with minimal squeaks, and the two crawled into the warehouse, closing the door behind them. Blaine wasn't sure exactly what he had expected to see inside, but he knew it wasn't this. The large building was completely empty. There wasn't so much as a crate or box or even a packing peanut. The place was swept clean.

The two stood from their crouching stances and walked to the middle of the empty warehouse. Brutus looked like he was about to say something, but he was interrupted by a loud sound.

The two looked toward the door they had come through to see that Tamina's four goons had busted in on them. Tamina was right behind the four, and the fashionista had the smuggest of smug looks on her face.

"Well, hello Brutus," the tall, slender woman greeted. "Funny running into you here. What are you doing in my warehouse?"

Brutus didn't answer because he knew Tamina wasn't asking a question.

Blaine, however, did. "We know you stole Aishaanya's fashion line that she was going to showcase this year at the Merlion Fashion Extravaganza! Maybe it's not here in your warehouse, but we know you stole it!"

As he spoke, Blaine elbowed his mentor for confirmation. "Isn't that right, Bruticus?"

Brutus didn't say anything. He stared at the four henchmen who were slowly inching toward them.

"You think I'm a thief?" Tamina laughed. "Funny you say that, because right now you're the ones who broke a lock and are standing in a warehouse that's not yours!"

Blaine folded his arms and tried to maintain a defiant look. "Oh, yeah, well . . . you . . . are . . ."

Tamina cut Blaine off with another laugh. "Maybe you can finish that sentence later, little boy. Right now, let me say: I want to let the two of you leave without any charges or any kind of incident. However, I'm not so sure my security detail is of the same mind."

The four massive bodyguards took Tamina's statement as their cue to pounce.

"Aishaanya truly is the best boss ever," Rosemary gushed authentically. "Plus, she's such an inspiration. She was born in a small fishing village and became a world icon not only in fashion but also in business. She's like a real-life Merlion. She has shown the world how amazing Singapore is and has let everyone know we belong among the world's elite in the fashion industry."

Tracey was listening to her friend talk even as more attendants surrounded her. Evidently, earlier in the day she had received her base layer makeover. Now it was time for her full makeover. The Sassafras girl was cooperating, but she was still a bit uneasy about where all this attention was leading her.

"More than being a great boss, she is a great mentor," Rosemary continued. "She has consistently taken the time to listen to all of us, build our confidence, and share invaluable ideas with us. However," Rosemary paused for a second before she said the next part, "ever since she had to fire Tamina, she's been a little . . ."

"Frustrated," Bisaam said for Rosemary. "She's frustrated. I'm sure it was a huge bummer to fire her former best friend. But can I be honest?" Bisaam added. "I don't know why she was so pessimistic about my silicon thread. I mean, c'mon, Rosemary, you have the best designs in here. When you couple that with my technology, how in the world could Aishaanya say no to your fashion line? It totally should've been chosen for tonight's extravaganza. And, no offense, but I think it's even better than Aishaanya's gold line!"

"Maybe," a new voice suddenly interjected. It was the CEO herself. She had stepped into the workspace unnoticed. Bisaam's face immediately flushed as red as a strawberry. Aishaanya stepped toward the embarrassed conceptual artist and put a gentle hand on his shoulder.

"It is my genuine hope that everyone who works for me would one day surpass me." She looked from Bisaam to Rosemary to Tracey and her attendants and then back to Bisaam. "You may be right about everything you said. And, yes, I was a little pessimistic about your silicon thread because I've tried myself to produce it before and failed, so I don't trust the element. However, Bisaam, I think you have surpassed me, which is a good thing!"

Bisaam's face seemed to become a little less red at this sincere statement.

"You know, silicon was used in the boots that Neil Armstrong wore as he took that first step on the moon," the beautiful designer informed. "The astronauts' silicon rubber boots protected them from both the extremely high and extremely low temperatures in space. Silicon has also been used in a myriad of products like lubricants, adhesives, and even clocks. So why couldn't it be used effectively in a conductive thread?"

Bisaam nodded, but he was still too embarrassed to say anything.

"The symbol for silicon is Si. It has an atomic number of 14 and an atomic mass of 28.09," Aishaanya continued. "Silicon is the second-most abundant element on earth. It is found in sand, quartz, and many other minerals. It has some of the properties of a metal, but in its pure form, it is a glossy, off-white lump. It is typically found in nature bound to other elements because it doesn't seem to like to be on its own. When combined with boron and phosphorus, silicon is a semi-conductor—the one that gave rise to the computer age via the silicon chip."

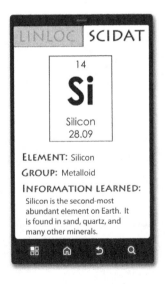

As the fashion CEO talked about silicon, she got more excited. There didn't seem to be any pessimism in her. "All that said, Rosemary and Bisaam, show me what you got." Aishaanya smiled. "I am still hoping that Brutus and Blaine find that missing gold line, but Rosemary, even as I look at some of your pieces now, I wouldn't hesitate to put them on the runway tonight. And Bisaam, let's see what your conductive silicon thread can do to enhance these gorgeous garments of Rosemary's. Oh, and Tracey, beautiful Tracey Sassafras, let's see what you look like in these stunning outfits!"

It was a thing of beauty. Brutus made one defensive move to protect himself and Blaine from the four muscle-bound attackers. And then he made one offensive move to push them all back, careening across the warehouse floor in four different directions. Blaine had been in the karate stance he'd learned in Japan. In his mind, he had been ready for the advance of the four goons. Regardless, he was impressed with the moves Brutus had made.

Brutus and Blaine walked to the door, passing Tamina on the way. Not looking threatened at all, and still wearing a smug look, the tall, skinny fashionista wiggled her fingers at the two in a sarcastic wave. "Ta-ta," she laughed as they exited into the Singaporean sunshine. The two silently walked the block to the car and got in.

Brutus sat still and silent for a second. Not Blaine. "What's our next move, Brutes-on-the-ground? Does Tamina have another warehouse we can storm? Does she have other associates who could've been involved? Can we go find them if she does? Should we go back in where we came from and teach these jokers another lesson?"

Instead of responding verbally to any of Blaine's questions,

Brutus responded physically by reaching over and using his huge hand to literally shut the boy's mouth. After pinching Blaine's lips together to keep his mouth closed, Brutus responded, "We are going back to Aishaanya Inc."

Blaine nodded and tried to say, "Sounds good, Brutes-R-us." But with his lips pinched, it sounded more like, "Sossgoobrumferus."

He wanted to forget it all. He wanted to forget all his failures. He wanted to forget all his losses. He'd set out to wreak vengeance on Cecil Sassafras by stopping the man's niece and nephew from learning science. But at every turn, he'd failed at that task.

Even in his failures, though, he had gained power, prestige, and even, dare he say, love. However, that was all gone now.

It was all broken, shattered, and in shambles like this underground lab he had lorded over for a short time. He had sat slumped and dazed in his disheveled lab for a day or two, almost in a catatonic state, at a total loss with how to move forward, but not anymore.

Now he was moving.

Yes, everything he had planned and done thus far had failed, but he had one last grand idea, an idea that had come from his heartache.

As he had sat in his coma-like state, the only thing left to stare at was the big, crumpled Forget-O-Nator. All the scientists were gone. All the Dark Cape suits were gone. And everything else was destroyed. So as he stared at the Forget-O-Nator and dwelled on wanting to forget, he had come up with one last-ditch idea. He would search through the wreckage in his lab and find materials he could use to make a huge harness big enough to fit around and secure the Forget-O-Nator. Then he would use his three-ringed carabiner, which was the only one left in the lab, to zip the Forget-O-Nator and himself back to 1108 North Pecan Street.

He knew for a fact that after Adrianna's arrest, his old house sat empty. He would spend the time needed to fix the large Forget-O-Nator, and then he would use it. He would enter the machine himself, and he would wipe all of his terrible memories away.

But it wasn't only his memories he wanted to be gone. He wanted to wipe away all their memories as well. All of them were going to forget everything: Cecil, Summer, those twins, those rodents, and even that robot, for good measure. Along with his own, he was going to wipe it all away.

He was going to kill two birds with one stone. He was going to eliminate his grief, and he was finally going to exact revenge on Cecil Sassafras.

Over the course of this science learning summer of theirs, Blaine and Tracey hadn't been apart much. When they had been, they'd had some pretty memorable reunions. However, none of the reunions had been as memorable as this one. Tracey had been shocked when Aishaanya had called her out to be a model. Then, throughout this day of being made over, she'd been a little on the insecure side, wondering if she had what it took to walk the runway or if people would see her as a fraud. But right now, as she looked at the awestruck expression on her brother's face, she knew she must look good.

Blaine and Brutus had walked into the workspace at the precise moment that Rosemary had looked at Tracey and said,

"OK, you're all done!"

Tracey's hair was curled, fluffed, and flowing. Her face was artistically highlighted with beautiful shades of makeup. Her ears and neck were adorned with fine jewelry. She had on gorgeous, yet surprisingly comfortable, high heels, and she was wearing the shimmering and stunning GPS dress.

"What's that look on your face all about?" Tracey asked her brother with growing confidence. "Never thought you'd see your twin sister looking all good like a supermodel?"

"I'm . . . just . . . you . . . how . . . golly . . . umm . . ." Blaine tried to respond, but the shock of seeing his sister like this was too much for him to take in at the moment.

Rosemary beamed, proud of Tracey and proud of the dress she'd designed. Basaam beamed, proud of the tech in the dress, and Aishaanya, who was also present, beamed with glee at Blaine's reaction to seeing his sister. "See, I told you Tracey; you have the poise and natural beauty it takes!"

Everyone agreed with gleaming smiles and nods of their heads.

Aishaanya turned toward her bodyguard. "What about you and Blaine?" she asked. "Did you find the missing line?"

Brutus silently shook his head.

Aishaanya responded with a smile that communicated she had almost expected that to be Brutus's answer and that she was content with the situation. The fashion queen turned back toward Tracey, Rosemary, and Bisaam.

"Well, it's official then," the beautiful woman announced. "Rosemary Rajan, your absolutely stunning and boldly unique garments, and Bisaam Sepat, your cutting-edge tech and conductive threads, and Tracey Sassafras, your poise and drop-dead good looks will be representing Aishaanya, Inc. tonight at the Merlion Fashion Extravaganza!"

Chapter 12: Great Britain's Carboxynitro Games

Menacing Nonmetals

"Hello, I'm Sadie Nichols with THE DROP, reporting live from the Merlion Fashion Extravaganza! This year's show has been a dazzling success! The best designers from Singapore and from all over the world have showcased for us their periodic table-themed fashion lines. We've seen all kinds of wonderful garments come down the runway, but once again, like she does year after year, it has been Aishaanya, our very own Singaporean fashion queen, who has stolen the show. She and her crew of young and exciting designers have been totally in their element as they've showcased a groundbreaking line made entirely with a new silicon-based conductive thread."

"Despite this morning's report of a missing fashion line and turmoil within the company, Aishaanya Inc. has graced the runway with two breathtaking dresses, a stellar pantsuit, and a sleek athletic outfit. To make Aishaanya's new fashion line even more stunning, all four of these amazing outfits came down the runway worn by a beautiful new model named Tracey Sassafras."

The heavily made-up Sadie Nichols frowned, and Grady brought the camera he was holding close in tight to her face.

"However, even in the midst of all the victorious glitz and glamour of this year's Merlion Fashion Extravaganza," THE DROP reporter continued, "there has been one dreary and dull spot. Great anticipation had built around Tamina and seeing what the former Aishaanya Inc. designer could come up with, having recently launched her own company. Yet all she did was send a humdrum gold line down the runway that fell flat with the crowd. The garments were uninspiring and arrested no one's attention. The most exciting part of Tamina's night was when she herself was arrested mid-show. Evidently, she had stolen her whole line from another designer. When we get more details on that, you'll be the first to hear it here on THE DROP."

Suddenly, Grady pointed with his free hand, motioning for Sadie to turn around and look. "Oh! Look everyone, look! It's Tracey Sassafras coming down the runway one last time!"

This time, THE DROP reporter and cameraman had successfully captured all the wanted and needed audio and video, as had every other news and media outlet in the place. Right now, bulbs flashed and voices awed as Tracey strode confidently down the runway wearing the Chameleon dress. Even though she had been insecure about being a model at first and terrified to walk the runway, she had chosen to face the fear. She had chosen to believe that she had real and authentic beauty to offer, not just outwardly, here on the runway, but also inwardly from her heart.

Aishaanya beamed, proud of her newest model. Rosemary gleamed, proud of Tracey and honored that her fashion line was being showcased. Bisaam nodded with a smile, excited that his silicon-based conductive thread had now been introduced to the world. Brutus, the big, stoic bodyguard, looked like he might even be smiling. However, it was Blaine Sassafras who had the biggest smile on his face in the whole crowd. He was so proud of his sister and was so happy she was feeling beautiful and as confident as she should be. Even yet he'd probably still poke fun at her later about this whole thing.

The Sassafras twins got a great night's sleep on some couches at Aishaanya Inc. and woke up refreshed and coherent. They successfully entered all the correct SCIDAT data from Singapore into their smartphones, along with pictures from the archive app, and here they were opening their LINLOC apps to see where they would be zipping off to next.

"Ooooh, Great Britain," Blaine said in excited delight. "Longitude 4 °44' 50.1" W, latitude 50° 21' 35.5" N."

"Where we will be studying the topics of nonmetals, carbon, oxygen, and nitrogen," Tracey added, "all with a local expert known as 'The Unseen One.'"

"Ooooh, the Unseen One," Blaine repeated in excited curiosity.

The twelve-year-old twins put on their helmets, cinched up their harnesses, and calibrated their specially designed carabiners to the coordinates that would take them to Great Britain. As soon as the carabiners snapped shut, the two were pulled up a foot or two in the air, securely attached to the correct invisible zip line. They would dangle like this for approximately seven seconds before whooshing away.

Blaine looked at his sister with a kind and thoughtful expression. She wasn't dressed up or made-up like a model anymore, but he was still proud of her for having the guts to walk down that runway.

"What?" Tracey asked, seeing the rare look on her brother's face.

"Nothing," he said, and then off the Sassafrases zipped at the speed of light.

It had taken several days, but he and President Lincoln had done it. They had successfully cleaned the basement. "Wowie whopping willikers, would you look at that!" Cecil exclaimed to his lab assistant. "This place isn't just spick; it's span as well. It's spick and span, and it's almost ready for the arrival of sweet Summer Thyme Beach."

President Lincoln grunted in agreement as the two stood at the top of the staircase with arms folded, looking at the basement in satisfaction. The knick knacks had been moved to closets around the house and the junk that had filled the open spaces in the attic stowed away. The floor had been swept and mopped to the point of sparkling. Soft songs of romance played on the speakers of the tracking screen, which was currently showing the green dots representing Train and Blaisey zipping from Singapore to Great Britain.

In the center of the basement was a table with two chairs, topped with a crisp, white linen tablecloth, candles, fine china, shining silverware, and placemats depicting the periodic table. Now all that was left to do was to figure out what the menu was going to be for this highly anticipated date.

"Welly well, well, well, Linc Dawg. What do you think? For this romantic meal at this romantic table, should we go light or hearty? Should we go sweet or savory? Should we go five course or single plate?"

A thoughtful look formed on the prairie dog's face. It looked like he was going to respond, but the moment was interrupted by the sudden sound of the front porch trapdoor opening up.

"Ohpity nopity," Cecil exclaimed with wide eyes and raised arms. "Is that sweet Summer Thyme already? I thought she wasn't supposed to be here for a few more days! We're not quite ready!"

Now the sound of someone coming down the porch to basement slide reached the pair's ears. Who was about to careen into the spick and span basement?

"What is this place?" Blaine asked with heightened curiosity. The Sassafras twins' sight and strength had returned to full capacity after their invisible zip-line landing. However, they were confused because it looked and felt like they had landed in some kind of small half dome made out of foggy glass. Surely this wasn't the correct landing spot. Had they gotten the coordinates wrong?

Tracey was using an index finger to see if she could wipe the haziness from the glass. Blaine was raising both hands and arms above him to see if he could lift or move the half dome. Neither were successful.

Tracey was about to repeat the exact same question her brother had asked when she was interrupted by a loud voice.

"Welcome to the first ever Carboxynitro Games!" the British voice creepily announced, not sounding welcoming at all.

CHAPTER 12: GREAT BRITAIN'S CARBOXYNITRO GAMES

The twins looked around to see where the voice was coming from. It had to be piped into their little half dome by some unseen speakers somewhere.

"I am the Unseen One!" the voice continued. "And I will be your host, your teacher, your referee, and your judge as you compete against each other in the games!"

Compete against each other? Both Sassafrases looked at each other in alarm.

"The Carboxynitro Games, or CON Games, will be held in their entirety here in the state-of-the-art Twin Biodome facility. One dome is a tropical rainforest. The other is a temperate rainforest. Both are packed with organic chemistry!"

Currently, nothing the Unseen One was saying was making sense to the twelve-year-olds. Why was he mentioning games, rainforests, and organic chemistry? All they could see was this small, foggy dome they were trapped in.

"The Carboxynitro Games comprise three intense challenges, based on organic chemistry," the unnerving British voice continued. "Remember, organic chemistry is a part of chemistry that looks at the science behind carbon compounds. It's often referred to as the chemistry of life because so many carbon compounds are essential to life as we know it. When this branch of chemistry was originally founded, it dealt only with compounds made by living organisms, but as technology has grown, so has organic chemistry. Now it includes the compounds of life plus man-made compounds such as plastics and other industrial products."

Not only had the Saassafras twins never had a zip-line landing spot like this, but they'd also never had a local expert like this. Who was this guy? Why was his voice so creepy? And why didn't he have a real name?

"Now, from my brilliant unseen mind, I will share a little bit about nonmetals," the Unseen One continued. "Nonmetals include elements from groups 14, 15, and 16 on the periodic table: carbon from group 14; nitrogen and phosphorus from group 15; oxygen, sulfur, and selenium from group 16. These elements are not metals. They lack the strength that metals provide. However, five of them are essential to life. The other one, selenium, is also needed in trace amounts."

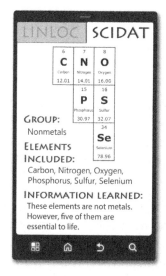

"Who all was the Unseen One talking to?" the twins wondered. "Are we the only ones here, or are there others?" At the moment, their questions remained unanswered as the strange local expert continued.

"Nonmetals are far more common on Earth than metals. Nonmetal elements can be gases, liquids, or solids. So, they behave differently in chemistry. They have significantly lower melting points and are poor conductors of heat and electricity."

Blaine and Tracey knew they needed to be committing all this SCIDAT information to memory so they could correctly enter it into their smartphone apps later, but they were having a hard time focusing in this little bubble, listening to the figureless voice.

"Phosphorus burns readily in the air and can be poisonous. However, it's a part of our DNA and is an essential part of our bones and teeth," the Unseen One continued pompously. "Selenium is used in photoelectric cells and to color glass red. It is also found in nature and is needed by humans for our metabolism and thyroid, although too much would poison us." The Brit paused to let out a minatory laugh.

"Why is he laughing?" the twins wondered.

"And now let me mention sulfur!" the voice bellowed after

CHAPTER 12: GREAT BRITAIN'S CARBOXYNITRO GAMES

the cackle. "Sulfur is the whole reason why I'm sharing all this information on nonmetals right now. Sulfur is found in proteins and enzymes in our bodies, but it can also be found oozing out of active volcanoes. Pure sulfur is bright yellow and is a key ingredient in gunpowder. Sounds pretty volatile, doesn't it?"

The Sassafras twins nodded.

"In ancient Greece, they burned sulfur to get rid of pests. New York City did the same in the late 1800s to prevent the spread of disease," the Unseen One shared, and then he started another unsettling laugh that he let run throughout his entire next statement. "And now, I will use sulfur to sanitize all of you! Before you start the Carboxynitro Games, I need you to be absolutely clean so as not to harm the somewhat delicate indoor man-made biomes here at the Twin Biodomes. Prepare yourselves for a smelly, yet cleansing, sulfur shower!"

At the precise moment he said the word "shower," a small sprinkler head appeared at the top center of the dome sprayed liquid all over. The warm liquid reeked of rotten eggs. It was amazing that such a small sprinkler could spray so much. Blaine and Tracey were immediately soaked, and even worse than that, they now smelled like compost.

All at once, the sulfur shower stopped, and to the Sassafrases' astonishment, the small dome's haziness cleared in a way that was almost like gray pixels falling from a screen, making the clear glass visible. Their astonishment deepened as they looked around at all they could now see. Their small dome was one of about a dozen little domes just like it, all of which were currently clearing up, like theirs. In every small dome there was a pair of people who looked to be about Blaine's and Tracey's age. However, the most astonishing thing wasn't the small domes, rather it was the gargantuan rotunda that rose above them. They were inside a huge dome, one that had to be the size of a baseball stadium, if not bigger. It looked to be constructed using steel support beams and an uncountable number of glass panes. The glass was glazed, much like their small domes had been, but it was translucent enough to let a good amount of sunlight in.

Under the dome, it looked like a rainforest with foliage covering the entire surface, rising up into the dome at different heights and exploding with all kinds of color. There were bubbling springs, gurgling brooks, and small, pristine pools. Blaine and Tracey could easily imagine this place looked like what the Garden of Eden might have looked like, with the exception of a few walkways and what looked to them like handrails made of rope and wooden posts. For a second the twins almost forgot how unpleasant they had felt a few moments earlier . . . until the Unseen One spoke again . . .

Bubbles of Carbon

"Look up. Look down. Look all around," the portentous voice commanded. "As you look up, you will see that you are in dome number one of the Twin Biodomes. This is the tropical rainforest. At the south end of this dome there is a tunnel connecting to the second dome, where the temperate rainforest can be found. The second dome is slightly smaller but just as spectacular."

Still trapped in their bubble, the twins took in a full circle view of their new science learning location. Sure, it was spectacular, but where was this unseen voice coming from?

At the top and center of the rotunda was something that looked like an upside-down dome or bubble. It was hanging, but at the same time, it was built into the structure. The tinted glass and steel framework of the bubble was about two or three times as big as theirs. It looked like it had a couple of catwalks leading to it. Was this sky bubble where the Unseen One was? Was he looking down at them from this hidden, lofty spot? The twelve-year-olds weren't sure.

"As you look down, you can see that you are not the only duo here," the Unseen One continued. "In every holding bubble is a set of twins. All of you will be competing against every other set of twins here in the Twin Biodomes for the Carboxynitro Games."

Blaine and Tracey lowered their gazes toward the other bubbles, which held those they would be competing against, and gulped. Suddenly, the other sets of twins looked bigger, stronger, and faster than they had the first time the Sassafrases had looked at them.

"As you look around," the invisible host continued, "you will see what you want and what you don't want."

"What in the world does he mean by that?" Blaine asked out loud.

"What you want is this," the voice immediately answered Blaine's question as a bottom section of the sky bubble opened up. Out of the opening a large see-through sphere was lowered by a mechanical arm. To the Sassafrases, it looked like the sphere was full of...

"Diamonds!' the Unseen One declared. "The pair of twins who wins the Carboxynitro Games will be given this cache of diamonds as a prize!"

Although Blaine and Tracey couldn't hear any of the other twins, they could see by their expressions that everyone was oohing and aahing.

"What you don't want is this," the explainer divulged as there was a small explosion of water in one of the pools of water directly in front of them. A whirlpool quickly formed and deepened. Then came a splash and a gurgle as the whirlpool disappeared and the pool returned to normal.

"That was a flush," the Unseen One explained, with a creepy laugh edging his voice. "The sets of twins who don't perform well in the challenges will be flushed out of the Carboxynitro Games."

The Sassafras twins gulped again.

"You've looked up. You've looked down. You've looked all around. And now if all of you will glance directly outside your holding bubbles," the Unseen One directed, "you will see a sizeable sphere and a small pile of equipment. The spheres are made from a carbon compound. The equipment comprises two harnesses, two quick draws, and a connector strap."

Blaine and Tracey peeked out of their little dome and saw the things their local expert was talking about.

"You will use these items for your first challenge," he shared. "However, before I explain the rules to the first challenge and release you from your holding bubbles, let me share a bit more from my brilliant unseen mind."

The faces of the other sets of twins looked much less enthusiastic than they had when the Unseen One had mentioned the prize of diamonds. Blaine and Tracey, however, were excited because they saw scientific knowledge as a sort of treasure in its own right.

"There are six elements common to all life, and thus considered essential."

The local expert began with this round of science. "These elements are carbon, hydrogen, nitrogen, oxygen, phosphorus, and sulfur. You could use the acronym CHNOPS to remember these. Humans also have the following elements present in their bodies: calcium, potassium, sodium, chlorine, and magnesium. Additionally, humans have a need for other trace elements like fluorine for strong teeth, zinc for enzyme action, selenium for metabolism, and iron to help transport oxygen in the blood."

The voice paused here, almost like he was giving everyone the chance to catch up and let their minds both process and be impressed with everything he'd said.

"I thought about having a challenge for each and every one of these elements," the Unseen One continued, "or at least a challenge for the six essential elements. Then I could have called these the CHNOPS Games. But instead, I decided to call these the CON Games to have three extremely intense challenges, focusing on my three favorite elements: carbon, oxygen, and nitrogen. After all, carbon is considered the backbone of life. Oxygen is considered the fuel of life. And nitrogen gives motion to the circle of life," the formless voice explained.

The Sassafras twins nodded in understanding.

"Let me share with you all about the element that is the focus of the first challenge: carbon. Carbon is the fourth-most abundant element in the universe. It is referred to as the king of elements because it is found in millions of different compounds, many of which are important to life. The symbol for carbon is C. It has an atomic number of 6 and an atomic mass of 12.01. Carbon is a nonmetal found in charcoal, graphite, and, yes, diamonds like the ones you see hanging above you as your grand prize."

With that, the unseen emcee let out an eerie laugh that was becoming all too familiar.

"Carbon can bond in several different ways," the voice continued, "meaning that it can form many different shapes and sizes of molecules. Because of this versatility, it is a part of almost all living matter. It is the primary component of fats, proteins, carbohydrates, and nucleic acids like DNA. All in all, there are more than nine million different compounds of carbon that we know about. On Earth, the carbon cycle shows how this element moves through the environment. It is released by animals and humans in exhalation and in waste. This carbon is absorbed

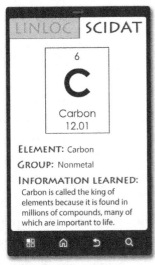

by plants, which are then eaten by animals and humans to begin the cycle again."

There was another pause, followed by another laugh, and then the invisible voice said, "Okay, enough of that for now. Let us get to the first excruciatingly intense challenge of the Carboxynitro Games!"

This time instead of gulping, the Sassafras twins attempted to gather their resolve for whatever was coming.

"The 'Carbon Sphere Obstacle Course' is our first game," the Unseen One exclaimed. "All of you will get cinched up in a harness. Each set of twins will be joined together by a connector strap. The connector strap is the longer strap you see in front of you, the one with carabiners at each of its ends. Clip a carabiner to your harness, and always stay connected to your twin by this strap. Next each of you will grab a quick draw. The quick draws are the shorter straps with carabiners at each of their ends. Attach a quick draw to your harness by one carabiner, and then the other carabiner of the quick draw will connect to a guideline. Each team's guidelines can be found in front of their holding bubbles. The guidelines consist of lengths of rope connected by intermittent wooden posts. These guidelines will lead each team in their set course for the challenge."

"Every team's course is approximately the same distance, faces approximately the same obstacles, and will lead from here to the temperate rainforest and back again. The goal of the challenge is to successfully get your carbon sphere through the obstacle course. But be forewarned—this is not a traditional obstacle course with completely man-made impediments. Rather, the lush rainforests will provide the majority of the obstacles."

The unseen host briefly paused his detailed instructions for an ominous cackle. Then he finished his explanation, "The only rules to this first challenge are as follows. You must stay connected to your twin by the connector strap at all times. At least one twin must be connected to the guideline by a quick draw at all times.

And at least one twin must have a hand on your team's carbon sphere at all times."

Another cackle and then a question came, "Does everyone understand the rules and the goal of the first challenge?"

Nods could be seen coming from all the teams in all the holding bubbles.

"Then, on your mark, get set, go!" the voice shouted.

In unison, all the holding bubbles lifted up, opening as if by unseen hydraulic motors and hinges. The teams of twins lunged forward into the challenge. The Sassafras twins immediately felt at a disadvantage, not only because the other sets of twins looked fit, athletic, and intimidating but also because they still had their backpacks, helmets, and zip-lining harnesses on. They knew they needed to follow the specific instructions, which meant they needed to quickly change out of their zip-lining gear and into the provided Carboxynitro Games gear. This was sure to put them behind from the start.

Blaine got his old gear off and his new gear on slightly faster than Tracey. Both were careful to follow the detailed directives. When they were successfully clipped to each other with the connector strap, they quickly jumped to get their hands on their carbon sphere. It was about the size of an exercise ball, but both Sassafrases could immediately tell it was much, much heavier. In a rush, they rolled the sphere toward the guideline in front of them. While rolling, they were careful to keep at least one hand on the orb.

Once they were at the guideline, Blaine and Tracey clipped onto the rope with their quick draws. Then they sprinted forward down the line and into the challenges. The rope the Sassafrases were clipped into led them straight into a pool of water. They splashed in without pause, relieved to find their carbon sphere could float. It looked like the other teams' guidelines had led them into the water as well. Most of the twin duos were well in front of

Blaine and Tracey. However, it became shockingly apparent that not all the twin duos had paid as much attention to the detailed instructions as Blaine and Tracey had.

Explosions of water went off, and the teams to both the left and the right of the Sassafrases were flushed. In the blink of an eye, two teams disappeared into gurgling whirlpools. The Unseen One's laugh filled the entire dome.

"Both of those teams broke the rules. One team didn't have a quick draw connected to their guideline," the shrouded voice said through a guffaw. "The other team had their hands completely off their sphere. Be sure to follow the rules. I am watching you."

Blaine and Tracey shuddered but managed to keep moving forward as the Unseen One's laugh continued to echo over these Carboxynitro Games.

Chapter 13: The Three Challenges
Never Mind, Oxygen

"Paul? Paul Sims?" Cecil questioned in surprise. "What in the wonderful wide world are you doing here? I thought maybe you were Sum—"

"Somebody else?" the museum curator and old junior high classmate of Cecil interrupted, breaking off Cecil's sentence as he stood and brushed himself off.

Sims had slid down into the basement from the front porch. With the basement now being clean and free from junk, including the old, musty pillows that used to serve as landing cushions for the slide, Paul had slid all the way across the basement floor and crashed into the romantic table that had been set up for Cecil and Summer's date.

"Sorry about that," Sims apologized. "Oh, and it looks like I broke a couple plates too. Sorry, old friend, but I mean, can you blame me? I didn't know there was a trapdoor on your front porch. And I sure didn't know I was going to slide so quickly down into your basement. But I guess I shouldn't be surprised by any of this. After all, it's Cecil Sassafras we're talking about here."

Paul smiled a smile that he was trying hard to make look kind. "To answer your question about what I'm doing here," the well-spoken curator responded, "I've simply come to reconnect, you know, maintain our friendship. It's been ages since we've seen each other. I got to see Summer Beach at my museum last week, and that got me thinking about how much I missed my other former junior high classmates."

Sims held onto his smile throughout his statement, and then he held out a hand toward Cecil for a handshake. The red-headed scientist looked at his old junior high classmate curiously at first, but he quickly took the outstretched hand and shook it, smiling

222 CHAPTER 13: THE THREE CHALLENGES

with an authentically kind smile. President Lincoln, however, remained in his spot at the top of the stairs with his arms folded, feeling mighty skeptical about this visitor of theirs.

Blaine and Tracey were both covered in dirt and sweat. To say this carbon sphere obstacle course was strenuous would be putting it way too lightly. The guideline that dictated their course had led them over both land and water. It had wound them around plants and logs, even up into trees. Yet the hardest part of the challenge had come when the guideline had led them under a fallen tree.

It didn't seem too difficult at first, but when the Sassafrases found their carbon sphere wouldn't fit under the log, they realized they were going to have to dig a hole in the dirt big enough to roll the sphere through. Of course, they knew they must keep at least one of their hands on the sphere and at least one of their quick draws connected to the guideline. Blaine and Tracey had accomplished this difficult task, but now they were exhausted. Even so they knew they had to keep going.

The other teams were navigating similar courses to theirs, with winding routes, plus climbing and digging elements. Surely, some of them must be tired as well. Blaine and Tracey had seen some of the other teams absent-mindedly break the rules. However, no one had been flushed since the beginning of the challenge. The Sassafrases wondered if the flushing could happen only in a place with water. Whatever the rhyme or reason, Blaine and Tracey were going to keep moving forward, and they were going to be careful to follow the rules while doing so. The two science learners could see that their guideline was leading them into the tunnel that connected the tropical rainforest dome to the temperate rainforest dome.

Even though they had started in last place, the Sassafrases had managed to claw their way into the middle of the pack. The twins raced toward the tunnel, swiftly and carefully rolling their sphere. They reached a post where their current section of guide rope ended and a new section was attached, starting on the other side of the post. Blaine was connected to the line ahead of his sister, as had been the case throughout the challenge. He unclipped his quick draw from the front side of the post and quickly clipped into the rope on the other side of the post. Once she knew Blaine was clipped in again, Tracey swiftly unclipped, went around the post, and clipped in behind her brother. Both were making sure to keep a hand on the carbon sphere whenever the other sibling was clipping and unclipping.

As they started into the tunnel, it became apparent the connecting passageway was going to become quite the bottleneck—every team's guideline ran through this way. It was almost like the lines were overlapping each other.

Without warning, Blaine was shoved to the ground by a team of twins to the right. He shuddered as his hand slipped from the carbon sphere when he hit the ground with a thud. The shudder was followed by a small amount of relief as he looked back and saw that Tracey was still standing upright with a hand on the sphere.

Both Sassafrases turned to their right. The identical twins who had shoved Blaine to the ground were tall, muscular, blonde-headed brothers. "You better stay down, little bloke," one laughed.

The other said, "This challenge is ours so stay out of the way."

"Oh, blimey, you daft, blonde-headed Davies twins. Don't be so gormless!" a voice said from the Sassafras' left.

Blaine and Tracey looked that direction to see a red-headed set of identical female twins who were also tall and athletic.

"Why did you knock this wee little guy down? Pick him up," one of the girls said.

Blaine smiled bashfully at the pretty, red-headed twins. Tracey mouthed a silent thank-you,'but the Sassafrases quickly realized the redheads weren't speaking out of compassion.

"You knocked him down directly in our path!" one of the girls continued. "Get him out of the way now! Or are you trying to block us because you're scared we're going to beat you?"

"Oh c'mon, Edwards twins," one of the blond-headed Davies boys huffed arrogantly. "You know very well there is no way you can beat us!" The two tall and fit brothers turned and raced through the tunnel.

The red-headed Edwards twins responded to that by pushing Blaine to the side and angrily rushing up the tunnel in pursuit. To make matters worse, during this brief argument between the blondes and redheads, several other duos sped past on their guidelines rolling their spheres. The Sassafras twins were squarely at the back of the pack again.

Tracey stepped forward to help her brother get up off the ground, but before she reached him, another pair of hands got there and pulled him up. "Don't mind the jiggery-pokery of those two teams," the boy who helped him up offered with a kind smile. "The last will be first, and the first will be last; am I right?"

The Sassafrases nodded, hoping that would prove true. They were standing side by side with a set of boy-girl twins who looked much like themselves, only a little older, a little taller, and a little more sculpted.

"We're the Clarke twins—Peter and Anne Clarke. It's a pleasure to meet you," Peter greeted as both he and his sister held out their hands, being careful to keep their other hands on their carbon spheres.

The American twins shook the hands of the British twins and responded with their part of the introduction. "We're the Sassafrases," Blaine shared. "Blaine and Tracey Sassafras. Nice to meet you guys. Thanks for helping me up."

"Of course, Peter smiled. "After all, we fraternal twins have to stick together, right?"

Cecil's niece and nephew nodded again.

"Okay, Sassafras twins," Anne said with a kind smile to match her brother's. "Best of luck to you then. Pip-pip and cheerio!"

"Pip-pip," the Sassafrases responded in unison, hoping it meant something nice and encouraging.

He held his hand over his nose and mouth, attempting to block the strong smell of bacon and mothballs as he awkwardly crawled into the creaky bed. Cecil had referred to this place as the guest room, but it sure didn't seem like a guest room. There were piles of scientific-looking junk stacked everywhere, including on the bed. Even more strange, though, were two mannequins leaning in the corner. They were dressed in togas and looked to be staring at him with their artificial eyes.

"What a nut," Paul Sims mumbled to himself as he dropped his hand, braving the smell. He shoved some things off the bed to make room for himself. He pulled a small portion of the covers up over his body.

The museum curator laid his head on the musty pillow, closed his eyes, and let out a long, uncomfortable sigh. The plan was still to flatter his way into a perceived friendship with Cecil and the other Sassafrases. But as he lay in this bizarre room, he wondered if it was worth it.

The temperate rainforest dome was a little smaller, cooler, and less dense than the tropical rainforest dome. It also had pines instead of vines and ferns instead of palms. But rolling their carbon sphere and staying attached to their guideline had proven to be as difficult in the second dome for the Sassafras twins as it had in the first dome.

Blaine and Tracey pressed forward in determination, and they found themselves back in the tropical rainforest dome and near the front of the pack. In fact, by this point, they had passed every team except for the considerate Clarkes, the unsympathetic Edwards, and the rough Davies. The Sassafras team was close enough to see the bubbles all the teams had started in. However, there was no telling what kind of swirls and loops this guideline might take them in before they got back to where they had started, which, according to the instructions, was also the end point of this challenge.

The Unseen One had been strangely quiet during this first competition. Other than an occasional eerie laugh, they hadn't heard much from him. The Sassafrases wondered if he'd been able to watch them during this entire competition. Were there unseen cameras everywhere? Had he been able to track whether or not every twin on every team had followed the rules? He had been so wordy when they had first landed that it felt strange for him to be so silent.

The two science learners followed their line around the trunk of a huge tree and then up and over one of its lower limbs, all while maintaining contact with their sphere. They raced over a tangle of roots to the next post. After they made it around that post, they saw that they had only one more post to go. The rope was leading them down a slanted bank toward their last post, which was located in a pool of water. It was the same exact pool of water they had started in. They were almost finished with this grueling challenge!

The twelve-year-olds stormed down the bank and plunged into the water. They pushed their floating carbon sphere vigorously across the surface of the pool, reaching the last post quickly. There were no more guidelines left to follow. There were no more obstacles in front of them.

The Sassafrases had finished their course in fourth place, after the first-place Davies, the second-place Edwards, and the third-place Clarkes. Blaine and Tracey breathed heavily after the extreme exertion. They each tried to catch their breath as they watched the other twin teams splashing into the pool and finishing behind them. The Sassafrases wondered how many teams were going to advance to the next challenge. How many teams were going to get flushed? Were they going to get flushed?

"Well done, everyone! Well done indeed," the Unseen One

finally spoke again. "Actually, 'everyone' is quite a stretch," he corrected himself. "Let me re-word that and say 'well done' to about half of the teams. The other half, I'm sorry. You broke the rules. Winning the cache of diamonds is no longer an option for you. And now, you will be flushed."

Blaine and Tracey tensed, fearing that they were about to be flushed. Simultaneously, five splashing explosions of water happened all around the Sassafrases as teams of twins disappeared into whirlpools of water. Then, as abruptly as the flushing had started, it was over. Now there were five teams of twins left standing in the pool.

"Oxygen is the most abundant element in the Earth's crust and the third-most abundant element in the universe," the Unseen One informed, not acknowledging the loss of competitors that had happened or allowing the remaining participants any time to process it. "The symbol for oxygen is O. Its atomic number is 8, and its atomic mass is 16.00. This nonmetal readily combines with other elements to release energy. It is a colorless and odorless gas, but it is the driving force behind many reactions that we call 'oxidation reactions.'"

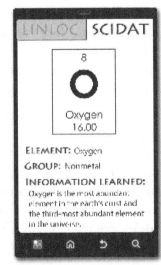

The Sassafrases stood completely still as they listened to the voice sharing about one of their topics for chemistry. They weren't sure if they cared about winning the diamonds, but they surely didn't want to be flushed. Right now, probably because of how shocked they were, they felt like any movement might result in the Unseen One flushing them. Also, they cared a lot more about the SCIDAT than the diamonds. However, whether they liked it or not, their strongest motivation to pay attention was fear.

"Oxidation reactions are what cause iron to rust and wood to petrify," the Unseen One continued. "It also causes different types of fuel to burn. It's the presence of oxygen that gives rocket fuel the power to burn with enough force to lift the rocket. Oxygen can be found up, down, and all around. It is high up in the atmosphere as ozone, helping protect us from harmful ultraviolet rays. At the same time, it is necessary to life down here. Our cells use it as fuel for the chemical reactions in our bodies. Indeed, oxygen cycles around our planet because all animals need oxygen to survive. They breathe it in, then release it as carbon dioxide, which plants need to survive. The plants use the carbon dioxide as fuel and then release oxygen, which in turn, animals use again."

The Unseen One paused long enough to release an eerie laugh. Then he said, "Aaah, oxygen. The fuel of life, but I'm not telling you this to showcase my brilliant unseen mind. I'm telling you this because oxygen is of utmost importance to our next simple challenge. So go ahead and take your hands off your carbon spheres and unclip from your guidelines."

The Sassafrases cast worried glances at each other as they followed their strange host's instructions. What kind of crazy shenanigans were coming next?

Iced-over Nitrogen

"All teams must now dip their heads under the water," the voice instructed. "Hold your breath as long as you can. The team who comes up for oxygen first will be flushed, taking them out of the running for the cache of diamonds. This is challenge number two, the Hold Your Breath as Long as You Can challenge. Does everyone understand?"

The Davies and Edwards nodded confidently. The Clarkes looked determined, confirming that sentiment with resolute nods. The Sassafrases hadn't yet met the other set of twins. They were unidentical boy twins, currently looking as nervous as Blaine and

Tracey felt. However, the four remaining contestants also managed to nod.

"Very well," the Unseen One cackled from his invisible spot. "On your mark, get set, go!"

The Sassafrases didn't want to go under the water, but they also didn't want to get flushed—so down they went, submerging their bodies and heads completely into the manmade pond along with the five other sets of twins. The water was a comfortable temperature, and it seemed clean, but it was not clear. Neither Blaine nor Tracey could see their hands in front of their faces, much less each other. Not being able to see anything was going to make it harder to hold their breaths for any substantial amount of time. Yet, they did hold their breaths because that was the name of the game.

"Thirty seconds," Blaine counted, actually mouthing the words underwater and using his fingers to count.

"Forty-five seconds," Tracey counted mentally. "I think I can keep going for a little bit, but I don't like this at all."

"One minute," Blaine counted. "Now the pressure is on. I know, lungs. I can feel you, and I know you need oxygen, but you've got to keep holding."

"One minute and fifteen seconds," Tracey counted. "Now I really don't like this. All I want to do is take a big gulp of oxygen. But I really don't want to get flushed!"

"Okay, we're at a minute and a half," Blaine was starting to feel a little panicky. "I wonder how Tracey is doing. I wonder how all the other teams are doing."

"Two minutes. Or is it...a minute forty-five," Tracey tried to count, but she was beginning to lose clarity of thought as her lungs screamed for oxygen. "This reminds me of Japan, when we had to swim through the underwater intake canal to enter the nuclear powerplant. I wonder how long we held our breaths that time . . .

how's Blaine doing? Is he still under the water?"

"Ahhhhhh!" Blaine gurgled. "I lost count! I don't know how long I've been down here. I've got to breathe! I've got to get some oxygen! But if I go up, and we're the first team out, we'll get flushed, and getting flushed would be worse than this. But I gotta breathe!"

"I can't do it anymore," Tracey's mind screamed. "I can't hold my breath one more second. I need oxygen!"

"Aaahhh!" Blaine gurgled again and shot up out of the water.

"Uuhhh!" Tracey screamed as her head broke out of murky water and into oxygen-filled air.

The Sassafrases had come up for air at the exact same time. Both quickly wiped the water from their faces and opened their eyes. They saw each other first and then looked around to see if any of the other teams had come up yet.

"Wow, Sassafrases!" Peter Clarke called out as he saw them. "You two were underwater the longest by far! Great job!"

Blaine and Tracey could see that Peter was right. Everyone else had already come up for oxygen. Blaine and Tracey had lasted the longest. Peter and Anne Clarke looked both impressed with the Sassafrases and also content with their own performance, so they must not have come up first.

The Davies and the Edwards twins looked mad. The other set of twin boys looked scared, so the Sassafrasses couldn't tell which duo had come up for air first. "Who is about to get flushed?" they silently wondered in alarm. An immediate answer to that question came as a small explosion of water engulfed the trepid unnamed twin boys. Down they went in a whirlpool to who knows where.

"And then there were four teams left," the Unseen One laughed, seemingly without one ounce of compassion for the team that had fallen. Then, like at the conclusion of the first challenge, he jumped right into the scientific data, not giving the remaining competitors time to process the loss of another team.

"Nitrogen makes up 78% of the Earth's atmosphere," he started. "The symbol for nitrogen is N. The atomic number is 7, and the atomic mass is 14.01. It was Daniel Rutherford who discovered this element in 1771, and he called it 'noxious air.'"

"You're noxious air," Blaine mumbled and immediately hoped the creepy invisible host hadn't heard him.

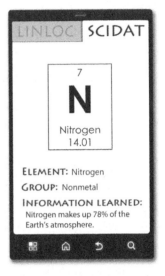

"And the human body is made up of 3% of this element. Like oxygen is a part of the cycle of life, nitrogen is also cyclical," the Unseen One continued like he hadn't heard the Sassafras boy. "Nitrogen from the air and soil is absorbed by bacteria and changed into a usable format for plants. These plants are then eaten by animals and humans. When the animals and humans die, the nitrogen compounds are returned to the soil and air again. This is called the nitrogen cycle. Nitrogen compounds, along with phosphorus compounds, are used in fertilizers because without these elements, plants would wither and die."

While Blaine was still breathing a sigh of relief that his comment hadn't been heard, Tracey was happily breathing in the oxygen she had been deprived of while underwater. The Sassafras girl was also thinking about all the cool science displayed in these Twin Biodomes and about how cool of a place this would be to visit if it was a field trip instead of a brutal competition or whatever this was.

"Nitrogen is essential to life on Earth, but liquid nitrogen is very cold," the invisible emcee continued. "It will freeze just about anything it comes in contact with."

"Even more interesting than that is how powerful nitrogen is," the Unseen One said with his familiar laugh. "Due to the strong bond between two nitrogen atoms, it is a fairly unreactive gas. However, when that bond between nitrogen atoms is broken, it releases a tremendous amount of energy, so much so that nitrogen is often used in explosives."

"Uh oh," the Sassafrases gulped. "Where is all this going?"

"And that leads me to the third and final challenge of these Carboxynitro Games," the snickering man declared. "I call this the Nitrogen Pip-Pip challenge. Don't worry. I'm not going to use nitrogen to blow anything up. I am, however, going to be pouring large amounts of liquid nitrogen down into the pool you are currently standing in. When the freezing-cold liquid nitrogen hits the warm water of the pool, it will cause a spectacular burst of steam. Liquid nitrogen has an extremely low boiling point of -196° Celsius (or -320° Fahrenheit). When it hits warm water it instantly boils, creating a fog of nitrogen vapor. The pool you are in is approximately 26.5° C (or 80° F), but it will quickly cool to freezing. Meanwhile, the steam burst you see will be a thick cloud of nitrogen. And as that cloud hovers over the pool, the nitrogen will push some of the oxygen away. So, it will feel like you're breathing regular air, but in actuality, you will not be getting all of the oxygen you need."

All four sets of twins began looking at each other with a new level of angst. This wasn't sounding good.

"Your goal in this challenge," the Unseen One continued, "is to see how many times you can push your carbon spheres in complete circles around your starting posts before you give up or faint because of lack of oxygen. The team of twins that can stay conscious the longest and roll their spheres around the posts the most times will win the cache of diamonds and be crowned the grand champions of the Carboxynitro Games! The other three teams will come just that close, but they will be flushed like the rest!"

The level of angst in the Sassafrases was now excruciating.

The Clarkes looked nervous, too.

The Davies and the Edwards were trying to look confident, but it was an obvious façade, masking real fear.

"As you have probably summated," the invisible man continued. "This third and final challenge is called the Nitrogen Pip-Pip challenge because we will be saying goodbye to every team but one. However, my favorite thing about this challenge is that it brings together all three elements of these Carboxynitro Games: the spheres representing carbon, the soon to be diminishing oxygen in the air, and the cold liquid nitrogen that's about to be poured down on top of you!"

The angst was turning to panic.

"Very well then," the invisible voice cackled. "You may begin the challenge the moment the liquid nitrogen hits the pond. On your mark, get set . . ."

Chapter 14: Iron Nails in the Chilean Desert

Fortuneless Halogens

The strong, blonde-headed Davies twin brothers flexed their muscles and pretended they were ready. The athletic, red-headed Edwards twin sisters did some shadow-boxing in place to act like they were ready to fight for the win. The benevolent Clarke twin brother and sister looked at each other and spoke some last encouraging words before the challenge's start.

The Sassafras twins were looking up, wondering where the liquid nitrogen was going to be poured from, wondering if their local expert was really up there at the apex of the dome in that sky bubble, and wondering if someone was really going to win all the sparkling diamonds hanging in the translucent sphere. They wondered if they were about to lose consciousness in a cloud of nitrogen before getting flushed.

The Sassafras Science Adventures

Chapter 14: Iron Nails in the Chilean Desert

"Get set," was the last thing the eight remaining contestants in the Carboxynitro Games had heard, and they were expecting to hear a loud boisterous "Go," but instead they heard loud, fast-paced footsteps banging on metal.

All eyes made their way to one of the high catwalks, where they could now see a man walking in an angry huff toward the sky bubble. He reached the hanging half-sphere and yanked open a craftily hidden built-in door. The flustered man quickly entered the sky bubble, and as soon as he did, the four sets of twins heard two voices broadcasting loudly throughout the large dome.

"Blimey, Aaron, you've gone and done it again!"

"Tom! When did you get here? Don't you try and stop me, Tom! I'm about to pour the liquid nitrogen down on top of them!"

"Oh, no you don't, Aaron. You gormless prat, I'm knackered to the collar with all of your jiggery pokery!"

"It's not jiggery pokery, Tom! It's my calling. It's my job! I must put on these Carboxynitro Games. I simply must pour liquid nitrogen onto the contestants."

"No, you mustn't! In fact, it is not your job. You don't work here anymore, remember? And they're not contestants, Aaron. They're adolescents competing here under false pretenses. They don't know these games are made up, and they don't know these diamonds are fake!"

"The games must go on, Tom."

"No, they mustn't, Aaron."

"Yes, they must, Tom."

"No, Aaron."

"Yes, Tom."

"No."

"Yes."

The back-and-forth was followed by the sounds of a muffled scuffle. Evidently, Tom, the flustered, cat-walking newcomer, and Aaron, the emcee known only to them before as the Unseen One, were wrestling for control of the sky bubble. It wasn't a long scuffle. Even as the four sets of twins listened in and looked up in shock and surprise, the glaze and haziness of the sky bubble pixelated away from gray and became clear glass much like the holding bubbles had done earlier. All could see that Tom had subdued Aaron—the Unseen One—who was now visible.

He had long, scraggly hair and an unshaven face. He looked defeated yet still defiant. Tom, who was taller, clean shaven, and in charge now spoke into the microphone to address the bewildered group of twins.

"To the remaining eight of you, I want to apologize on behalf of the Twin Biodomes. Although Aaron is no longer an actual employee of the Twin Biodomes, he did work here in the past. He was fired and is considered by us to be a con man. The Carboxynitro Games, or the CON games, were totally made up by him and are not a real or actual competition. Aaron drew you here as competitors to win a prize on the only day of the week the domes are closed to the public. The games do not have our stamp of approval, and these diamonds you see hanging in the sphere are fake. They're plastic."

The Davies and Edwards twins looked frustrated upon hearing this news. The Clarke twins looked neutral. But Blaine and Tracey were feeling relieved. However, the Sassafrases were worried about all the other sets of twins who had been "flushed." Did Tom know anything about that?

"The Twin Biodomes were designed to introduce people to the wonders of science and nature in a safe, beautiful, and sustainable environment," the level-headed man continued, "not to scare, hurt, harm, or deceive anyone."

"Oh, c'mon Tom, I just—" the Seen One tried to cut in.

"No, Aaron. No more words from you," Tom stated authoritatively.

He continued addressing the twins. "So, if any of you have been hurt by this charade, on behalf of the domes, I am sorry and I sincerely apologize."

"Excuse me, sir. What about all those who were flushed?" Anne Clarke asked, wondering the same thing Blaine and Tracey were. "What happened to them? Are they okay?"

Tom looked at the remaining eight twins in empathy. "I am so sorry that Aaron made flushing seem like a scary and bad thing. In all actuality, flushing is one of our most beloved features here at the Twin Biodomes."

The eight adolescents were confused.

"The flushing whirlpools are actually the exciting entrances to hidden waterslides. These slides lead downstairs to the locker rooms, the gift shop, and the exit."

Moments later, the Sassafras twins found themselves swishing, sliding, and careening wildly through a cylindrical tube. It was not a tube filled with rushing water, rather it was a tube filled with rushing light! Blaine and Tracey were back on the invisible zip lines, swishing, sliding, and careening from one science learning adventure to the next. They had indeed gotten the chance to slide through the waterslides at the Twin Biodomes, and although being "flushed" at first seemed scary, it had turned out to be fun, not as fun as sliding through light, of course, but fun nonetheless.

For a while, England, had felt like a creepy and weird place, but in the end, everything had been resolved. Their questions had been answered, four scientific topics had been learned, and Blaine and Tracey had actually had some fun. Now, they were zipping to the South American coastal country of Chile, longitude 69° 28' 45.9" W, latitude 24° 25' 31.5"S. The LINLOC app had told them

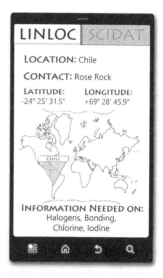

they would be studying the topics of halogens, bonding, chlorine, and iodine with the help of a local expert by the name of Rose Rock.

All at once, the swishing and sliding of the zip-line journey came to an abrupt end with the customary jerk. Blaine's and Tracey's bodies slumped, devoid of strength or sight.

"Where exactly have we landed this time?" they both wondered as they waited for their eyesight and physical strength to return. However, it was their hearing that returned before any of their other senses as they heard a strong Spanish-accented female voice talking about halogens.

"The halogens include all the elements from group 17 on the periodic table," the voice said. "These are fluorine, chlorine, bromine, iodine, astatine, and tennessine."

"That must be Rose Rock, our local expert here in Chile," thought Tracey as color and form began to come to her eyes. She quickly lost her excitement because Tracey could see she was face-to-face with some kind of hairy, strange-looking animal.

"The halogen elements are all nonmetals, and they all react strongly," the voice giving scientific information continued, but Tracey was finding it hard to concentrate because of this animal staring at her.

Suddenly the beast opened its mouth and let out a terrible screeching, trilling scream. Tracey wanted to react with a scream of her own, but shock kept her silent.

Blaine, in contrast, did scream. The twelve-year-old boy's scream was so high pitched and terrified that it sounded much like the noise that had come out of the animal.

"The name 'halogen' literally means 'salt-giver,'" the female voice continued, seemingly unaffected by the screeches that had rung out. "However, this name is a little misleading, considering the fact that halogens easily 'steal' electrons from metals, especially the alkali metals, bonding together to form salts."

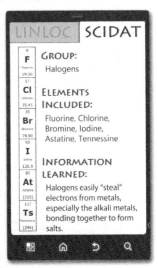

Another scream rang out. Tracey couldn't tell if it had come from the animal or her brother. The beast inched closer to the twins, and it looked mad. Tracey jerked to her left, but it was then that she realized they were in a cage. She and Blaine were stuck in a smallish wood crate with this animal.

"The halogens often appear as brightly colored gasses, liquids, or solids when all by themselves," the science-giving voice continued, evidently completely unaware of the twins' presence or predicament. "For example, fluorine is a yellow gas. Chlorine is a green gas. Bromine is a purplish liquid, and iodine is a dark purple solid."

Tracey looked around in every direction, trying to see where the voice was coming from. At first, all the Sassafras girl saw was a wide, barren, steaming desert. Then she saw a few more cages or crates with animals in them. She saw a small village in the not-too-far distance. Finally, she saw where the voice was coming from.

"There she is!" She had spotted her, a strong and tall Chilean woman, standing at a distance to their right, talking to a group of ragamuffin children who were seated next to a dilapidated adobe structure of some kind.

"*Una pregunta*, Rose Rock," one of the boys spoke. "Can you give us some examples of how these halogens are used?"

"*Por supuesto*! Of course I can, *niño*," Rose Rock responded. "Fluorine, for instance, was used during World War II in different weapons, so that's not good, but an ion of this halogen called fluoride is used to strengthen teeth. Many countries add fluoride to their water supplies. They certainly do in the big cities on the coast here in Chile."

Upon hearing this news, many of the kids shook their heads in disbelief. After the brief looking around she had done, Tracey wondered if there was running water in this new location, much less fluoride-infused water.

"The Phoenicians were the first to use a purple dye from sea snails," Rose Rock gave another example. "Turns out, this dye gets its color from bromine. This halogen is also used in making furniture flame resistant."

Again, the children shook their heads in disbelief. Accompanied with chuckles like these were far-fetched facts from far-off lands.

There were no chuckles coming from the Sassafras twins, however, as the beast was not only face-to-face with the twelve-year-olds but nose to nose.

"Tracey," Blaine managed a whisper. "I think maybe this thing is—"

But before the boy could finish his sentence, the animal let out another horrible scream. The Sassafrases could feel the heat from the animal's mouth and smell the regurgitated cud on its breath. Blaine opened his mouth to scream in terror again, and as he did, the animal spit at him. Something about this action seemed to relax the beast because it backed up, giving the humans some space.

Tracey, who had not been in the line of fire, looked over toward her brother and finished his rudely interrupted sentence. "Llama," she said with certainty, which was Blaine's exact conclusion as to what kind of animal this was and what he had intended to say.

He couldn't respond to his sister, however, because he was too busy gagging and extracting what had gone into his mouth.

"Two more halogens that I'll mention are astatine and tennessine," Rose Rock continued, seemingly unaware of the Sassafrases. "Astatine is one of the rarest elements on Earth because it is so radioactive and unstable. It wasn't isolated until 1940. Tennessine is one of the heaviest elements on Earth—the second heaviest to be exact. It is also known as element number 117. It is not naturally occurring, having been created only briefly in a lab."

As the local expert finished what she was saying about halogens, a small group of people walked around the corner of the adobe structure and joined the eagerly listening children. This new group of people were older, some much older. Some had smiles, and some had frowns. Some were empty-handed, and some were carrying well-used handmade tools like shovels and hammers. All of them looked to be worn, weathered, and hard-working villagers.

"Okay, *niños* and *niñas*," Rose Rock said. "*Los aldeanos* have arrived. It is now time for us to discuss . . . the race."

Chemical Bonding

The children nodded like they understood, but an elderly woman who'd just arrived interjected with a smile. "No, no, Chiquito Jara, Rose Rock, please finish your lesson, *por favor*."

The tall, strong woman with beautiful brown skin returned the smile and continued teaching. "Okay, let me say a little about bonding then. In chemistry, atoms form molecules by bonding together with other atoms."

This time as Rose Rock spoke, Tracey noticed she was using not only her voice but also her hands. Tracey nudged Blaine and pointed to see if he also thought this was a little curious. Blaine noticed nothing because his sole focus was to not have any more llama spit in his mouth. The boy continued vigorously working at this task with gags, clawing, and purposeful spitting of his own.

"All atoms want to be stable," the local expert continued, "which means they want a full house of electrons. Some atoms, like helium, for instance, are like this naturally. However, most are not, and this is why atoms bond with each other—to give each other a full house of electrons. Atoms can do this by donating and receiving electrons or by sharing them."

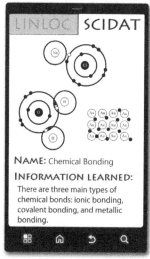

Another thing Tracey noticed as she watched the woman teach was that although Rose Rock was dressed much like the villagers and the children in tattered clothing, there was something different about her appearance. She seemed smoother, cleaner, and less weathered than the others. She had better posture and wasn't hunched over like some of the men and women were.

"Hmmm," Tracey mused.

"Hack, yuck, ohhh!" Blaine screeched next to her.

"The three main types of bonds are: ionic bonding, covalent bonding, and metallic bonding. Ionic bonding is one atom, usually a metal, donating an electron to another atom that receives it," Rose Rock went on with her lesson. "This results in a positively charged ion—the one that gave the electron away—and a negatively charged ion—the one that took the electron. The two ions then attach to each other and stay together because of the charge that was created. This is the type of bond that halogens tend to make."

As Tracey continued to observe with deep interest, she noticed some of the villagers were also making a few motions with their hands. "Is she teaching in two languages at once?" Tracey mused. "Is she using sign language?"

"In covalent bonding, two or more atoms get together to share electrons so that they can all have a full house together," the brilliant woman taught. "They can share one pair of electrons to form a single bond or two pairs of electrons to form a double bond, and so on. The atoms that make these types of bonds are typically nonmetals. And finally, in metallic bonding, metal atoms line up together, and then their electrons float around in between them. These mobile electrons are what makes metals good conductors of electricity and heat."

Tracey was making an extra effort to remember everything the local expert was saying about these two topics. She knew that because of the llama-spitting incident her brother probably wasn't going to be much help later when they needed to enter all the SCIDAT information into their phones.

"All in all," Rose Rock said in closing. "The way a molecule bonds together determines the properties of that molecule."

The children exhaled as though they were content and happy with what they had learned. Then most of them stood and skipped or ran away from the area, leaving a few to linger in the area with the adults who'd showed up mid-lesson. One man among the Chilean villagers, the tallest and strongest looking of them all, stepped forward and put his right hand to his mouth with four fingers extended, moving his hand back and forth several times. He then put both fists in front of him, palm to palm with thumbs extended, and then moved each thumb forward and backward in an alternating pattern.

Rose Rock's face became stern, and she responded, "Yes," with a hand motion of her own. It looked like she was reaching up to knock on a door.

"Let's talk about the race." The villagers took seats against the old adobe building where the children had been, all except the strong man, who remained standing, the sternness of his face matching Rose Rock's.

The tall, intelligent woman took a deep breath and began again, using her hands to communicate. She spoke out loud at the same time. "We have to race," Rose Rock started.

This statement was immediately met with grumbles from most in the small crowd.

"I know, I know," she responded by reaching up with a flat hand and touching the side of her forehead with the tips of her fingers. "I know that by agreeing to race, not only do we expose our racers to immense dangers, but we are also seemingly succumbing to Ring Finger's hubris. But at this point, to race is our only option."

Now the grumbles became audible words of fearful disagreement. The standing man remained silent, keeping his hands still. However, his sternness seemed to deepen as Rose Rock continued to communicate with the people.

Tracey nudged Blaine. "What do you think all this is about? And have you watched our local expert talk? Do you think she's using sign language?"

Blaine, still keeping an eye on the spitting llama, ventured his first glance over toward Rose Rock. "I think she's smart. I think she's an ace at chemistry. And yes, she is definitely using sign language."

"What about the race? What's that all about? And who do you think Ring Finger is?"

"I don't know, Trace," Blaine answered and turned his attention back to the llama. "What I'm more interested in is getting out of this cage and getting away from this crazy animal."

Tracey agreed that being free from the cage was important. Still, she was more interested in the conversation that was continuing off to their right next to the adobe building.

"I've talked to the chiefs of nearby villages," Rose Rock continued with both her hands and her voice. "I've pleaded with them not to race, but none of them would listen. They are all preparing buggies. They are determined to race. I argued with them that if we band together, put aside our differences, and cooperate, we could overcome Ring Finger and his Iron Nails. We could unseat him from his made-up throne and made-up position as the War Lord King of the Atacama. I've told them this, but none would listen."

The people of the village were grumbling, but even from their cage, the twins could see it wasn't because the villagers disliked Rose Rock. It was because they disliked whoever this Ring Finger character was.

"You are a resilient people," the Chilean woman encouraged the people in front of her with a twinkle of pride in her eyes. "For generations, you have successfully made a living here in one of the harshest environments on the planet. You have subdued the Atacama by herding, farming, mining, and raising families."

She paused after saying the word "families" with her thumbs and index fingers touching on both hands creating circles, with the other three fingers on each hand extended, then bringing her hands around toward the front until her pinkies touched.

"I know some of you may not see me as a part of this village anymore, nor do you see me as part of this family. I know that when I was a little girl, many of you viewed me as the spoiled daughter of the chief. And when Papa Jara sent me off to college in Antofagosta, some of you thought I would never come back. However, it was always my aim to acquire worthwhile tools and knowledge, then to bring that back to my home, my village, my people, and use what I'd learned to help. It's true: I am the chief's daughter; God rest his soul. It's true: I haven't had to do the backbreaking work that all of you have had to do. It's true: I am a chemist and not a herder, farmer, or miner. But I love this desert, and I love this village. I love teaching the children, and I'm appreciative of those of you who have taken the time to listen to me rave about my love of chemistry and about all the wonderful minerals that can be found in our desert."

"Because of deposition, right?" exclaimed the same elderly man who'd encouraged Rose Rock to continue her lesson with the kids' moments earlier.

The college-educated woman nodded. "The desert contains many different minerals thanks to deposition. Minerals can be deposited in the desert through evaporation. Rain falls, and then as it evaporates in the sun and the heat, the minerals are left behind. These minerals can be found close to the surface of the desert sand. Minerals can also be left behind when groundwater leaches into areas near the water table. When it recedes, it can leave behind minerals. These minerals have to be dug out (or mined) from the desert. So, as you can see, here in the Atacama, we live in the middle of a mineral-rich treasure trove, not some sun-scorched wasteland."

"And now," she continued, "Ring Finger has come in here by force with his marauding group of henchmen and has kidnapped our herds, drained our wells, laid claim to our mineral deposits, and has threatened to strip us of every bit of our resources."

There was another pause. "And now he says we must compete in a race, a dune buggy race. It's a race against the other villages and one that he says is to become an annual race. It will be a race from a predetermined starting line and go to the Hand of the Desert, where he says the winning buggy will win a year's worth of resources for its village, as though he is benevolent. The villages that don't win will receive nothing, and so they are desperate. When presented with the chance to join together in an attempt to collectively take down Ring Finger, they say no. Why? Because they are scared. They choose fear instead of cooperating to take back what is rightfully theirs."

Now her face didn't just show deepening sternness, but it was rising resolve that Tracey noticed in Rose Rock's demeanor as she spoke. "But I say instead of choosing to fear Ring Finger and his Iron Nails, we choose instead to defy this unsanctioned king. And if the other villages won't join us, then we'll do it alone!"

The strong man who had remained quiet for a long time, spoke again, emphatically using his hands to communicate. The Sassafrases couldn't tell if he was agreeing with Rose Rock or disagreeing with her. They were certain, though, that the man was deaf. He finished with a slap of his hands together then balled them into fists.

"Yes, I know, Vicente," the valiant woman responded with emotion to the big man. "I know the other villages might try to destroy us during this race. I know they will more than likely create dune buggies that are weaponized both offensively and defensively. I know the Iron Nails will set up traps and pitfalls all along the race route. I know that Ring Finger is a cheat and a scoundrel. I know it's dangerous, but we must race. We must come together as a village and build ourselves a dune buggy that can race and win. As we race, we must not harm any of the other racers even if they try to harm us. And we mustn't race, but we must win! For if we survive the race and win, we can not only receive our needed resources, but we can take down Ring Finger and his henchmen. We can get back all the resources. Then we will not only get back what's ours, but we will also return to all the other racers and their villages what's been stolen from them!"

No more grumbles were coming from the small crowd of Chilean villagers. They sat silent as if deeply considering what Rose Rock had proposed. Vicente, too, was obviously weighing in his mind all that the woman had said.

"I know you may not see me as one of you, much less as your chieftess," Rose Rock said in a softer voice. "But I am. I am yours, and you are mine. Please stand and fight with me. Let us fight to take back all the enemy has stolen. Let us win this race."

Chapter 15: The Desert Dune Buggy Race

Chlorine Buggies

The invisible zip lines were designed to drop the Sassafrases off at every location as close to their local expert as possible without their landing being detected. Here in Chile, not only had their landing not been detected, but their presence in this place had still not been detected. Blaine and Tracey were stuck in the small crate with the llama all night. There had been no more spitting incidents with the animal, and unlike the twins, it had calmed enough to fall quickly asleep. Both Blaine and Tracey had weighed the decision of whether to call for help but had decided not to because most of the villagers had moved out of the immediate area. The twins weren't sure what was worse: being stuck in the crate or being this close to an animal that would potentially spit all over them when it woke up. Yes, it was true that the villagers might not hear them if they cried out, but the villagers had surely heard the request of their young chieftess.

Chapter 15: The Desert Dune Buggy Race

Rose Rock had asked the villagers to join her in the desert resource race. At first, they seemed skeptical, but in the end they had collectively responded with shouts of solidarity and determination. She was their leader, and they would join her in the race. They believed with her that they could take down this terrible Ring Finger fellow. They believed with her that they could win the race and win back the stolen resources, not only for themselves, but for all the victimized desert villages.

Morning sunlight crept over distant mountains, bringing light to a desert that had been dark but not sleeping. Blaine and Tracey had heard sounds coming from the village all night. Strange clinks and clanks had been ringing out, seemingly nonstop. From their vantage point in the crate, it had been too far away and too dark for them to see exactly what was going on.

As the sun ushered in a new day's light, everything was becoming visible, and the twelve-year-olds were amazed at what they saw. Driving from the village toward the adobe structure, where the chemistry lessons had happened yesterday, was the most interesting-looking vehicle the twins had ever seen—at least since Oklahoma City, where they had ridden Lucille, the storm-chasing vehicle. This was no storm-chasing vehicle, however. This was a dune buggy that was being piloted by Rose Rock and copiloted by Vicente.

The people of the village had worked through the night to build the dune buggy. Its engine was loud and guttural, and the vehicle looked to be made completely with spare parts and knickknacks the people had found lying around the village and the desert. All four of its wheels were different sizes. Its body was comprised of metal scraps and lengths of rebar that were welded together. Its two seats were sections of a broken couch. Its steering wheel was an old, rusty basketball goal rim. Its front grill and the cage around the seats were made from the same wooden crating that the Sassafrases found themselves in.

Blaine and Tracey didn't know what the other dune buggies were going to look like, but they couldn't imagine a more scrappy-looking vehicle than the one they were looking at now. They weren't sure this thing could withstand speeding through the desert, much less any attacks from other buggies or traps set by Ring Finger. The buggy didn't seem to have weaponry built into the design unless the huge, arm-like contraption sticking out from the back was for that purpose.

"Hey, Trace, what do you think that big, long thing sticking out of the back is?" Blaine asked, engaging in something other than his fear and disdain for the llama. "Do you think it's a catapult? It looks kind of like a catapult to me."

Tracey responded with a slight nod as she watched one of the young villagers run up with a white, gallon-sized plastic container and offer it to Rose Rock as the chieftess was opening up the cage door and alighting from the vehicle. "Rose, Rose," the teenage boy said excitedly. "I found some chlorine! We can use this in the engine to keep things clean and working correctly. *Sí o no?*"

Rose Rock took the container from the boy with a kind but wry smile. "Good idea, *chico*," she responded, "but no. We shouldn't add any chlorine to the engine. Chlorinated hydrocarbons were used in the past by the oil industry in engine-oil additives. But this practice stopped when it was discovered how corrosive chlorine compounds can be to an engine."

Rose Rock looked at the boy and then at the dune buggy with its roaring engine. Then she looked back at the boy and laughed. "I know it probably sounds like the engine could use some help, but that's actually the part of this buggy I'm most confident about."

The boy took the container of chlorine from the woman and responded with a chuckle of his own.

"The symbol for chlorine is Cl. The atomic number is 17. And the atomic mass is 35.45. It is mainly found in salt compounds such as sodium chloride," the local expert talked about the chemistry topic at hand. "It is a greenish gas that is very toxic. In fact, it has even been used in chemical weapons dating back to World War I. It is reactive, so it's not often found on its own in nature. That said, poison dart frogs secrete a chlorine-containing compound as a part of their defense."

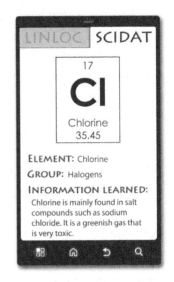

This fact about chlorine took Blaine's mind all the way back to the first time they'd landed in South America. He and Tracey had learned about poison dart frogs while studying zoology in Ecuador. This made Blaine wonder if there was toxicity in llama spit. "Surely not, right?" Blaine thought to himself as he looked at the animal that was moving and awake again, probably because of the noise happening all around them.

"That's not to say there aren't some positive things about chlorine," Rose Rock continued. "Chlorine is another trace mineral that we need in our bodies. It helps with digestion, muscle movement, and immunity. In small amounts, chlorine compounds help make water safe to drink because it is deadly to bacteria and viruses. Chlorine is also used to make PVC, which is a lightweight and strong plastic used for pipes, windows, and much more."

The boy from the village nodded as the chieftess spoke. He looked like he was learning as much as the Sassafrases were.

"And while we're talking about chlorine, let me add a bit about electrolysis," Rose Rock said. "Electrolysis is the method of separating compounds by passing an electrical current through a solution with a compound. Chlorine gas is produced by the electrolysis of a sodium chloride brine solution."

"Tracey. Tracey." Blaine immediately followed the end of

their local expert's giving of SCIDAT with an alarmed and irrational question for his sister: "You don't think llama spit is toxic; do you? Like chlorine gas or the poison from a dart frog?"

Tracey looked at her brother to study whether he was serious or not. He was. "Of course not, Blaine," she answered flatly.

Now the whole village gathered around Rose Rock, their Chilean chieftess, and Vicente, the big, strong, deaf man. They celebrated and encouraged the duo by dancing in a circle around them with cheers in Spanish and sign language. They were shouting something like, "*lanzador de llama*," and were making signs with their hands that looked like llamas with their pointer and pinky fingers extended and their middle and ring fingers bent touching their thumbs and with another movement added at the end that made it look like the llamas were floating into the sky. "They sure are excited and hopeful," the twins thought as the villagers moved from dancing to ushering the two to the buggy they had collectively built. Evidently, Rose Rock and Vicente were going to be the drivers. They would be the two to represent this village in Ring Finger's race.

Rose Rock climbed back into the driver's seat, and Vicente sat next to her. These two were the hope of the village. Even Blaine and Tracey felt their hearts daring to hope from their crate. Surely these were the ones who could win this despicable race and get back the resources for the whole desert.

But then something happened that made the twins' lose hope. A group of villagers ran over, grabbed the crate they were in with the llama, hoisted it over their heads, and carried it to the buggy. The villagers placed it on the back of the vehicle on top of the contraption that looked like a catapult.

The twins looked at each other with wide eyes. What was happening? Were they being loaded up for the race? They freely called out for help, but the llama was also wide-eyed and screeching, so their voices were drowned out—none of the villagers noticed them. Every villager's full attention was focused on the front of the buggy where their chieftess was. They were a group of people in desperate need of a win. They were disheveled, marginalized, stolen from, and tired. Their hope was resting squarely on the shoulders of the woman in the dune buggy.

"Onward to the starting line," Rose Rock shouted valiantly and loud enough to be heard over the roar of the engine and the cheers of the villagers. She sat in the driver's seat next to Vicente and immediately used her foot to hammer down the accelerator. Off the buggy jolted into the desert toward the starting line of the resource race.

"Okay, Cecil," Paul smiled with outward peace but with inner impatience, "we've fixed the table and chair I slid into and broke. We've replaced the shattered china. Everything in your basement looks perfect for this special dinner of yours, but you still haven't decided what the menu should be. This is our 20th trip to the supermarket over the last couple of days. Have you made up your mind? Is there anything here at the Left-Handed Turtle that will suffice?"

"Hmmm, hmmm, hummidy hmmm," Cecil mused as he paced the pasta aisle with arms folded and eyebrows bobbing. "It needs to be perfectly perfect because she's perfectly perfect. I know she's not that picky when it comes to vittles, but it's still got to be perfect."

Now Paul Sims's eyebrows bobbed. Cecil had said "she." He'd suspected Cecil's basement was set up for a romantic date, but now he knew for certain.

"So who's the lucky girl?" the museum curator asked the

research scientist, trying not to sound sarcastic.

"Sum . . . Sum . . . Somebody who . . . welly well . . . really I'm the lucky one, not Sum . . . Sum . . ."

"Summer?" Paul exclaimed with real interest. "Summer Beach?"

Cecil's face suddenly turned as red as a floating tomato.

"Of course," Paul nodded. "Summer Beach. That makes perfect sense. Our old junior high classmate. Your lab partner in Mr. Womberfraggle's chemistry class, if I remember correctly. Yes, Cecil, that does make sense. You two would be quite the couple. But does she know how you feel about her? Do you think she feels the same way?"

"Well . . . uh . . . I . . . geeze little weeze, I . . . the equation . . . works out . . ." Cecil stammered through a response but was suddenly interrupted by a side swipe.

"So sorry, Mr. Sassafras sir," Preston, the teenage supermarket clerk, apologized as he rushed by. "I didn't mean to bump you, Mr. Sassafras. I'm trying to rush to the lunchmeat aisle to do a cleanup. One of the other clerks accidentally knocked over the tower of tuna they were building."

"No problem," Cecil responded with kind eyes. "No problem at . . . sandwich!"

"Sandwich?" Sims asked, confused at Cecil's exclamation.

"Sandwich," the red-headed scientist confirmed. "That's the perfect meal for sweet Summer Thyme!"

Ring Finger was a giant of a man. He stood about a foot

taller than any of his henchmen—a group called the Iron Nails who themselves stood a foot taller than most of the village racers who'd shown up. Ring Finger stood at the top of a dune with his elaborate robe flapping in the wind, his expensive jewelry shining in the sun and his arrogant smile casting both disdain and intimidation on the racers who faced him. His Iron Nails stood in a menacing circle around the racers and their buggies, each man holding some kind of metallic weapon and wearing some kind of metal or iron helmet.

The Sassafrases gulped from their spot in the llama crate. "So this is the starting line for the resource race," Tracey whispered to Blaine. "Maybe it's good that we're stuck safely in this crate after all." The twins didn't know how many villages there were in this part of the Atacama Desert, but only about a dozen or so dune buggies were here. They wondered if every village was represented or if some had been too scared to come or too poor to scrap together a buggy.

The dune buggies ranged in size and style, but all looked rugged and handmade. All appeared to be cobbled together from spare parts like the one the twins currently found themselves on. There was a buggy with rusty bulldozer parts and one with blades from an old helicopter. There was a buggy with big, weathered tires that looked like they came off a monster truck and one that had a body made from old billboards. There was a buggy equipped with huge sails of tattered cloth and one that was belching more black smoke than a coal factory. Even in their hodgepodge nature, most of the dune buggies looked well fortified. Additionally, most looked equipped with some kind of weapon, be it sling shot, spinning blade, cannon, or otherwise.

The dune buggy to the right of the twins looked like it was covered with anything and everything the villagers had been able to find that was sharp and/or pointy. Its entire body seemed to be made of protruding objects, all designed to poke, prod, or pierce.

"*Buenos dias*, Rose Rock!" the driver of the scary, sharp dune buggy shouted with a snarl. "Your buggy looks like it was put together by llamas, not people. Do you think you can win with that piece of junk?"

Instead of answering the man's question, the twins' local expert responded with a couple questions of her own. "Do you want to join us, Maximiliano? Don't you think it would be better if we all cooperated and worked together?"

The driver stared intently at Rose Rock for a moment as if contemplating but then shook his head no.

Vicente returned Maximiliano's intense stare and then made motions with his hands.

"Who is that? What did he say?" Maximiliano scoffed, asking about Vicente.

"He asked what you call your dune buggy," Rose Rock translated.

Maximiliano smiled a smile nearly as cocky as Ring Finer and answered. "It's called Running with Scissors, and don't you come near me during the race, or I'll be forced to impale you." He smiled another arrogant smile and asked, "What are your calling your buggy?"

"Lanzador de Llama," Rose Rock answered, both vocally and in sign language.

"Really?" Maximiliano laughed, unimpressed. "Lanzador de Llama? Huh? The Llama Launcher?"

Blaine and Tracey again looked at each other with wide eyes. "Uh oh," they both gulped.

"Racers of the Atacama," the giant man standing on top of the dune suddenly called out in a loud, booming voice. "Welcome to the first annual Desert Resource Race!"

The surrounding Iron Nails reacted to this announcement

with loud shouts and metallic clanging of weapons. No reaction at all came from any of the racers, however.

"Ever since I have become your protector and king," Ring Finger continued, "I have been carefully compiling and storing resources to be dispersed according to my will."

"Stealing is a more accurate term," the Sassafrases heard Rose Rock say. They watched her speak in sign language to her partner by raising both forearms in front of her, with the right arm in front of the left. She extended the index and middle finger of her right hand into hooks and pulled those fingers along the raised left forearm from the elbow toward the hand.

"That grand dispersion will happen today at the Hand of the Desert," Ring Finger continued. "As the *Mano de Desierto* rises mysteriously out of the sand and towers into the sky, I will rise and provide for the winner of this race and their village from my mighty hand."

Vicente, though deaf, easily and clearly understood Ring Finger's words and the hubris they were drenched with, thanks to Rose Rock's translations. The deaf man shook his head as the tyrant continued.

"You now find yourselves at the starting line. The racecourse will lead you through the Atacama and its terrain to the Hand of the Desert, where the winner, and only the winner, will win a year's worth of resources for their village. The route is clearly marked with iron flags that have been planted by my men. Rest assured that the Iron Nails will be stationed along the entire course, ensuring that every buggy follows the correct route."

The towering man paused and smiled smugly. He snapped his fingers, and immediately from the unseen other side of the tall mound of sand he was standing on, a dune buggy appeared, driven by an Iron Nail. This buggy was no hodge-podge, mix-and-match, thrown-together buggy like all the villagers' were. This dune buggy was glimmering and sleek with an engine that purred instead of grumbled.

"The race starts when I take off in my buggy," Ring Finger declared, putting one large hand on his buggy, preparing to climb into the passenger seat. "I will see at least one of you at the finish line." The smile got smugger. "Maybe. If any of you survive the course."

The big man took his seat in the pristine buggy. The Iron Nail behind the wheel revved the perfectly calibrated engine. All the racers from the villages of the Atacama revved their engines as well—the machines moaning, gurgling, clanking, and grumbling for the start of the race. The village racers looked around at each other nervously, each desperately hoping and needing to win. They each hoped their dune buggy would have what it took to finish this race. They all needed the resources that waited at the Hand of the Desert.

All at once, the driving Nail punched the gas of Ring Finger's sleek buggy. Its wheels threw sand up into the air like a starting flag. The Resource Race was on. Ring Finger's dune buggy disappeared over the dune as fast as a fennec fox. The other 12 dune buggies immediately accelerated and muscled their way up to the apex of the first dune. Before them stood the wide, hot Atacama. Who was going to overcome and survive this race? Who was going to win?

Healing Iodine

He was going to win. He was going to overcome and survive. He was now certain of it. However, what would not be surviving were his memories—his or anyone else's.

Thaddeus Wazeezy, the Man With No Eyebrows, now made his way to his backyard at 1108 North Pecan Street. He had watched through the blinds of his front window as Cecil and President Lincoln had walked by his house. He was pretty sure Paul Sims had been with them too. Paul was an old classmate who used to live in the neighborhood. Thaddeus wasn't sure why Paul was back, but no matter, he could have his memory wiped as well.

He heard Cecil and Paul talking as clearly as day about how Summer and her crew would be arriving soon, along with that niece and nephew of Cecil's.

"Perfect. Just perfect," Thaddeus mused to himself as he stepped from his back door into his fenced backyard. "Everyone will get here in time to be forget-o-nated!" the eyebrow-less man exclaimed loudly enough for only himself to hear.

The invisible zip-line trip of the mobile home-sized Forget-O-Nator from Siberia to his backyard had gone surprisingly well, so had the repair of the machine. After being smashed by whatever that monster-looking machine had been, the Forget-O-Nator had looked irreparable.

However, it looked much worse than it actually was. It had taken Thaddeus only a few days to get it up and running again.

Here it was now, in his backyard, waiting to wipe away everyone's memories.

Cecil's memories would be gone.

Summer's memories would be gone . . . again.

That niece and nephew of Cecil's would forget everything they had learned about science this summer.

Even Paul, that robot, and those rodent lab assistants would lose their memories.

Then he himself would step into the Forget-O-Nator with them and wipe his own memory away.

This was what he wanted. He didn't want to remember all the losses, mistakes, and shortcomings. The loss of his eyebrows would be avenged. This is how he wanted it. This is how he would secure his victory of vengeance.

"Is there any victory at all to be secured here for anyone?" the Sassafrases mused from their spot in the llama crate. This race was despicable. It was horrible that Ring Finger was hoarding stolen resources and making desperate people compete for them. It was unbelievable that the different villages wouldn't come together and cooperate to take Ring Finger down. It was despicable how the racers were treating each other out here on this treacherous course. Blaine and Tracey had watched with clenched teeth and grimaced expressions as the different dune buggies had used their weaponry against each other. Tires had been shredded. Engines had been destroyed. Frames had been dismantled—all by the terrible designs of other villagers' dune buggies.

So far, some way, somehow, the Lanzador de Llama had been left untouched. Maybe that was solely because of the stellar driving and navigation of Rose Rock and Vicente. The two could communicate seamlessly with sign language over the screaming of the engines and the rush of the race, where others could not communicate with their mere vocally communicated words. Not only had their vehicle not been hit by any other, but they also had not fired upon any other vehicle. For that the Sassafrases were extremely grateful. It was crystal clear to them that they were sitting on the launcher of the llama launcher. So, if Rose Rock or Vicente decided they needed to launch the llama, the twelve-year-olds knew that meant they would be launched too. They didn't want to be launched.

There were now only four dune buggies left. In addition to their buggy, the buggy with monster truck wheels, the buggy with helicopter blades, and the buggy named Running with Scissors were the only vehicles still operable, moving forward. These had not only made it through the infighting of the other buggies, but they'd also made it through everything Ring Finger and the Iron Nails had thrown at them.

The iron flags Ring Finger had mentioned in his starting line speech were just that. They were iron flags on iron flagpoles, unaffected by the wind and clearly marking the route. And, as mentioned, big, imposing Iron Nail men were stationed all along the route, ensuring that every buggy stayed on course without deviation. The marked route had first led the racers over a stretch of wide, rising and falling sand dunes, which was to be expected. But then the unexpected had come back to back to back.

They had been led through a gauntlet of quicksand. It had been next to impossible to tell the difference between normal sand and quicksand. That is where the bulldozer buggy had been lost. Next, they had been directed into what could best be described as a predator zone. In this place, the Iron Nails had released caged pumas to chase the buggies. No person had been hurt by the predatory cats, but the animals had attacked most of the buggies. The dune buggy with the sails got the worst of it. The pumas had rendered it undriveable. While in this zone of the race, the llama sharing the cage with the twins had screeched and spit with insane fear. But Rose Rock had gotten the llama and the rest of them out of the predator zone unscathed.

The iron flags then led the remaining dune buggies into a maze. But the maze walls were not made of mortar, stone, or hedge; they were made of fire. Upon the racers' arrival, the Iron Nails had lit pre-poured lines of fuel with torches, creating walls of fire that could not be driven through. Blaine and Tracey hadn't seen what happened to all the other buggies, but they had watched their two leaders drive and navigate the flaming maze with skill.

Now, here they were, after all that, racing alongside Big Wheels, Helicopter Blades, and Running with Scissors down into a rocky canyon. With only four dune buggies remaining, how much

Volume 7: Chemistry

longer would this race last? Would someone actually overcome and win? The racing path narrowed as the four remaining buggies entered the canyon, causing the vehicles to race uncomfortably close together. Big Wheels and Running with Scissors surged into the lead, forcing Helicopter Blades and Lanzador de Llama to follow behind. There was not room to make a pass.

The deeper into the canyon they went, the narrower the path became, and not only that but the canyon walls also seemed to get higher on each side. All at once, a horrifying sight reached the Sassafrases eyes. Ahead, huge boulders were being pushed down into the canyon by a group of Iron Nails who were stationed at the canyon's rim.

"We're going to get smashed!" Tracey's mind screamed.

"We'll get flattened like a pancake!" Blaine shouted silently.

Rose Rock and Vicente saw the falling boulders too, as was evidenced by their emphatic sign language. They had both of their hands balled into fists with palm sides down. Then they were smashing the top fist onto the bottom one, clearly communicating the word "rock."

Big Wheels, however, either didn't see the falling rocks or wasn't able to avoid them because, faster than one could shout "Rutherford B. Hayes," the vehicle's front left tire was crushed by one of the huge boulders. This sent the buggy into a front flip, landing back on its remaining three tires. As big as the tires were, it was obvious this buggy could not continue.

Maximiliano speedily steered Running with Scissors ahead, leaving both Helicopter Blades and Lanzador de Llama to swerve and careen past not only the fallen buggy but more falling boulders. The Sassafrases held their breaths as rocks landed all around them like overweight raindrops. But as she had done the entire race, Rose Rock skillfully steered their buggy through the geological barrage without even one nick. Slightly in front of them, Helicopter Blade also made it through without a scratch.

The Sassafras Science Adventures

The canyon widened out again, and the three remaining buggies had the corridor's exit in their sites. Maximiliano leaned his head out and looked back at his pursuers with an arrogant wag of the tongue. But what he didn't see, something that everyone else saw, was an Iron Nail pushing one last boulder directly toward him.

In the split second they had before the falling boulder would crush Running with Scissors, Rose Rock decided to do something that both delighted and terrified the Sassafras twins. The Chilean chieftess pulled the lever for the catapult.

It delighted the twins because it was clear that out of the goodness of her heart, she was aiming not to hit Maximiliano's buggy but to hit the falling boulder that was about to crush it. She was attempting to launch her llama on a trajectory that would knock the boulder off its course and therefore save Maximiliano.

This also terrified the twins because they, of course, were in the llama crate being launched to accomplish this good deed.

In that split second, everything that happened seemed to be in slow motion. The catapult thrusted powerfully upward, launching their crate. Their crate soared through the air, over the blades of the helicopter buggy, which was racing in between Lanzador de Llama and Running with Scissors. The terrified llama again chose to spit directly into Blaine's open mouth. A disgusted Blaine once more gagged and tried to extract llama saliva. Next their crate made impact with the boulder, knocking it enough off course as to miss Running with Scissors. Their crate smashed and splintered into a million pieces. Then everything went dark for the twins.

"The symbol for iodide is I. Its atomic number is 53, and its atomic mass is 126.9."

"What is this sound? What is this voice?" Tracey wondered,

totally at a loss for what was happening around her. "Where am I? Why can't I see anything? Who is that talking?" The girl's brain was firing off question after question.

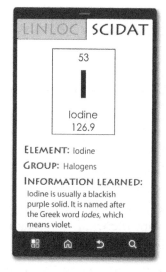

"Although what I have here is a liquid, iodine is usually a blackish purple solid. It is named after the Greek word *iodes*, which means violet. When iodine is heated up, it quickly turns into a purplish gas without becoming a liquid. This process of a solid turning directly into a gas is called sublimation."

"Is this science? Is someone teaching science?" Tracey blindly mused.

"Iodine is almost never seen on its own," the voice continued. "It is usually paired together with itself or with another element to form a compound. Compounds with iodine can be found in seawater and fish."

Tracey blinked her eyes, but she could still see nothing. In addition to the voice, though, she could also hear the grumbling of an engine.

"Iodine is a trace mineral necessary for humans, which is why it's often added to table salt. Our bodies use this halogen for help in making hormones in the thyroid."

"Wait a second. I know this voice," Tracey thought. "That is Rose Rock, our local expert! Blaine and I are in Chile learning about chemistry. We were in a dune buggy race. But what happened?" Tracey still couldn't see, but she could feel some kind of liquid running down her face.

"The yellow-brown liquid I am now applying is an iodine-containing compound," Rose Rock continued. "It is used in starch tests because it turns blue-black in the presence of starch. But more importantly, for our situation right now, it is used to treat cuts. It is also often used during surgery as an antiseptic. I'm glad we loaded some in the buggy. It can sting, but iodine is effective at preventing infections."

Even as the local expert said the word "sting," Tracey felt a tinge of pain on her forehead. Instinctively, the girl reached toward the spot, and as she did, she knocked off the piece of cloth that had been covering her eyes. Bright desert sunshine lit everything around Tracey. She and Blaine were in the dune buggy with Rose Rock and Vicente. They were out of the canyon. Vicente was behind the wheel, and Rose Rock was dabbing at some kind of wound on Tracey's head. Blaine was on the outside of the buggy and was hanging on with both hands with the wind whipping at his clothes. He looked like he as having the time of his life.

The boy smiled at his sister. "Don't worry, Tracey. You're in good hands with Rose Rock. You've got a pretty good cut on your head, but she's fixing it right up with a cloth and some iodine."

Tracey looked from her brother to her local expert. "Thank you," the girl acknowledged and meant it.

Rose Rock responded with genuineness of her own. "I am so sorry I launched the llama with you two in the crate. Neither Vicente nor I had any idea you guys were in there. I'm also sorry I had your eyes covered with that cloth. I was trying to clean your wound a bit."

Tracey smiled in a way that let the chieftess know it was all okay.

"It was crazy, Tracey! Absolutely crazy!" Blaine shouted over the whipping wind. "Our crate hit that boulder and exploded! The boulder landed out of the way, and both you and I bounced off the canyon walls a couple of times and somehow landed in here with Rose Rock and Vicente. Can you believe it? And the llama, golly golly goodness, Tracey, the llama landed in the seat right next to Maximiliano!"

Rose Rock confirmed all that Blaine had said with a slight smile and nod.

"But even after we helped him, Maximiliano raced on!" Blaine continued. "I'm not sure what happened to that helicopter buggy. He must have gotten caught in the canyon or something, but Maximiliano races on."

Tracey sat straighter and looked around a little more. They were racing across flat, wide-open desert. There was no buggy racing beside them or behind them, but there was indeed one up in front of them: Running with Scissors with Maximiliano and the llama sitting next to each other. However, she noticed something much more captivating than the dune buggy in front of them: a huge stone hand that was rising up out of the desert floor.

"*Mano de Desierto*," Rose Rock informed. "The Hand of the Desert. The finish line of this race."

Chapter 16: On to Morocco
Mysterious Noble Gases

It had been a photo finish. The buggy with the spikes and the buggy with the catapult had screamed toward the finish line neck and neck, but it had been Running with Scissors that had clearly won. Maximiliano had prevailed in Ring Finger's despicable race and in doing so had secured a year's worth of resources for his village. Rose Rock and Vicente had lost. They would receive nothing. Their village would remain in desperate need.

With the race over, the engines of the two dune buggies clinked off at the base of the Hand of the Desert. The sculpture towered in front of them like a hand coming up out of the sand to give the winner a high five. Although to the losers it felt a little more like the hand was coming up out of the sand to slap them in the face.

Towering up seemingly even higher was Ring Finger with his ever-present arrogant smile. The big man's sleek dune buggy had surely long since arrived at the Hand of the Desert, and here he stood, with his band of Iron Nails and the winnings for the race's champion. There were crates full of food and supplies. There were pens full of animals. There were humungous containers of water. And it was all for Maximiliano. The winning driver stumbled out of his buggy covered in desert sand and llama spit, but he was victorious.

"Congratulations to the winner of the First Annual Desert Resource Race!" Ring Finger's loud voice boomed in acknowledgment of Maximiliano. "Come and receive your reward!"

Maximiliano glanced at his dune buggy to make sure the llama was going to stay put. He looked toward Rose Rock and her troop as they climbed out of Lanzador de Llama.

"Is he going to say thank you?" Tracey wondered. If it wasn't for Rose Rock, he would have been smashed instead of being the winner.

The driver of Running with Scissors did not say thank you. Instead, he turned his gaze toward Ring Finger and all the resources he'd won. At first Maximiliano was quiet, but then as if the joy of winning suddenly hit him, he happily shouted and skipped around to put his hands on all that he'd procured.

The shoulders of the Sassafras twins slumped. This was no good. How was it right that Maximiliano had won and Rose Rock hadn't? How was it right that Ring Finger and the Iron Nails could wield this kind of deplorable power?

After a few minutes of celebration, Maximiliano came to another pause. He again looked toward Rose Rock and the three with her. His face filled with a sudden resolve as if he'd made a decision he'd been wrestling with.

"I am going to share my winnings with chieftess Rose Rock and her village," the Chilean man announced.

The Sassafrases' shoulders popped back up. This was great

news! Vicente put a hand to his mouth and moved it forward, saying thank you in sign language. He followed with another sign where he made a hook shape with his index finger and moved his hand forward and down.

"Yes, indeed," Rose Rock voiced while at the same time signing, "Thank you. We need this."

Maximiliano was about to say something when he was interrupted by the angry, booming voice of Ring Finger. "No! There will be no sharing of resources! There is one winner and one winner only. If the winner plans to share their resources, then there will be no winner!"

As the warlord king shouted, his Iron Nails took intimidating steps closer toward Maximiliano, whose face betrayed his immediate regret. All at once, Vicente rushed up and stood to face Ring Finger. The warlord was much taller than the deaf man, but Vicente's confidence somehow made him look taller. Vicente pointed at himself, then made a C shape with his right hand and put it over his heart.

Ring Finger, along with his Iron Nails, who were standing at attention and ready to strike if need be, were momentarily shocked. However, the slight shock didn't stop Ring Finger from looking at the man in front of him and laughing arrogantly. "Who do you think you are, coming up to me like this? Don't you know who I am? Get out of my face. Don't you fear me and my authority?"

Not shaken in any way, Vicente stood his ground in front of the towering man. Rose Rock joined him in his brazenness, speaking boldly to Ring Finger with both voice and hands. "It is you, Ring Finger, who should fear the man of authority who is now standing in front of you. Yes, he is deaf, but he so happens to also be the chief of police from Antofagasta."

Blaine, Tracey, Maximiliano, and possibly even the llama, gasped at this sudden revelation.

THE SASSAFRAS SCIENCE ADVENTURES

"And we do not stand here alone," Rose Rock continued. "Lift up your eyes and look around! You are surrounded by the entire Antofagastan police force!"

Ring Finger did as Rose Rock directed, as did his Iron Nails. Blaine and Tracey also looked out at the surrounding desert to see an army of armed Chilean police officers encircling them.

"Your short reign of terror is over," Rose Rock declared to the self-proclaimed warlord king. "*Estás terminado*! You are finished."

Sometime later, the Sassafras twins found themselves sitting alone at the base of the *Mano de Desierto*. They had finished sending in some cool pictures from the archive app to go along with all the SCIDAT they had learned on topics of halogens, bonding, chlorine, and iodine. Next, they would open the LINLOC applications on their smartphones. Both twins took long, deep breaths. Chile had been a trying location, but thankfully in the end everything had worked together for good. Ring Finger and the Iron Nails had given up without a fight. They had been arrested by the Antofagastan police force and were now on their way to jail. All the resources Ring Finger had stolen had been recovered and were being hauled by dune buggy to be dispersed among the villages of the Atacama.

To everyone's surprise, the helicopter dune buggy had reappeared with the big-wheeled buggy. Evidently, after seeing Lanzador de Llama help Running with Scissors, he had decided to stop and help repair the fallen buggy. Big Wheel was now an operable trike dune buggy. This made a group of five buggies able to carry and disperse resources—Helicopter Blades, Big Wheel, Running with Scissors, Lanzador de Llama, and Vicente driving Ring Finger's sleek new dune buggy.

Rose Rock had met and become friends with Vicente during her time living in Antofagasta. The twins wondered if maybe their local expert and the brave deaf police chief were an item.

The twelve-year-olds took another breath. It was time to see where they would land next.

"Morocco is the next location, longitude 6° 27' 37.8" W, latitude 31° 26' 50.2" N!" Blaine exclaimed. "We'll be learning about noble gases, helium, neon, and air! I hope we don't land in a llama crate this time around," the boy huffed.

Tracey agreed with a wry smile. "Our local expert's name is The SAM Collective," she read and then repeated as a question, "The SAM Collective?"

"I know, right?" Blaine retorted, reading the name listed there on LINLOC. "A lot of the names of our local experts during our chemistry study have been kind of different; haven't they?"

"No matter," Tracey responded as she grabbed her carabiner, preparing to calibrate it. "They've all been great. Well, I guess, with the exception of the Unseen One."

"They have been great," Blaine nodded as he too handled his carabiner. "But Summer is still my favorite!"

Tracey agreed wholeheartedly.

"Summer is still my favorite!" Cecil Sassafras stated excitedly as he sliced some salami. He and Paul Sims were in his kitchen at 1108 North Pecan Street preparing all the stuff they were going to use to make sandwiches for the upcoming date.

"Okay," Paul responded with a nod. "She is still your favorite, but are you her favorite?"

"Ummm, welly wee willikers, I don't know," Cecil murmured with sudden seeds of doubt threatening to be planted.

"Because you know Summer is a pretty accomplished and classy gal," Paul continued. "I mean she's got that sleek space-worthy lab with all the latest and greatest equipment. She rubs shoulders with the likes of Triple S, an organization comprised of some of the finest humans on Earth. With all of that in her life, do you think an old junior high classmate of hers is still her favorite?"

Cecil was suddenly speechless. Summer was certainly his favorite person, but was he hers?

"I mean, Cecil, I know you were her lab partner all those years ago in Mr. Womberfraggle's chemistry class, but there were lots of kids in that classroom she was friends with," Paul kept on. "Summer is a friendly person. She's always been nice. She's nice to everyone, right? Can you remember all the people who were in that class of ours? There was you and me. There was the Chinese exchange student, Yang Bo, who is now a successful astronaut. There was that other guy, oh, what was his name? Thad or Thaddeus. Yeah, Thaddeus Wazeezy, right? I mean, Summer was nice to all of us. She's a nice person. Toward you, maybe she's just being nice. Maybe there's nothing more there. I don't want you to put yourself out there and potentially get your heart broken. You know what I'm saying, old buddy?"

Cecil stopped his slicing as his face clouded. The seeds of doubt had been planted.

THE SASSAFRAS SCIENCE ADVENTURES

"Oh, you've got to be kidding me!" Blaine exclaimed in frustration. "We did land in a crate again!"

"Well, at least there's not a llama in this one," Tracey offered, trying to be optimistic.

"Yeah, I know there's no llama, but it's still a crate. A crate, Tracey! I don't want to be in a crate again!"

"You know, all in all, I ended up liking that llama," Tracey declared.

"What?" Blaine couldn't believe it. "How could you like that terrible, spitting llama?"

"It kind of ended up saving the day."

"Whatever. You wouldn't say that if it had spit in your face."

Now Tracey laughed at her brother.

"Stop laughing, Tracey. Getting spit on by a llama was quite possibly the worst thing that's ever happened in my life!"

"If you say so," Tracey giggled.

Blaine was about to continue his tantrum, when suddenly the twins heard approaching voices. The twelve-year-olds hushed themselves, trying to see where the voices were coming from. This was going to be fairly hard to do considering the fact they had landed at night in Morocco.

There was enough moonlight peeking through the slowly passing clouds to see each other and to see they were in the mountains. They could make out ubiquitous outlines rising and falling in shadowy moonbeams peppered with the black outlines of trees at different distances. Still, darkness invaded much of the landscape.

"Can we all agree that hydrogen was a terrible idea," one voice questioned in a kind of loud whisper.

"Fine, I'll admit it," another voice answered in the same

manner. "I brought it up because they had tanks of it lying around."

"It's way too reactive. Way too risky, hydrogen, that is," a female voice added the the mix. "We needed something just as light but much nobler."

"True, but they didn't have anything like that on the compound," the second voice rebutted, sounding a little defensive.

The three voices were close enough to the twins' crate that they could see the shadows of the figures belonging to them. Moving slowly, in a close cluster, the three shadows walked right past the twins' spot then stopped in a small clearing beyond the Sassafrases. Although they were moving somewhat stealthily, the three conversationalists continued quietly chatting.

"Ahhh, the noble gases," the first voice said. "The elements from group 18 on the far right of the periodic table. These include argon, krypton, xenon, radon, oganesson, neon, and helium."

"Now, if they would've had some helium, that might've presented some interesting possibilities," the second voice commented.

"When Mendeleev created his periodic table," the female continued the conversation almost as if she hadn't heard the second voice's comment. "He did not predict the existence of the noble gases as a group of elements, even though he did say other elements would be found."

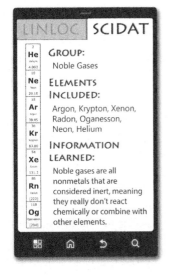

"That's right," the first voice agreed. "Many of the noble gases are found in the atmosphere. These elements are all nonmetals that are considered inert, meaning they don't react chemically or combine with other elements. This is because they have a full outer shell of electrons. The rare exception is xenon, which will make a few compounds.

"Argon was the first noble gas to be discovered," the woman explained. "It was found by Scottish chemist William Ramsay, who separated it from liquid air in 1894. It is named after the Greek word for lazy because it is so inactive. It is used to create a safe atmosphere for arc welding and as an insulation between window panes."

"You know William Ramsay was also a part of discovering another noble gas," the second voice interjected excitedly.

"Oh, yeah, that's right—krypton!" the first voice interrupted, stealing his thunder. "He discovered this gas in 1898, along with an English chemist by the name of Morris Travers."

"On top of that," the female added, "in 1904, William Ramsay was awarded the Nobel Prize in chemistry for discovering a total of five noble gases: helium, neon, argon, xenon, and krypton."

And like argon, krypton is named after a Greek word," the first voice expounded. "'Hidden' is where the Greek word *krypton* comes from because it is so hard to find. It is used in fluorescent lights and in monitors for radioactive elements."

As the three talked, they weren't standing still. They seemed to be collaboratively working on something because they would crouch and stand back up, grabbing at something on the ground with their hands. In the provided light, the twins couldn't exactly tell what the trio was doing.

"Xenon is used in bulbs, giving off a blue glow," the woman continued sharing information about noble gases. "It is also used to sterilize surfaces and as a propellent in ion thrusters."

"Radon is produced when uranium and thorium decay. It is a heavy gas that can be toxic in high quantities," the first voice gave details on another noble gas and then another. "Oganesson is a lab-created noble gas that is thought to be similar to radon. It was made in 2002."

"Then we have helium," the female voice started again. "It makes up about a quarter of the—"

"No, no, now it's my turn," the second voice interrupted. "You two will hardly let me get a word in!

Gaseous Helium

The combined sound of good-hearted chuckling came from the other two, and then the woman said, "Okay, Sami, no problem. Go for it."

"Helium makes up about a quarter of the weight in the universe. I believe that's what you were about to say, right, Samirah?" the second voice, evidently belonging to a man by the name of Sami, said to the woman named Samirah.

"That's right, Sami, go on," Samirah answered.

"Helium is produced in massive stars when four hydrogen atoms fuse together, releasing tons of energy," Sami happily obliged with more scientific data. "Helium is a colorless, tasteless gas with no smell, and even though it's present in the atmosphere, you don't know it's there. The symbol for helium is He. Its atomic number is 2 and its atomic mass is 4.003."

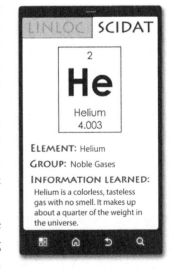

The Sassafras twins were listening, but they were beginning to get a little restless in their crate, especially Blaine. They had been in a crate for the majority of their time in Chile, and he didn't want to be in a crate anymore. He wanted to be learning science face-to-face with his local experts, not crate to face. He didn't want to be hearing about helium from a small, cramped spot. He wanted to be hearing about it over in that clearing with the three people who were talking about it. He also wanted to know what they were working on over there. He wanted to be out of this crate!

"Like argon, helium is also used in welding because it's so inert and unreactive," Sami continued. "Liquid helium is used as a coolant for superconducting magnets in MRI machines. But here's where it starts to get exciting, and here is why I wanted to share about it."

Sami's voice got louder and more enthusiastic. "Helium is lighter than air. Yes, it's the noble gas that if inhaled will make your voice high and squeaky. It is used to blow up balloons because it's lighter than air! And it's not just for small balloons; it's also used for large weather balloons and airships!"

"But, Sami, they didn't have any," the first voice said.

"Just a second, Samir, let me finish."

The first voice, which the twins knew belonged to a man named Samir, tried to cut in, but the conversation was immediately taken back by Sami. "To escape using helium, there are three main components we would need to take into consideration: the size of the balloon, the weight of the payload, and how much positive lift we would need. If there were a plethora of small balloons, we could even use those instead of needing to construct one large balloon. Each basic party balloon can hold about five liters of air when fully inflated. We would also need to take into account that each balloon has a mass of about two grams. The density of air at standard temperature and pressure is 0.011143 pounds per cubic foot."

"Next we would need to calculate the weight of the payload. In our case, we each weigh, what, about 150 pounds?"

"Speak for yourselves, boys. I only weigh 125 pounds,"

Samirah answered, still chuckling but sounding somewhat offended.

"Okay, so that's a total of 425 pounds when adding the three of us. We would also need to add the weight of our riding basket plus potential supplies from those crates, which could be an additional 150 to 200 pounds. That would put the total weight of our payload at roughly 600 pounds. Now we would take that 600 and divide it by the difference of density per cubic foot in air and helium, which would be 0.06956, right? Okay, let me do a little math in my head."

"Okay."

"Wow, that would put us at approximately 8,625-ish cubic feet. Next—"

"Get on with it, Sami," Samir said, his chuckling gone.

"Well, the Avagadro constant tells us that a mole—"

"We know, Sami, we know," Samir interrupted again. "A mole, not the burrowing animal mole, of course, but the measure word "mole," which is the base unit amount of a pure substance in the International System of Units that is defined by having exactly $6.02214076 \times 10^{23}$ indivisible units of that substance. We understand the math; just finish up and tell us how many small party balloons it would take to give us the positive lift we would need to escape."

"Approximately 90,000," Sami answered, "not taking into account the mass of any strings used for attaching the balloons."

"Well, that was a fun little science experiment, or rather a math problem, in your head regarding helium," Samir quipped. "But what we physically have our hands on is propane, so let's fill up this balloon with that, and let's get out of here."

"Boys, boys," Samirah cut in, her good-hearted laughter still present. "It's good for us to keep our minds sharp with math and science. So, Sami, that was a good exercise, but Samir is right. It's time for us to get going."

At that, the conversation among the three stopped, but their movement did not halt. They continued diligently working on whatever it was they were hovering over.

"What is going on over there, and what are these three talking about?" the Sassafras twins wondered. They understood and committed to memory all the SCIDAT information about noble gases and helium.

However, they had been unable to follow the rest. They had no idea what all this talk of escape was about. One thing was for sure, they were ready for escape themselves—an escape from this crate.

After a few minutes, Blaine and Tracey heard Samir say, "Okay, now it's time for the propane!"

One of the three shadows stood and came toward them. As the shadow got closer, the twins could see by the gait and square frame that it was a male shadow. He reached their crate and worked to get it open, but then he spotted the twins and stopped with a gasp.

"Oh, no! Samirah! Sami! You're not going to believe this. There are kids in the propane crate!"

"What?" Samirah called as she and Sami shot up from their spots in the clearing and rushed to the crate. As the three looked at them, Blaine and Tracey remained quiet, not knowing what to say.

"Oh, no," Sami said in a grave tone. "Now they're not only stealing goods and imprisoning adults. They're capturing children, too!"

All three let out disheartened sighs. Even in the dim light, the Sassafrases could see the compassionate looks on the faces of these three people who'd moments ago been only voices. All three were draped in dark clothing, with only their faces and hands showing.

"This will bump our payload up another 150 to 200 pounds," Sami spoke again. "But obviously, we have to take these two with us."

Samirah and Samir nodded in agreement. Samir got the crate all the way open. He then helped Blaine and Tracey get out from the cramped spot and up to their feet.

"Thank you so much," Tracey said gratefully.

"And hello," Blaine added. "We are the Sassafrases. Blaine and Tracey Sassafras."

"Nice to meet you, Blaine and Tracey," Samirah greeted. She then gestured toward herself and her two companions. "We call ourselves the SAM Collective. I am Samirah, this is Samir, and that's Sami."

The two men gave small waves as they were introduced.

"We call ourselves this," Samirah continued, "because our names all start with 'Sam' but also because of what the S, the A, and the M stand for."

"That's right," Samir jumped in. "We're not just all Sams; we're also all scientists, activists, and mathematicians."

"Wow, that's cool," Tracey responded. "We overheard you talking about noble gases. We also heard some of your calculations."

"Uh oh," Samirah chuckled. "Maybe we should've been talking a little quieter."

"Why all the hush hush?" Blaine asked.

"Well, that's because of our activism," Samir answered.

"Your activism?" Tracey queried.

"That's right," Samir confirmed with a serious face. "The A.S.M. captured us and put us in this prison because we spoke out against their ancient, cruel practice of imprisoning snakes for snake-charming."

Blaine and Tracey weren't following what the SAMs were saying, and their faces showed it.

"The A.S.M. group is not a collective of three," Samirah explained, "but a ruffian gang of hundreds. The A.S.M. stands for Anonymous Snake charmers of Morocco, and they are a menace."

"A few months ago, we staged a protest in Jemaa el-Fnaa to speak against them," Samir informed.

Sami emphatically agreed with a nod of the head, passionately adding, "Yes, we did! Are the two of you aware the snakes that rise from the charmers' baskets are captured and often mistreated?"

The Sassafrases shook their heads no.

"Most people don't know that," Sami continued. "Most people also don't know that not only are the snakes not magical or charmed; they are simply trying to defend themselves. Many of these reptiles have their fangs taken out, or their mouths are sewn shut so they can't strike the charmer."

Blaine and Tracey did not know any of this. They'd never seen a snake charmer before, so they were unfamiliar with the practice. Snakes, in contrast, were a different story altogether. They'd nearly fallen into a pit of snakes when studying zoology in Egypt with Princess Talibah. All in all, they didn't necessarily love snakes, but they also didn't like the idea of the reptiles being mistreated. Really, the whole concept of snake charming was confusing to them. They were curious about several other things the SAM Collective had mentioned. One, they had no idea what Jemaa el-Fnaa was. Two, they couldn't tell how anything about their current location would classify as a prison. And three, they were still wondering what the three had been working on over in the clearing.

Luckily for the twins, the SAM Collective was a talkative bunch. "Yes, our protest at Jemaa el-Fnaa was over almost the moment it started," Samirah explained. "We started walking the rows of the market with our anti-snake-charming posters, and almost immediately the A.S.M. thugs emerged from the hidden corners, narrow alleyways, and vending stalls of the crowded market. Escape was not an option because we were outnumbered and surrounded on all sides."

"Jemaa el-Fnaa is the most vibrant market in all of Marrakesh, and there is a strong police presence," Samir jumped in. "However, the anonymous snake charmers struck so fast. The police didn't have a chance to respond. Before anybody knew what was happening, we were blindfolded, thrown in the back of a vehicle, and headed somewhere out of town fast!"

"Hours later, the ride stopped. Our blindfolds were ripped off. And we found ourselves in the Atlas Mountains!" Samir exclaimed, the most animated of the three. "And not only in the mountains but in a prison in the mountains!"

"Well, a prison of sorts," Samirah clarified. "Somehow, the anonymous snake charmers of Morocco had claimed a large, abandoned facility and were using it as a storage compound for all kinds of stolen goods as well as a makeshift prison for people they deem as enemies."

"The first month or two we were watched like hawks," Samir remembered. "A slew of guards forced us to stay inside the facility, not allowing us to go outside. They used us as free labor. We basically served as warehouse lackeys, forced to perpetually move stuff around the facility."

"However, as time passed, they saw us as less and less of a threat," Samirah explained. "They began to allow us more freedom to roam around the facility at our own accord. They even let us occasionally go out of the building. We found there was a large wall encircling the entire perimeter, hammering in the point that this was indeed a prison. However, one fateful day we also found that there was a decent-sized hole in the wall that the guards didn't seem to know about."

"Even with the hole in the wall sparking ideas of escape,"

Samir expounded, "we knew there was no way anybody could get away on foot because the facility was so far out in the mountains away from any and all cities."

"It's true," Samirah agreed. "It would be too far and too dangerous to walk to Marrakesh. Plus, as soon as the guards noticed we were gone, they would use everything at their disposal to chase us down."

"But then our science and math kicked in!" Sami interjected. "We started paying a little more attention to some of the different items they were storing in this facility. After some brainstorming and calculations, we realized we had everything we needed to escape right at our fingertips!"

"You did?" Blaine and Tracey asked in unison.

"Yes, we did!" Sami confirmed. "We decided we were going to escape by building a hot-air balloon!"

Now the twins gasped. Everything was starting to make sense, but the revelation of all of it was still shocking.

"So over the past few months we have been secretly gathering the needed supplies for our balloon. We've been sneaking it through that hole in the wall, and we've been stashing it out here near this clearing," Samirah shared. "Slowly but surely, our balloon began to take shape as we've worked together to build it."

"We found the components we needed to build the burner," Sami began a list. "We found plenty of hammocks and old parachutes to build the envelope, otherwise known as the balloon, plus all the thread we needed to sew it together. We found some lightweight wicker material we used to make the basket. We found some rope for tethering and some sandbags for anchoring. We found some—"

"Propane," Samir interrupted his collective member with a chuckle. "Not helium and not hydrogen but propane. We found some propane tanks. Although it is not a noble gas, this is the best gas to use when flying a hot-air balloon."

"We carried the propane out here in crates just like the one you two were in." Samirah pointed at the crate the Sassafrases had zip-lined into. "We are so sorry the anonymous snake charmers captured the two of you and put you in that crate. That is terrible."

"Well, actually," Blaine began to explain but was interrupted by Samir, who was now pointing to another nearby crate.

"See right there. There is the propane we need to inflate our balloon."

"Inflate the balloon?" Tracey clarified.

"That's right," Sami confirmed. "It's the middle of the night, so the guards shouldn't notice we are gone. The balloon is built. It's in this clearing far enough away from the facility as to not be detected. It's time to inflate this thing!"

"You mean it's . . ." Tracey started to say but was too nervous and excited to finish.

"Yes!" Sami finished for her. "It's time. Tonight. Right now. It's time to inflate this handmade hot-air balloon. It's time to escape! And Blaine and Tracey, you're coming with us!"

Chapter 17: Just a Bunch of Hot Air
Neon Outbreak

Just a bunch of hot air, that's what President Lincoln thought Paul Sims was full of. The cocky museum curator had just whisked in here unannounced, and ever since his arrival, he'd been speaking down to Cecil, filling his head with falsehoods and doubts. Paul had Cecil doubting his skills and purpose. He even had Cecil thinking that Summer Beach might not like him, much less love him.

On top of that, Paul Sims couldn't help but take charge of everything. The authoritative guy had been reorganizing things, cleaning up this house at 1104 North Pecan Street to his liking. He'd totally hijacked the romantic table/dinner date project that Cecil had been preparing for Summer. It was like Paul was the one hosting Summer, not Cecil. President Lincoln did not like it, not one bit.

At the moment, the prairie dog scurried through the tunnels in the house's walls, from the immaculately cleaned basement up to the kitchen, where Paul was shelving the buffet of sandwiches that Cecil had prepared for Summer, replacing it with a spread of fancy hors d'ouevres.

The Prez was flustered. He wanted to get rid of Paul and help Cecil. He just wasn't sure how to do that yet.

Just a bunch of hot air, that's what Thaddeus Wazeezy, aka the Man With No Eyebrows, thought this whole summer up to this point had been. He had set out to exact revenge on Cecil

Sassafras for taking the eyebrows off his face back in junior high. He originally had hoped to accomplish this revenge by stopping that niece and nephew of Cecil's from learning science. It was a goal that, if it had proven successful, would have crushed the red-headed scientist. However, everything Thaddeus had tried had failed. It had all added up to a bunch of hot air.

Now he had the new, improved, enlarged, and empowered Forget-O-Nator right in his backyard—no more failing, no more hot air. Now he wasn't only going to stop those little Sassafrases from learning science, but he was going to stop everyone and everything. He was going to usher everybody inside this memory-taking machine, including himself, and he was going to wipe it all away.

No more failing.

No more hot air.

No more memories of anything.

However, just because it was the end didn't mean it couldn't be poetic. Seeing Paul Sims with Cecil had sparked an idea in his mind, one last grand idea of poetic vengeance. He wasn't only going to use his Forget-O-Nator. He was going to organize a class reunion. Because so many of his old junior high classmates were involved, it would be perfect.

He would move the Forget-O-Nator from his backyard to the old junior high school building. It was summertime, so no classes were in session. The building would be empty, and no one would notice. He would send out invitations to all his old classmates, inviting them to a reunion at the school. He was certain they would all RSVP.

Once they arrived, he would somehow get them all to enter the Forget-O-Nator. Then he would wipe everything away. "How poetic," he thought to himself even now. It will end right where it all began.

Just a bunch of hot air, that's what Paul Sims was throwing at Cecil Sassafras. He didn't actually care about his old junior high classmate. He didn't care about the red-headed scientist's niece and nephew learning science. He didn't care about the prairie dog that scurried around the house and was treated like a human. And he certainly didn't care how this romantic dinner date with Cecil and Summer went. If anything, he thought it much more likely that Summer would fall for a guy like him than Cecil. He didn't care. But he had to act like he cared.

He had to make Cecil and all of Cecil's entourage think he was a genuine friend. He had to make them think and feel that he was a good guy who could be trusted. That way, if or when Triple S came calling to question everyone about his involvement with all the crimes committed around the Rotary Club, the moon, and the museum, Cecil's entourage would be on his side.

He knew the Swiss Secret Service respected Cecil. Obviously, they respected Summer. If it seemed as though he was squarely on the right side, then maybe that would cause Triple S to question any involvement of his in the nefarious activities of the past few weeks. Paul wasn't sure all this effort would be enough, but he had to try. So he would continue to blow hot air. He would get this house cleaned up and this dinner perfected so Cecil and Summer saw that he "cared."

Just a bunch of hot air, that's what Summer T. Beach was exhaling from her lungs right now as she finished her paperwork. She wasn't a fan of paperwork. She much preferred lab work and field work, but she knew that pushing papers was sometimes a necessity. This had been paperwork dealing with the arrest of the Rotary Club. Summer had been asked by Captain Marolf to write a report about all that had happened on the moon with Alexander, Graham, and Belle Slote and the equipment they'd stolen from the National Air and Space Museum. Now she was finished. The report had a few curious holes in it, but Summer was finished with it.

It was time for what was next on the docket, which was currently turning the scientist's hot air-exhaling sigh into a high-pitched squeal of delight and anticipation. It was finally time to go see Cecil again! For so long, Summer had wondered if maybe, just maybe, Cecil felt the same way about her as she did about him.

Then they'd had their moment under the sparkling disco ball at the Ambidextrous Octopus bowling alley, a moment when she thought she'd see love in his beautiful blue eyes. It was a moment that was interrupted far too soon by a call back to work.

Summer squealed. It was almost time! Time to zip back to 1104 North Pecan Street! Time to look into those blue eyes again and see what was there!

Just a bunch of hot air, that's what Yang Bo was looking forward to basking in. He was about finished with his six-month mission aboard the International Space Station. It had been wonderful, challenging, eye-opening, difficult, and a dream come true.

However, after being surrounded by dark, cold space for so long, he was ready for some hot, bright sunshine! A beach vacation sounded good, and maybe a trip to visit some old friends. Right now, the Chinese astronaut did a zero-gravity flip just thinking about it.

Just a bunch of hot air, the twins had found out. That's what it takes to inflate a hot-air balloon. It had taken about 30 minutes for the handmade burner to burn up enough of the liquid propane from the tanks to turn it into a gas that filled the balloon, or envelope as they'd heard the SAM Collective call it. Currently, the three SAMs and the two Sassafrases stood snugly inside the riding basket underneath the fully inflated balloon. It was just a matter of cutting the tethers and releasing some of the sandbags. Then they would be home free, soaring through the starry night with the cooperation of the wind on their way out of the Atlas

Mountains, toward the city of Marrakesh. Although the twins had not been incarcerated with Samirah, Samir, and Sami, they too were excited with the hope of escape.

"Okay," Sami was saying, "now we just need to—"

"STOP!" an unseen and unfamiliar voice suddenly shouted out. "Stop where you are! Don't move!"

"Oh no!" the Sassafrases' hearts sunk. Shadows were now emerging out of the shadows—dozens of them. The guards of the makeshift prison were coming toward them. The thugs from the anonymous snake charmers were chasing them.

Sami did not heed the orders given but instead worked double-time to cut the ropes and drop the bags. Samir jumped in to help him. To the Sassafrases it didn't look like release and lift were going to happen fast enough.

Snap! Snap! Whoosh! Whoosh! Whoosh!

The tethers were cut, and the sandbags dropped. Still, the angry guards were approaching faster than the balloon was lifting. Samirah, who was working the burner, fully opened the valve, releasing a large flame of burning propane, filling the envelope with more gas, therefore causing more lift. The balloon was off the ground and climbing, but to Blaine and Tracey, it still appeared it was too little too late.

The fastest of the guards reached their spot and lunged for the basket of the escaping balloon. He missed. Maybe they had gained enough altitude after all. The next guard reached them. Instead of lunging for the basket, this guard jumped for one of the dangling tether ropes that had been cut.

Oh, no! He got it! And he was successfully hanging on! Blaine and Tracey leaned out of the basket enough to see him. The moon cast enough light to see the man's face. He looked determined. His eyes said he was certain he was going to catch these escaping prisoners.

However, the hot-air balloon was still climbing in elevation. It was reaching the height of the surrounding treetops. As the Sassafrases looked down at the man, his eyes went from communicating confidence to fear, as if saying, "Oh, my cow! What am I doing hanging onto a flying balloon this high off the ground?" Even now, his fellow guards on the ground were yelling for him to let go.

He did. And lucky for him, he landed in the top of a tree instead of flat on the ground.

A collective gasp of joy and relief released from the collective. They had done it! They were free! They had meticulously built a hot-air balloon. They had carefully planned an escape. And it had worked! They were soaring on the winds of freedom!

As they now lofted above the treetops, the Sassafrases got their first glimpse of the facility turned prison. It was a huge place, surrounded by a wall like the SAMs had said. Only a few lights illuminated its grounds. However, that was the only electric light the twins could see in any direction. They truly were in the mountains out in the middle of nowhere.

"Ahhh, what a beautiful night to be free!" Sami exclaimed. "Look! The clouds are parting open even more. The moon and the host of stars are greeting us and wishing us bon voyage! Now, onward we go out of the Atlas Mountains, down to desert plains, back toward home, back toward Marrakesh, the Daughter of the Desert, the Red City."

Blaine and Tracey closed their eyes and felt the evening breeze as it blew across their faces and through their hair. What an adventure this was—this night in Morocco and the science-learning summer as a whole.

"Do you think they'll chase us?" Tracey asked as she opened her eyes. "Do you think the guards and the anonymous snake charmers will chase our balloon all the way back to Marrakesh?"

"Probably," Samir answered. "But no matter. The breeze is good tonight, and it's blowing in the right direction. We should get back to Marrakesh much faster by air than our former captors will be able to on the precarious and curvy mountain roads."

"And when we do arrive home," Samirah added, "the city is full of friends and a truly wonderful police force on top of that."

The Sassafras twins were impressed with the SAM Collective's optimism and their lack of anxiety. Even after living through such a terrible experience, the three of them knew how to think free and be free.

"What the anonymous snake charmers of Morocco did to us was wrong," Samirah continued. "But it's not only us they wronged. They've also wronged the other prisoners who are still at the facility. And, of course, they've wronged the reptiles, which is where this whole thing started for us."

"And it's not finished," Sami stated emphatically. "It's not over for us. It's only beginning. We must fight to right all these wrongs. Yes, we are scientists, and yes, we are mathematicians, but we are also activists. So, our activism will continue. It will continue on peacefully so that it will be effective. We will fight darkness with light."

Onward the hot-air balloon floated on streams of air and wind and over the mysterious dark of the nighttime Atlas Mountains. As the gentle journey progressed, Blaine and Tracey thought they were remaining awake, but they both suddenly jerked and opened their eyes. The twelve-year-olds realized they'd fallen asleep. Tracey blinked and stretched. Blaine rubbed some slobber from the corner of his mouth.

"Well, good morning, Blaine and Tracey!" Sami greeted with a smile. "Welcome to Marrakesh!"

"Marrakesh?" Tracey asked. "How long were we asleep?"

"A little more than two hours," Samir answered. "And it's a

good thing we've reached the outskirts of the city because we are running a little low on propane."

"Are we about to land?" Blaine asked.

"Well, our aim is to land on the other side of the city, closer to where we live," Samir explained. "But windspeed and fuel will heavily play into where the actual landing spot will end up being."

As the Sassafrases looked out over the edge of the wicker basket, they no longer saw shadowy mountains. Instead, they saw the buildings and lights of a large city about to wake up. The sun had not risen yet, but its glow was edging the eastern horizon. Soon after launch, the twins had heard Sami call Marrakesh the "Red City," but as they looked down on the African city now, it didn't look ancient to them. Many of the buildings looked modern, and much of the light they could see looked neon.

Blaine decided he would ask about it. "We were kind of under the impression that Marrakesh was, well, sort of an old city. If that's the case, what's with all the neon lights?"

"Neon comes from the Greek word *neos*, which means new," Samirah answered for the collective. "Marrakesh is indeed an ancient city, dating back to Neolithic times, but it's also a neon (or new) city, here in the 21st century."

"Neon is the fifth-most common element in the universe, but it is rather rare on Earth," Samir said, jumping into the science of the topic at hand. "It has a symbol of Ne, and its atomic number is 10. Its atomic mass is 20.18. Neon is the least reactive element on the entire periodic table. It does not form compounds or react with any other substances."

LINLOC SCIDAT

10
Ne
Neon
20.18

ELEMENT: Neon
GROUP: Noble Gases
INFORMATION LEARNED:
Neon is the least reactive element on the entire periodic table.

THE SASSAFRAS SCIENCE ADVENTURES

"Neon is a colorless gas," Sami began.

"Except when you pass electricity through it," Samirah interrupted. "Then the gas will glow bright red. It is what fills many of the glass tubes of those neon lights you can see right down in the city. However, any color other than red means that different gases or a mixture of gases was used. The very first neon light display was illuminated on December 11, 1910, in the city or Paris!"

"Neon is used in all kinds of things," Sami said, hopping in. "In fluorescent tubes, yes, but also in television sets, indicator lights, lasers, and even those barcode scanners they have at the checkouts in many shops."

As the five continued to float over the city, the Sassafrases did began to recognize more ancient-looking buildings and landmarks, as well as some candlelight, dotted in with the neon. Marrakesh was indeed a city that represented quite a large time span. The rim of light on the horizon was becoming brighter as morning continued to introduce itself. Soon it would be daytime in Marrakesh.

Air Below

"Oh! Oh!" Sami suddenly exclaimed, while at the same time pointing. "Radio towers! Not too far in the distance! Let's make sure we don't hit those!"

Everyone looked in the direction Sami was pointing and saw that he was indeed correct. They were coming up to dozens of radio towers. If their balloon made even the slightest contact with any one of these towers, it would certainly spell disaster.

With zero panic in her movements, Samirah calmly and quickly worked the burner, opening the valve, releasing more propane, and filling the envelope with more hot air. They were far enough away from the radio towers that there would be plenty of time to gain altitude and go over the towers, that is, if they had enough propane in their tanks. Samir had mentioned that the tanks were a little low.

The Sassafrases looked at Samir's face. If he was nervous about the diminishing fuel, his expression wasn't revealing it.

"Blaine and Tracey," the man addressed them. "Do you two know how the air in a hot-air balloon works?"

Tracey gave a half nod, half shake. "Well, we did hear you guys talking a little bit about it when we were still in the crate."

Samir now gave a nod with no shake. "That's right. We were talking a little about that last night; weren't we?"

"Do you mind reviewing it for us?" Tracey asked, preferring to think about science as opposed to thinking about possibly crashing into any obstructions.

"To put it simply, hot air is lighter, or rather less dense, than cool air," Samir started. "Therefore, warm air will rise in cool air. The design of a hot-air balloon is based on this foundational scientific principle. To break it down a little more, a cubic foot of air weighs roughly 28 grams. If you heat air by 100 degrees Fahrenheit, it weighs about seven grams less. Thus, each cubic foot of air in a hot-air balloon can lift about seven grams. Of course, this can vary with the ambient temperature and pressure, but these calculations are close enough for what we need."

"So, that's why the envelopes have to be so big, right?" Blaine put two and two together.

"That's right," Samir confirmed. "And then, as you have seen during our flight, to gain altitude you have to reheat the air, and to lose altitude you release air through the deflation port at the crown of the envelope."

Both twins understood, but Tracey had another question. "What about air itself? Can you three tell us more about that?"

"Sure can!" Sami spoke with a smile. "Air is a mixture of

gases that form a protective layer around the Earth that we call the atmosphere. In fact, there is enough air to breathe up to six miles above the Earth's surface. These gases are held loosely in place by gravity."

Samirah nodded even as she continued to man the helm. "Air protects us from UV radiation from the sun and is essential to life on Earth," the woman shared. "Carbon dioxide in the air traps heat from the sun and keeps the Earth at a temperature that supports life. This is known as the greenhouse effect. This all works together to help plants make their food and gives animals what they need to breathe."

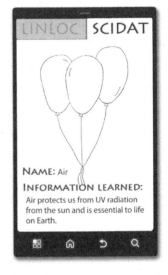

"The two main gases in the air are nitrogen and oxygen," Samir picked up the information trail. "But there are also traces of noble gas elements and carbon dioxide. Air is about 78% nitrogen, 21% oxygen, and 1% other gases. Additionally, air holds water vapor, dust, pollen, and pollutants."

"Yes and those noble gases can be separated from air by fractional distillation," Sami spoke again.

"Fractional distillation?" Blaine asked.

"Yes," Sami confirmed. "Fractional distillation is a process where a mixture, such as air, is separated into its components. This can be done physically, such as heating it, or chemically. Air is cooled and compressed into a liquid. Then, it is heated again, and the different gases are collected."

The twelve-year-old science learners looked from their collaboration of local experts back out over the edge of the riding basket. They saw that while the group was sharing the SCIDAT data they needed about air, their balloon had completed its safe passage over the tops of the tall grouping of radio towers.

"Yes! We made it!" the twins exclaimed.

"Yes, it is true that we made it," Samirah agreed. "But it is also true that we used our last bit of fuel to get over those towers."

"Oh no, does that mean . . . ?" Tracey started to ask but then stopped because she assumed she already knew the answer.

"Yes," Samirah confirmed. "We are going down."

"Down? As in down down?" Blaine asked. "It doesn't feel like we're going down."

"It won't be a fast descent," Samir clarified, knowing the details of the current situation as well as Samirah (and Sami). "But without propane, we no longer have the ability to create lift. The only direction we can go is down."

Blaine and Tracey looked at each other briefly and then out over the rim of the basket. What had moments ago seemed like a serene voyage now felt slightly tumultuous.

"Do you think we'll make it to the side of town we were hoping to get to?" Blaine ventured another nervous question. "You know, the place close to where you guys live?"

"I do not," Samirah spoke without mincing words. "At this point we are pretty much free-floating at the mercy of the wind."

"I am not a betting man," Sami spoke up, his voice excited but with an edge. "Mainly because it's not mathematically reasonable. But if I were, I would bet that we are going to land right in the middle of that!" He pointed.

The Sassafrases followed the trajectory of Sami's finger and found the largest concentration of electric light in all of Marrakech. "What's that?" they both instinctively asked.

"That," Samirah answered, "is Jemaa El-fnaa."

THE SASSAFRAS SCIENCE ADVENTURES

Chapter 17: Just a Bunch of Hot Air

The twins' eyes widened. They had been wondering exactly what Jemaa El-fnaa was, and now they could see that it was a massive, sprawling outdoor market. Brightly lit vendor stalls lined the square with row after row of stalls. They couldn't see exactly what was being sold because they were still too far away, but they could see lots of bright colors in and around the hubs of business. The edge of the market was outlined by ancient-looking, red stone buildings that almost seemed to be glowing in the approaching dawn. Even at this early morning hour, there were lots of colorfully dressed people moving around the market. Jemaa El-fnaa was a beautiful place but definitely not a good place to land a hot-air balloon.

With no more propane in the tanks, Samirah let go of the handmade burner and joined the others in looking over the balloon basket's edge. Where would the wind take them? They had escaped from the obscure mountain prison, but where would they land?

With a brilliant flash of light, the sun finally revealed itself, exploding up over the African horizon. By all accounts, it looked like they were indeed headed straight for the heart of Jemaa El-fnaa.

As they got closer to the ground, they could see people pointing at them. Some were smiling at the sight of a hot-air balloon headed straight for the market. Others were not.

There were clothes and jewelry being set out to sell. There were orange juice stands and grills for food being prepared. There were ornately dressed gentlemen carrying golden cups that they were filling with water poured from leather bags.

Everything they saw was interesting to the Sassafrases, and they didn't want to crash into any of it. But what took the twins' breath away was a gathering of people at one of the edges of the market. It was a group of snake charmers. They too were setting up for coming customers by laying rugs on the ground where they were placing baskets, instruments, and live snakes!

The breeze continued to push their balloon forward. Gravity continued to pull their balloon down. A crash-landing in Jemaa El-fnaa was inevitable. The five in the basket braced themselves. Those on the ground took cover. The handmade balloon of the SAM Collective touched down.

Blaine and Tracey closed their eyes as the wicker riding basket bumped, banged, and scraped. The twelve-year-olds could hear the shouts and screams of bystanders, but the landing had not been as violent as they'd been expecting. Had their balloon hit or destroyed anything?

Only after the wicker basket skidded to a stop did Blaine and Tracey venture to open their eyes. Within the basket, which was somehow still standing upright, everyone was okay. Samirah, Samir, and Sami were all whole and scratchfree. Outside the basket, there didn't seem to be any destroyed stalls or collateral damage. Above them, the envelope of their balloon had somehow gotten torn and ripped open, which actually might've been a good thing because it was deflating so fast that the wind couldn't move them anymore. Had they somehow landed without any serious wreckage?

Blaine sure thought so, and he let everyone know it. "We did it! We landed the balloon without hitting anything."

Tracey thought her brother might be right, but the three faces of the SAM Collective showed they did not share the Sassafrases' sentiments. They pointed to a sight behind Tracey and Blaine.

"We didn't hit any stalls," Sami said for the group, "but we must've hit some vendors. Look!"

The twins turned slowly to see what their local experts were pointing at. When they saw, they shuddered. Six or seven snake charmers were standing in threatening stances, staring at them. At their feet lay wrinkled rugs, crushed baskets, and broken instruments—snakes were slithering off in different directions.

Blaine wiggled his fingers in a nervous wave. "Hello, there . . . ha, ha . . . friendly snake charmers . . . whoops . . . did we land on your ummm . . . stuff?"

Deep, dark scowls formed on the charmers' faces. "Get them!" one of them suddenly pointed and yelled.

The SAM Collective's response to this was to jump out of the basket and flee. This immediately became the Sassafrases' response as well. There are times to stand and fight, and there are times for flight. According to the three that the twins trusted, this situation called for the latter response.

The flight of the five took them around a few stalls. They found themselves at the edge of Jemaa El-fnaa. Ahead, they saw an alleyway that cut between two buildings. The quintet headed straight in that direction. However, they quickly found out that the pursuing snake charmers were not only angry, but they were also fast. Looking over their shoulders as they ran, the twins were certain they would be caught before they even reached the alleyway.

All at once, something happened that the twins had not been expecting. Three backpackers—one guy with dreads, one guy with a mohawk, and one girl with heavily pierced ears, accidentally stepped in between the pursuing snake charmers and the fleeing five. The collision was magnificent, and it resulted in a pile of humanity made up of flailing arms, kicking legs, and grunts galore.

"Dude! We are so sorry! We didn't see you coming!" One of the backpackers apologized.

"Our fault, man!" another said.

"Totally our fault," the female backpacker added. "Sick way to start out the day in Morocco, though! Nothing like a full-on tackle to wake you up in the morning! Sick!"

Blaine and Tracey looked at each other as they fled. "Those three," they asked each other without words, "was that . . . ?"

Chapter 18: Zipping Back to Pecan Street

Bonus Data

"The chase through the alleyways of Marrakesh surely would've been epic," thought Blaine and Tracey. The narrow passages throughout the ancient stone buildings would've afforded sharp and abrupt turns. It would've included tumbles down steep stone ramps and hops up rock-hewn stairways. There would have been heart-pounding skips through hidden openings and jaunts over short connecting bridges. But alas, the chase had ended almost as soon as it had begun.

The SAM Collective and the Sassafrases had fled for a minute or so through the maze of alleys but had stopped when they realized no one was chasing them. The snake charmers' collision with the backpackers must have permanently halted their pursuit of the hot-air balloon riders. Even now, as Samirah, Samir, Sami, Blaine, and Tracey returned to the market from the alleyways, they saw that any pursuit from the snake charmers had been stopped. The three backpackers, who Blaine and Tracey were pretty sure had been Skip, Gannon, and Gretchen whom they'd met in Peru during their study on zoology, were nowhere to be seen.

However, what could be seen was a swarm of Moroccan police officers. The uniformed men and women were checking out the crashed hot-air balloon, and they also seemed to be apprehending the snake charmers.

Samir turned to his friends. "We must confess to crash-landing the hot-air balloon here in Jemaa El-fnaa," he said.

"But we didn't mean to—" Samira started to say.

"I know," Samir stopped her. "But it's the right thing to do."

"But it was the anonymous snake charmers of Morocco who

started thi—" Sami began to urge.

"I know," Samir consoled. "But we mu—"

"Samir?" Now it was Samir who was interrupted.

Everyone turned to see an approaching police officer. "Samir, is that you? And Samirah and Sami as well? You guys are alive?"

The SAM Collective nodded.

"I know you don't know me," the officer said with a smile. "But I was put in charge of your case."

"Our case?" Samir asked.

The officer nodded. "Yes. We knew you were kidnapped from the market here, and we knew it was the anonymous snake charmers who did it. But we had no idea where they took you or if you were okay. We have been looking for you since your disappearance."

The policeman looked over his shoulder to where their crashed balloon was lying and where the group of bad guy snake charmers were currently being rounded up. He chuckled as if he were beyond surprised. "Did you guys escape from the snake charmers in a handmade hot-air balloon?"

Samirah smiled and spoke for the group. "Have we got a story for you!"

A couple hours later, Blaine and Tracey Sassafras were soaring again. This time they were not gently floating in a hot-air balloon. Rather, they were zipping over invisible lines at the speed of light!

They had started their time in Morocco stuck in a crate near a prison, but they had ended their time free and profoundly wiser. The SAM Collective, who had also ended up completely free, had been wonderful companions, friends, and local experts. The twins had said goodbye to the scientists, activists, and mathematicians. Then, they had taken the time to enter everything they'd learned

about noble gases, helium, neon, and air into the SCIDAT app on their phones. They'd found some incredible pictures in the archive app, which they submitted along with the data.

Then, opening their LINLOC apps, they found their next destination was their uncle's basement! They'd done it! They'd successfully completed another scientific subject! Chemistry was firmly implanted in their brains and hearts.

Magnificent light swirled around them until their zipping came to a jerking stop; then the light went from multicolored swirls to bright white and back into the colors of their actual surroundings, which they thought was supposed to be a basement. However, as Blaine and Tracey stood and looked around, they weren't sure they were in the basement.

This place didn't look like the laboratory of a pseudo-famous research scientist. This place looked like a five-star restaurant! The walls were draped in black satin curtains. The floor was so clean that there was a shine to it. There was delicate jazz music caressing the room from unseen speakers. The subtle scent of fennel, clove, and cedar danced through the air. Soft light gently illuminated the space with flickering candles, elegant sconces, and even a small chandelier. At the center of it all, there was a table set for two. It was topped with a crisp, white tablecloth and set with perfectly organized fine china. It had an exquisite centerpiece made from real flowers, and one rose-colored candle. To finish it off, there were colorful place mats that looked to have a classy rendition of the periodic table on them.

Where in the world had they landed? Both twins instinctively pulled out their smartphones to see if maybe they had gotten the longitude or latitude coordinates wrong because this was not Uncle Cecil's basement.

It couldn't be. There was no mess here, no musty smell. And there also wasn't a cluttered desk or a tracking screen. At the precise moment they grabbed their phones, both devices vibrated.

"It's the bonus data," Blaine said, puzzled. "We always get bonus data when we land back in Uncle Cecil's basement after completing a subject, remember? But are we in Uncle Cecil's basement? We're not; are we? This can't be his basement; can it?"

Tracey knew how the bonus data worked, but she was with her brother in thinking this didn't seem like Uncle Cecil's basement. Something was off. The Sassafras girl took a wide look around their new landing spot and walked in her memory back through all the other times they had returned to their uncle's basement after successfully completing a subject.

"Well, you know, bro," Tracey said, still looking around, "Uncle Cecil has transformed his basement for us before. Remember all the wacky welcome-backs we've had. Once, there was a rock-climbing wall. Once we landed in a jungle. And remember the time we were greeted by Socrates and Aristotle?"

Blaine remembered, but he still couldn't fathom that this space could actually be their uncle's basement. He took a wide look around, while Tracey looked back at her phone. The bonus data shown on the screens were about hydrocarbons. The Sassafras sister went ahead and read it out loud.

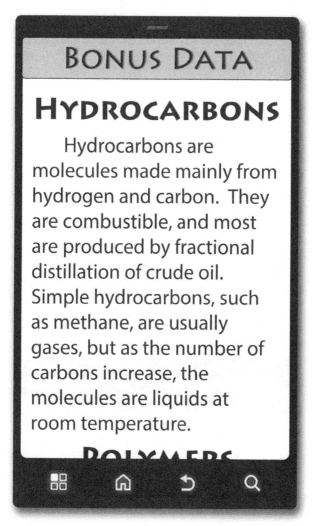

BONUS DATA

HYDROCARBONS

Hydrocarbons are molecules made mainly from hydrogen and carbon. They are combustible, and most are produced by fractional distillation of crude oil. Simple hydrocarbons, such as methane, are usually gases, but as the number of carbons increase, the molecules are liquids at room temperature.

Blaine looked at his phone too and read the rest of the bonus data, which was about polymers.

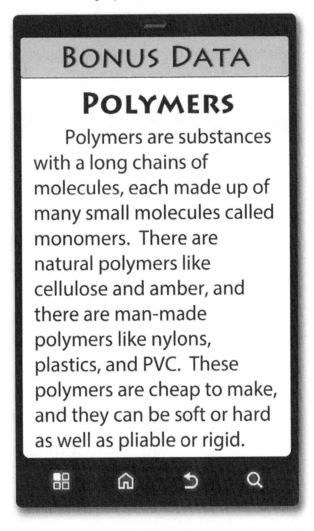

BONUS DATA

POLYMERS

Polymers are substances with a long chains of molecules, each made up of many small molecules called monomers. There are natural polymers like cellulose and amber, and there are man-made polymers like nylons, plastics, and PVC. These polymers are cheap to make, and they can be soft or hard as well as pliable or rigid.

Blaine took a pause to sigh and looked up from his phone. "Well, that's our bonus data, and it's good stuff, but Trace, I'm still wondering where in the wo—"

"Whoa! Wowie!"

Blaine was suddenly interrupted by a triumphant voice coming from a top corner of the room. The twins looked in that direction to see a section of the black satin curtain that was moving, being pushed and jabbed at by someone behind it.

"Wow! Wowdy wooty! Wowie wee willikers! It's Train and Blaisey! They've made it back! They've done it again! They've successfully soared through another subject of science!" The excited voice—it was obvious now—belonged to Uncle Cecil, but what was he doing up there behind the curtain? And where were they?

After more wrestling around with the black cloth, one of their uncle's arms finally poked out from behind the curtain, and then a bunny house slipper, and then his whole body. However, the red-headed man did not come out from behind the curtain with balance intact. Instead, he popped through on wobbly legs out onto an case of stairs the twins were just now spotting in the dim light. But what was even more shocking to the twins than the impending fall down the staircase, was Uncle Cecil's appearance. Yes, he still had fluffy slippers on, but he was not wearing his messy white lab coat. Instead, the man was wearing a suit! A tuxedo, by the looks of it. On top of that, he was carrying a loaded shiny silver tray, which looked to be currently sliding out of his white-gloved hand.

"Whoopsy whoop! Loopity loop! Dupity doop! Watch out, Train and Blaisey! I'm a coming!" the scientist shouted out as he danced with gravity.

Cecil's legs and feet went over his head and arms in an accidental cartwheeling motion. There was a bump and thump, but miraculously no crash. Their uncle somehow completed the flip and landed on his feet, almost like a cat saving one of its nine lives. The contents of the silver tray, though, flew up in the air in all directions.

Immediately, with more cat-like reflexes to showcase,

Cecil straightened the silver tray in his hand and dashed about, successfully catching every plate and every dish before they crashed to the ground.

"Wowzers! That was a close one!" the elder Sassafras said to the younger Sassafrases with a smile. "Welcome back to the basement, you two! You did it! You aced your chemistry leg of summer learning! Congratulations!"

"This is your basement?" Blaine asked, still not believing it.

Instead of being fixated on whether this was the basement or not, Tracey was more impressed with the magical dish-saving move Cecil had made. This was compounded by the fact that he had done it in a suit. "Uncle Cecil, you're . . . you're . . . wearing a . . . tuxedo." the Sassafras girl stammered in curious delight.

"This is your basement?" Blaine asked again, unable to move on.

Cecil did a giddy twirl toward the table at the center of the room, the tails of his tuxedo flying up as he did. He happily slid the dishes off the silver tray onto the elegant table, then he answered his niece and nephew with a smile. "Yessity yes, Train and Blaisey, this is indeed my trusty old basement, and in factly-o-fact, I am wearing a suit."

"Why?" Blaine finally asked a question that didn't include the word "basement."

Cecil sighed dreamily. "Ahhhh, It's all for Summer."

"Summer?" Tracey now added a one-word question.

A Periodic Setup

Their uncle nodded silently, his gaze awash with the googly eyes. The Sassafras twins looked at each other, and as they did, they remembered what had happened right before they zipped off to study chemistry at the Ambidextrous Octopus Bowling Alley.

VOLUME 7: CHEMISTRY   311

They remembered the glittery light from the twirling disco ball and the long, deep gaze into each other's eyes that Uncle Cecil and Summer had shared. It was a gaze that had been cut off by an untimely phone call from Captain Marolf of Triple S. It was no secret that Summer had a thing for their uncle; the twins had known that since their study of zoology at the beginning of the summer.

However, it had never been clear to them if Uncle Cecil felt the same way. Yet, during that gaze under the disco ball at the bowling alley, Blaine and Tracey were pretty sure they had seen a mutual feeling between the two scientists—a very strong feeling, a feeling that could be described as . . .

"For the love of all things orderly, Cecil!" a new voice shouted out in the basement. "You put the hors d'oeuvres in the wrong place on the table."

The twins looked over to see a man they knew walking down the stairs into the basement.

"Paul Sims?" Tracey exclaimed.

THE SASSAFRAS SCIENCE ADVENTURES

Blaine added, "What are you doing here?"

"Hello, Tracey. Hello, Blaine. Good to see the two of you again," the museum curator greeted as he approached the twelve-year-olds and their uncle. He looked at the twins with a professional smile. "You do remember that your uncle and I are old junior high classmates, right?"

Blaine and Tracey nodded.

"Well, I thought I'd stop by the old neighborhood for a visit with my old friend. It had been too long, you know. It's a good thing to keep up with old circles of friends, to keep the relationships current and kindled."

The Sassafras children kept nodding, not knowing what to say or if they were supposed to respond or not.

"But when I got here, I found out that your uncle thinks he's in love." Paul tilted his head toward Cecil. "Isn't that right, Cecil?"

The twins' uncle nodded, although the look on his face showed he wasn't paying attention to Paul and that his mind was somewhere else.

Sims continued as he looked at Blaine and Tracey. "Yes, this man is in love. And the woman he's in love with is none other than Summer Beach! When I got here, he was in the middle of planning a romantic date for Summer, but by my estimation his plan was a little sloppy. So, over the past few days I have made it my ambition to polish the plans and help Cecil pull a perfect date off without a hitch."

Paul turned his attention toward the table. "And to do that, we need the hors d'ouevres in the correct places." The man proceeded to reorganize the dishes on the table in a manner that looked pretty much the same way Cecil had placed them.

"No way!" the twins thought with wide-open mouths. This was both expected and unexpected at the same time. Even though they'd suspected it for a while, it was still quite stunning to hear it out loud. Uncle Cecil was in love with Summer! This was a wonderful thing! Blaine and Tracey loved their uncle. They loved Summer Beach, and they loved the two of them together!

They weren't quite keen on Paul Sims being around, but he was an old junior high classmate of Cecil's and Summer's after all. So although his timing seemed a little random, he was here to help, and that was a good thing, right? Wow! Uncle Cecil and Summer Beach in love! This was the best and craziest return to the basement yet!

"Uncle Cecil, is there anything we can do to help?" Tracey asked. "Is there any more that needs to be set up?"

"Where is Summer?" Blaine added. "Is she supposed to be here soon?"

"Sweet Summer Thyme could be arriving at any moment," Cecil swooned. "Manny oh manny, I can hardly wait! Everything is in its place, and the romantic table is set!"

"B-T-dubs, what do you guys think about the table?" Cecil asked his niece and nephew. "You two were the inspiration after all."

"What? How do you mean? How could we be the inspiration for all this?" Tracey asked, surprised.

Blaine scrunched his nose and said, "This whole place is kind of fancy-shmancy, and the table is covered with tiny little finger foods that look too pretty to eat. I mean, I'm saying if I were any sort of inspiration for a table, it would be full of things like pizza, burgers, sandwiches, and oh, what are those little things called that have the hot dog inside of the bis—"

Tracey nudged her brother in the ribs hard enough to get him to stop.

"You inspired it by studying chemistry!" Cecil said through a smile. "When you two zipped off and started sending in the SCIDAT about chemistry, it confirmed something I probably should've already known. Sweet Summer Thyme and I have chemistry together!"

Even though this statement from their uncle made them happy, it still caused the twelve-year-olds to blush a little bit.

Cecil continued, "When you sent in your SCIDAT on the periodic table, it sent my mind and heart into creative loopity-loops . . . the equation . . . CS + SB ->L_2F_2 . . . I thought, Train and Blaisey are learning about the periodic table. Hey! I should prepare a romantic table here in the basement to reveal my love to Summer! So bega—"

"He was twiddling his thumbs and spinning his wheels!" Paul Sims interrupted with a smile, but in a way that felt rude to the twins. "He was walking back and forth day after day from here to the supermarket. He was having trouble making up his mind about everything from menu to décor. He had cleaned this basement, but the rest of the house was a wreck. It was looking like the impending date could end up being a disaster. My heart went out to my old friend. Who knows if Summer reciprocates these feelings of love for him? But we at least need to pitch in and give the guy a fighting chance; am I right?"

Sims maintained his professional smile as he talked, and he was speaking as though he truly wanted to be a good friend, but Blaine and Tracey couldn't help but have an uneasy feeling about this guy.

"I mean, after days of wavering," Paul continued, as he patted Cecil on the back, "this guy had decided on a sandwich buffet as the main course for the date! Ha! Can you believe that? A sandwich buffet!"

The Sassafras twins could believe it. And not only that, they were certain Summer would absolutely be down for a date like that. The woman loved sandwiches more than anyone they knew.

"A sandwich buffet in a five-star setting like this," Paul

repeated with a laugh. "Preposterous, right? So, I helped my old buddy out by suggesting hors d'oeuvers."

Blaine and Tracey still weren't sure if or how they were supposed to respond to Paul Sims. However, they were sure that Summer did indeed reciprocate Cecil's feelings of love and that she would truly enjoy any romantic date their uncle set up for her, wacky or not. The two were a perfect match.

Blaine and Tracey were about to express this sentiment out loud when suddenly there was the sound of others entering the room. Everyone looked to the top of the stairs where three new individuals had entered the basement. It was President Lincoln, the prairie dog lab assistant, with Socrates and Aristotle, the stalwart trusty mannequins. And to the Sassafras twins' delight, all three were decked out in their own tuxedos!

"Meet the rest of the wait staff," Cecil said with an exuberant smile.

"Linc Dawg! Socrates! Aristotle! What's up?" the twins exclaimed in unison. "You guys look great!"

President Lincoln chattered happily in response, puffed his chest out a bit because he knew he looked good, and then nudged the two unresponsive mannequins down the stairs. However, before the three could even get halfway down the staircase, Paul Sims was on them like a duck on a June bug.

"No! No! No! Oh, no you don't! Cecil, I know you want these three things to be involved in your date, but I just can't let that happen. As a friend, I can't!" Paul forcefully grabbed ahold of Socrates and Aristotle and jerked them off the steps. "This is ridiculous, Cecil, ridiculous. These are mannequins! Mannequins! Honestly, it's a little disturbing to me that you even have these weird statues at your house."

Sims pointed at President Lincoln. "And this guy here, he's a rodent, Cecil, not a lab assistant, not an inventor—a rodent. How are you going to impress Summer and pull off a perfect date with all of this craziness around? You don't need these three things to be waiters. What you need is a dumpster and an exterminator!"

Cecil had no response. Neither did the twins. However, President Lincoln did. And what happened next would probably best be described as fury—or chaos—in a basement.

The fiery and offended prairie dog jumped from the stairs onto Paul Sims's head and attacked the man. The museum curator screamed, flailed, and knocked Socrates in Blaine's direction, who was then knocked in Tracey's direction, who in turn was knocked in Aristotle's direction, who bumped Cecil, who fell headlong into the perfectly pristine table in the center of the basement, sending its every content upward and outward.

It was then, when so many things were literally up in the air, that the seven heard another sound. The front porch trapdoor had opened, and someone was now careening downward about to enter the basement via the slide. The someone who was coming was letting out an extremely happy and high-pitched squeal as they approached. This squeal distinctly belonged to only one person in the world—Summer T. Beach.

Follow the Sassafras Twins on their Physics Leg!

The adventure doesn't have to end just because you've finished this book! The summer-long, science-filled, adventure-packed journey heats up as Blaine and Tracey look at the world of physics.

In *The Sassafras Science Adventures Volume Eight: Physics*, you and the twins will meet a variety of local experts who help them to learn about the different physical topics along the way.

Don't miss a moment of the final leg of their journey. Start reading today to learn about physics in a way you'll never forget!

Visit ElementalScience.com/Sassafras
Start your next adventure!

The Sassafras Science Adventures